World Civil Aircraft
Since 1945

Michael Hardy

Charles Scribner's Sons
NEW YORK

1 3 5 7 9 11 13 15 17 19 I/C 20 18 16 14 12 10 8 6 4 2

Printed in the United States of America
Library of Congress Catalog Card Number 79-53087
ISBN 0-684-16266-0

Photo Credits

Introduction

This book gives salient details of the origins, history, development and commercial use of 117 different types of postwar transport aircraft, ranging from small single-engined STOL types such as the de Havilland Beaver and Pilatus Porter up to the long haul intercontinental jets. As well as the products of the United States, Canada, Britain, France and Russia there are details here of indigenous designs from the aircraft manufacturers of Israel, Czechoslovakia, Switzerland, Brazil and Peru, amongst other countries, covering a very broad spectrum both of national needs and of different national approaches to a particular air transport requirement.

The year 1970 has been taken as a cut-off point, as this marked the beginning of the wide body and supersonic era in air transport, with Pan American inaugurating the first services by Boeing 747 jumbo jet across the North Atlantic on 21 January that year, and both the Concorde, which had flown in March 1969, and the Tupolev Tu-144, which flew on the last day of 1968, moving ahead with their lengthy test programmes. So, although the TriStar and DC-10 had made their first flights in the latter half of 1970 and the 747 and the two SSTs before that, it was felt logical to exclude them from this volume; full details about them may be found in the companion volume *Civil Aircraft of the World 1978*. Also, the manufacturer's name under which a type is described is the one under which it is best known rather than the one reflecting the latest industrial reoganisation. Thus the Comet, Trident and Argosy will still be found under 'Hawker Siddeley' rather than 'British Aerospace', and other British types will be found under their original manufacturers.

Some real old timers, such as the Ford Tri-motor and Junkers Ju 52/3m, are included where they have earned their bread and butter in postwar airline operations; this the Ju52 continued to do until the last one was retired in New Guinea in 1960, and the Ford continues to earn its keep in the USA by flying sightseers over the Grand Canyon. And of course there are those types such as the Rapide and the DC-3, which age cannot wither nor custom make stale, and which seem to go on forever. Sheer longevity is likely to be a characteristic of today's jets just as much as for some of their forebears of the 1930s, for in the economically lean 1970s, when so few airlines or manufacturers can afford to sponsor or embark on a major new airliner project, it is the theme of product improvement that is being pursued in the major design offices, and which firms like Boeing in particular have developed to a high degree. This takes the form of offering actual and prospective customers progressive increases in operating weights and engine thrust, better hush kits for the engines, wide body cabin interiors for the narrow body jets and such special items as modification kits for operating from gravel or unpaved runways. For many of today's types, it is product improvement rather than a major fuselage stretch or new engines, that remains the most feasible avenue of development.

No compiler of a book such as this can fail to be struck from time to time, as his work progresses, by the element of luck present and how this can, as much as the most careful market research, design work and engineering skills, make or mar a type's sales prospects. If the Britannia had not had its early engine icing problem or the Electra those two fatal accidents which led to speed restrictions being imposed on it, how much more securely might the turboprop have become established? For the short-haul jet made a very sideways entrance into the airline buying scene; the Hunting H-107 small jet project would probably never have been developed into the One-Eleven but for the formation of BAC and its takeover of Hunting Aircraft. And Douglas went ahead only reluctantly with the DC-9 in 1963 because they realised that unless they did so, the One-Eleven would have the US market to itself. In the early days, Douglas feared losing money on the DC-9 programme yet now more than 900 have been sold and the type has been stretched more than any other airliner in history.

Again, there would have been no civil 707 programme if the USAF had not ordered the KC-135A tanker-transport from Boeing, which did not break even on its jet transports until 1964, when about 1,000 707s, KC-135s and 720s had been sold. If Boeing had been a year or more later in reaching break-even point, and BEA had not had the Trident project scaled down in size and re-engined with Rolls-Royce Spey instead of Medway turbofans, there might have been no Boeing 727 and the British jet would have been sold in hundreds. Good luck as well as bad has played its part; Fokker had no home market to speak of for the Friendship, yet it became the most widely sold turboprop airliner almost entirely on the basis of small orders, hardly any for more than 10 aircraft at a time. And both the Caravelle and Viscount success stories are due not least to the right powerplants being available at the right time. 'The profession is overcrowded and the struggle's pretty tough' wrote Sir Noel Coward many years ago in advising Mrs Worthington not to put her daughter on the stage, and how true this is of airliner design and manufacture, as well as of show business!

Aero Spacelines Guppy, Super Guppy USA

Photo: Super Guppy
Data: Guppy 201

Engines: Four 4,912shp Allison 501-D22C
turboprops
Span: 156ft 3in
Length: 143ft 10in
Height: 48ft 6in
Wing area: 1,965sq ft
Weight: 100,000lb (empty)
Max payload: 54,000lb
Max take-off weight: 170,000lb
Speed: 288mph at 20,000ft (max cruising)
Initial rate of climb: 1,500ft/min
Service ceiling: 25,000ft
Range: 505 miles with max payload

The concept of a freighter version of the Boeing
Stratocruiser, incorporating a very large diameter
fuselage to cater for outsize cargo loads, was
conceived jointly by John M. Conroy and Lee
Mansdorf, in particular to meet NASA's needs for the
transport of very large rocket assemblies from
California plants to Florida testing grounds such as
Cape Canaveral. These rocket sections had to be
transported by barge through the Panama Canal
because they were too big for overland routes or any
existing freight aircraft. Conroy completed design of
an outsize fuselage for the original conversion,
known as the B-377PG Pregnant Guppy, which
made its first flight on 19 September 1962 and a
new company, Aero Spacelines Inc, was formed to
transport outsize missile and space components for
NASA and the US Department of Defense under
exclusive contract; 25 Stratocruisers and C-97
Stratofreighters were acquired and from these six
Guppy and Super Guppy conversions were
eventually produced. The lower fuselage, wings, tail
unit and cockpit of the original Stratocruiser were
retained and on the lengthened fuselage a new
outsize upper section was built giving an internal
cargo hold diameter of 25ft 6in for the Super Guppy
or 15ft 6in for the Mini Guppy; this reduced the
Super Guppy's cruising speed by 80mph compared

with the normal fuselage. On the Pregnant Guppy
the entire rear fuselage and tail were made
detachable at the wing trailing edge for loading and
unloading the 29,187cu ft cargo space.

The Super Guppy, which first flew on 31 August
1965, was made up from four aircraft based on the
YC-97J test bed for the Pratt & Whitney T34
turboprop; in addition to T34 engines it had a taller
fin, new inner wing sections increasing the span by
15ft and a larger diameter fuselage lengthened to
135ft 6in giving a cargo volume of 49,790cu ft. The
entire fuselage nose could be swung open to port for
loading and unloading. A second B-377PG Pregnant
Guppy was also produced with auxiliary underwing
turbojets for improved take-off, and the Mini Guppy
reverted to the Stratocruiser's Pratt & Whitney
R-4360 Wasp Major piston engines and had a
smaller fuselage than the Super's, lengthened to
144ft and featuring swing tail loading; it first flew on
24 May 1967.

It was followed by two Guppy 201s, which first
flew on 24 August 1970 and 24 August 1971
powered by four 4,912shp Allison 501-D22C
turboprops, dimensionally similar to the Super
Guppy. These two were both acquired by
Aérospatiale to fly major components of the A-300B
Airbus between the various factories in the A-300
manufacturing group, and to perform similar services
for British and French firms in the Concorde
programme. The first entered service in January
1971; both being operated by the UTA subsidiary
Compagnie Aéromaritime d'Affrêtement SA.

The original Pregnant Guppy and Mini Guppy
were acquired by American Jet Industries Inc in
1974 for use as 'pick-up trucks' to ferry damaged
aircraft out of a crash site for repair, as well as for
flying outsize cargo loads. Aero Spacelines also
studied a version of the Super Guppy with six Allison
turboprops and a 25ft maximum cargo hold width,
but the most outlandish project of all was for a
conversion of the Boeing B-52 eight jet bomber to
have been known as the Colossal Guppy, with a new
40ft diameter fuselage and a payload of 200,000lb!

Aérospatiale (Nord) 262

France

Photo and Data: Nord 262A

Engines: Two 1,065ehp Turboméca Bastan VIC turboprops
Span: 71ft 10in
Length: 63ft 3in
Height: 20ft 4in
Wing area: 592sq ft
Basic operating weight: 15,496lb
Max payload: 7,209lb
Max take-off weight: 23,370lb
Speed: 239mph (max)
233mph (max cruising)
Range: 605 miles with max payload
1,095 miles with max fuel

Better known as the Nord 262, this twin-engined pressurised light transport for commuter airline and feederline use had its origins in the Max Holste MH-250 Super Broussard, a twin-engined successor to the MH-1521M Broussard single-engined 6-8 seat utility transport used by the French Army and Air Force, and by several civil operators. The MH-250 Super Broussard first flew on 20 May 1959 powered by two 600hp Pratt & Whitney R-1340 Wasps and was intended to seat 17-23 passengers. It served in effect as a prototype for the MH-260 Super Broussard, which differed in having two 986ehp Turboméca Bastan IV turboprops and a fuselage lengthened by about 4ft 7in; it first flew on 29 July 1960 and could seat 20-30 passengers. The MH-260 aroused some airline interest, but it was realised that the addition of cabin pressurisation would greatly enhance the sales appeal, and the MH-262 was planned as the pressurised version. But while this was being developed a production batch of 10 MH-260s, or Nord 260s as they were to be known, was commenced; the state-owned Nord Aviation, under an agreement of 23 November 1960, having assumed responsibility for the development, production and sale of the Super Broussard. The first production Nord 260 flew on 29 January 1962 and the 10 production aircraft were operated on a trials basis by Air Inter on French domestic routes and by

the Norwegian operator Wideroe's Flyveselskap A/S. But there were no further orders, and the Nord 260 was succeeded by the pressurised Nord 262, design work on which had started in the spring of 1961.

This had a circular-section fuselage typically seating 24-26 passengers three-abreast, instead of the square section fuselage of the MH-260. The prototype Nord 262 first flew on 24 December 1962 powered by uprated 1,080ehp Bastan VIB2 turboprops, and was followed by three pre-production aircraft. French certification of the type was granted on 16 July 1964, and the first production aircraft (identified by a dorsal fin) had flown on 8 July. The first four aircraft were designated Nord 262B, the fifth, incorporating further small improvements, being the first to full production standard and being designated Nord 262A; altogether 67 of this version were built. Air Inter began scheduled services with the Nord 262 on the Paris-Quimper route on 24 January 1964, operating six in all. An important early customer was the US local service carrier Lake Central Airlines, which ordered 12, beginning Nord 262 services in May 1965; these 262As had a two-part airstair door for the passengers, and they continued in service with Allegheny Airlines after the latter had taken over Lake Central in 1968, being used more recently in third-level routes flown by the Allegheny Commuter Consortium. Only a few more 262s had been sold in the States following the Lake Central order, due in part at least to Nord not having offered a version with Pratt & Whitney PT6 turboprops. This was not remedied until 1974, when work began on converting nine Allegheny 262s to have 1,180shp PT6A-45A turboprops and updated systems instead of the Bastans; this version developed by Frakes Aviation, being known as the Mohawk 298 — the number being taken from FAR 298, the US airworthiness regulations covering third-level operations. The PT6s drive five-blade airscrews and the Mohawk 298 first flew on 7 January 1975, finally going into service with Allegheny in April 1977.

Meanwhile a new version with uprated 1,145ehp

Bastan VII turboprops driving four-blade airscrews in place of the earlier Bastan VICs had been developed as the Nord 262C, this also featuring revised wing tips that increased the span by 2ft 3¾in. This first flew in July 1968 and was named Frégate, the Nord 262D being the military version. The Armée de l'Air ordered 18 262Ds to supplement six Nord 262As it had acquired earlier, and the French Navy had also bought 15 Nord 262As, but only a few Frégates were ordered by airlines and governments. Altogether 110 Nord 262s of all versions have been ordered, of which about 40 are in airline service, mostly in Europe and the USA, although several African and Asian airlines, such as Air Comores, Air Madagascar, Tunis Air and Air Ceylon used to operate one or two examples.

Aérospatiale (Sud) SE210 Caravelle   France

Photo: Mk 6
Data: Mk 6R

Engines: Two 12,600lb st Rolls-Royce RA29/6 Avon 532R or 533R turbojets
Span: 112ft 6in
Length: 105ft 0in
Height: 28ft 7in
Wing area: 1,579sq ft
Basic operating weight: 63,175lb
Max payload: 18,395lb
Max take-off weight: 110,230lb
Speed: 525mph at 25,000ft (max cruising)
488mph at 35,000ft (best economy cruising)
Range: 1,430 miles with max payload

The Caravelle was the first short/medium haul airliner ever to be designed for turbojet power, and it set a new fashion in rear-mounted engines. More than any other civil type it established the postwar French aircraft industry as a major force in the world's international markets, and Caravelles were to be ordered by almost every European national airline outside the Communist bloc and by United and TWA in the States. The Caravelle had its origins in an official specification issued by the French government agency SGACC in November 1951 for a 'moyen courrier' (medium range airliner) for routes in the French Empire, especially those to North Africa. The specification suggested a payload of 6-7 tonnes to be carried over stage lengths of 1,000-1,200 miles at a block speed of over 380mph, this allowing two Paris-North Africa return journeys to be made in 24 hours.

SNCA du Sud-Est did design studies of two-, three- and four-engined layouts with turboprops, jets and ducted fans for their X210 'moyen courrier' project, and the final design study had three rear-mounted 6,600lb st SNECMA Atar 101D jets, two in pods and one with a central fin intake. But at this time the 10,000lb st Rolls-Royce RA16 Avon became available, and two of these engines were chosen in place of three Atars. In September 1952 the SE210 was chosen as the design contest winner, and construction of two prototypes and two static test airframes was put in hand early in 1953; at this stage the SE210 was a 52-seater with a wing area of 1,580sq ft. The first prototype made its initial flight on 27 May 1955 with 10,000lb st RA26 Avon 529s; it had a forward freight door and was followed by the second prototype on 6 May 1956.

Air France had placed the first order, for 12 (later doubled), in February 1956 and the first export order, from SAS for six with 19 on option, was placed in June 1957. French certification of the Caravelle was granted on 2 April 1958 and Air France had initiated proving trials with the prototype as a freighter over the Paris-Algiers route in June 1956, finally beginning regular passenger services over the Paris-Istanbul route on 6 May 1959, followed by SAS nine days later on a multi-stop Copenhagen-Cairo route. Initial production aircraft were Caravelle 1s with 10,500lb st RA29 Avon 522s, of which 20 were built, and Caravelle 1As, of which 12 were built, with RA29/1 Avon 526s; both these versions were 4ft 7½in longer than the prototype, with a maximum gross weight of 97,000lb and seating typically about 64 passengers in a two-class interior, or a maximum of 99. These 1s and 1As were all subsequently modified to Caravelle III standard with 11,400lb st RA29/3 Avon 527s and a gross weight of 99,210lb; the Mk III had a longer range and higher cruising speed. In addition, 78 Mk IIIs were built as such, beginning with the 24th production aircraft, the first Mk III being delivered in April 1960 to Alitalia.

The next version was the Caravelle 6 with

Above: *Chilean 3006 Caravelle*

12,200lb st RA29/6 Avon 531s without thrust reversers, gross weight increased to 105,820lb, with some structural stiffening, more powerful brakes and improved performance. The first Mk 6 was converted from the Mk III prototype, flying on 10 September 1960, and the first Mk 6 was delivered to Sabena in January 1961. The Caravelle 6R had 12,600lb st RA29/6 Avon 532R or 533R engines with thrust reversers, unlike the Mk 6, and had certain features to meet FAA requirements such as a modified windscreen, larger cockpit side windows and additional lift spoilers on the wing trailing edges. United Air Lines ordered 20 Mk 6Rs and began Caravelle services between New York and Chicago on 14 July 1961, thus becoming the first US domestic airline to operate a European jet. The Mk 6 without thrust reversers was now designated Mk 6N, and 53 of the latter and 56 Mk 6Rs were built.

With US sales in mind General Electric had acquired a Mk III and fitted it with 16,100lb st CJ805-23C aft fan jets; as the Caravelle VII this first flew on 29 December 1960. These engines would have powered the projected Caravelle 10, which had a 3ft 4in longer fuselage, and the Mk 10A, also known as the Caravelle Horizon or Super A. Twenty of the latter, plus 15 on option, had been ordered by TWA in September 1961 but this order was later cancelled because of the airline's financial problems at the time. A prototype Mk 10A first flew on 31 August 1962 and this version had a number of aerodynamic improvements, such as a wing root leading edge extension, redesigned flaps, a fin/tailplane 'acorn' fairing and a wider span tailplane; an APU was fitted in the tail. The Caravelle 10B, or Super Caravelle, was very similar to the 10A, with the same fuselage stretch and 14,000lb st Pratt

& Whitney JT8D-1 turbofans; the 10B prototype first flew on 3 March 1964 and 25 were built for Finnair, Syrian Arab Airlines and Sterling Airways. The latter operated 10Bs at a gross weight of 119,050lb and ultimately at 123,460lb, with an additional centre section tank, instead of the original 114,640lb. The 10B could seat from 68 to 105 passengers, and was the first version to have the Sud/Lear-Siegler autoland system as standard; several operators of earlier versions, such as Alitalia, had this system fitted retrospectively. The Caravelle 10R, also known as the Mk 10B.1R, was a Mk 6R fitted with 14,000lb st JT8D-7 turbofans with Sud-designed cascade thrust reversers, giving better payload/range capabilities; the prototype 10R first flew on 18 January 1965 and 20 of this version were built. The Caravelle 11R is a mixed passenger/freighter version similar to the 10R and with the same engines, but with a 3ft 0½in longer fuselage, a 10ft 10¾in × 6ft 0¼in cargo door forward and a strengthened freight floor. The prototype 11R first flew on 21 April 1967 and seven were built for Air Afrique, Air Congo and Trans Europa of Spain. Final stretched version is the Caravelle 12, first flown on 29 October 1970, which has a 10ft 6in fuselage stretch over the 10B, enabling it to carry up to 140 charter or IT passengers in a high-density layout. Engines are 14,500lb st JT8D-9 turbofans and gross weight went up to 119,050lb and later to 123,450lb with structural provision for operating at up to 127,870lb. Seven Mk 12s were built for Sterling Airways and five for Air Inter, and when the last of these was delivered in 1972 altogether 282 Caravelles had been built.

Airspeed AS57 Ambassador

UK

Photo: BEA Elizabethan
Data: AS57 Ambassador

Engines: Two 2,625bhp (max take-off) Bristol Centaurus 661 18-cylinder 2-row radials
Span: 115ft 0in
Length: 82ft 0in
Height: 18ft 3in
Wing area: 1,200sq ft
Weight: 36,304lb (empty)

Capacity payload: 11,645lb
Max take-off weight: 55,000lb
Speed: 288mph at 19,000ft (max cruising)
Range: 470 miles with 9,950lb payload
1,200 miles with max fuel

One of the most elegant airliners ever built, the Airspeed AS57 Ambassador, better known by its BEA class name 'Elizabethan', was designed to meet the Brabazon Type IIA specification for a medium

range inter-city airliner, and its clean lines and careful streamlining resulted in a high performance on low cruising power. The prototype, to Spec C25/43, made its first flight on 10 July 1947 and was followed by a second prototype, which was pressurised and had a fixed 'bumper' tailwheel, on 26 August 1948. The prototypes were powered by 2,400bhp Bristol Centaurus 631 engines with single-speed superchargers; the second prototype's demonstration of a single-engined take-off was one of the highlights of the 1948 SBAC show.

When BEA ordered 20 Ambassadors it required a 47-passenger interior instead of the 36-40 seat layout of the prototypes; this resulted in the Ambassador 2 production version with more powerful Bristol Centaurus 661 engines with two-speed blowers and an all-up weight increased from 45,000lb to 52,500lb. A pre-production aircraft very similar to the Mk 2 first flew in May 1950 and the first prototype flew for a time with a Centaurus 661 on the port side. BEA started route proving flights between London and Paris in September 1951 and, after some delays, regular Elizabethan services over this route began on 13 March 1952. In 1953 BEA's Elizabethans underwent a modification programme, after which the all-up weight was increased to 55,000lb. The Elizabethan's economics were better than the Viscount's on short routes such as London–Paris, and the type had been designed from the start for the eventual installation of turboprops (a version

with four Rolls-Royce Darts was at one time projected). But BEA's full-scale commitment to the Viscount, and Airspeed's merger in 1951 with de Havilland's, themselves committed to the Comet, meant that production ended with the last BEA deliveries and only 23 were built. BEA flew its last Elizabethan service on 30 July 1958.

In 1957 three Elizabethans were sold to Butler Air Transport of New South Wales but returned after Butler's takeover by Ansett the following year. The others of BEA's fleet were sold off to BKS Air Transport, Dan-Air Services and the Swiss charter operator Globe Air, Jordan's Royal Arab Air Force also acquired two which were later sold to Dan-Air while those of Globe Air were sold to Autair International. Some of the BKS aircraft had a forward freight door fitted; two Elizabethans were also used by Shell and one by the Decca Navigator Co. The second prototype was used as a turboprop test bed, being fitted successively with two Bristol Proteus 705s in 1954, two Rolls-Royce Tynes in 1958 and in 1966 a Dart 525 on the starboard side and a Dart 201P to port. The first production aircraft was fitted with two Napier NE1.1 Elands in 1955, and later the NE1.6 version, with a view to obtaining a C of A for freighting. BEA considered re-engining its Elizabethans with Elands but abandoned the idea, and the first production aircraft was later re-engined with Centaurus 661s for Dan-Air.

Antonov An-2   USSR

Photo: Polish An-2
Data: An-2M

Engine: One 1,000hp Shvetsov ASh-62 IR 9-cylinder radial driving a Type V509-D9 4-blade airscrew
Span: 59ft 8½in
Length: 42ft 6in
Height: 13ft 9¼in
Wing area: 769.6sq ft
Max payload: 3,300lb (crop spraying chemicals)
Max take-off weight: 12,125lb
Speed: 157mph (max) at 5,750ft
124mph (best economy cruising)
Range: 562 miles with max fuel

This big single-engined biplane had its origins in a specification of the Soviet Ministry of Agriculture and Forestry, and the prototype first flew in 1947 powered by a 630hp Shvetsov ASh-21 engine. It was at first known as the SKh-1 (*Selskokhozy-yaistvennyi* or SKh, meaning agricultural-economic) but went into production as the An-2 with a 1,000hp ASh-62 radial. Designed to operate out of small semi-prepared airfields, the An-2 rapidly took on a a multi-purpose role as a replacement for the elderly Polikarpov Po-2 biplane, being used not only as a light utility transport for passengers and freight, but for rescue and ambulance work, parachute training, photographic and geophysical survey and forestry patrol, as well as aerial agriculture. It does much the

same sort of jobs as the DHC-3 Otter, probably its nearest equivalent in the West, and has a cabin very similar in size, but is much more powerful and heavier, although with similar overall dimensions. Over 5,000 An-2s were built between 1949 and 1962 for the Soviet armed forces, Aeroflot and other civilian organisations. The Soviet Air Force used it as a light freighter carrying up to 3,000lb, a radio and navigational trainer and for training paratroops. The An-2, codenamed Colt by NATO, has been exported to all the Communist countries and serves with many of their air forces, while Aeroflot employs many hundreds on aerial agriculture and other duties.

Basic general purpose variant is the An-2P, which accommodates up to 10 passengers on lightweight folding seats, or 14 paratroops or freight or six stretcher cases and four sitting casualties and a medical attendant. In airline service either seven individual forward-facing seats may be fitted or four bench-type seats for two people and there are cupboards for food and drink, as well as a wardrobe and toilet. A glider-towing hook is standard, and the flight deck seats two pilots, with provision for a flight engineer. The An-2S agricultural version has a long-stroke undercarriage, permitting the fitting of a propeller-driven pump under the fuselage discharging liquid through underwing spray bars. This was succeeded by the An-2M, which has more efficient dust and liquid dispensing systems driven off the engine, and a hopper capacity increased from 308 to 431 Imperial gallons. Dispersal rates when crop dusting or spraying are increased and the An-2M can be operated by a single pilot. The M has a number of other improvements and is identifiable by a larger tailplane and more square-cut fin and rudder; it began to enter service early in 1965 and is convertible to passenger carrying or other duties. The An-2V, which has the Antonov design bureau

number An-6, is a seaplane version of the An-2P developed in 1954-55, with the usual curved-blade airscrew replaced by a reversible-pitch prop with straight square-tipped blades; floats or skis can also be fitted to other versions of the An-2. The An-2L water bomber is similar to the V, and drops water on fires from the bottom of each float. The An-2ZA (design bureau number An-4) is a special version of the An-2P for high altitude meteorological research, with an extra cockpit built into the fin leading edge from which such phenomena as ice accretion could be studied. The engine is an ASh-62 IR/TK with a turbosupercharger mounted externally on the starboard side to maintain 850hp up to a height of 31,000ft; the airscrew spinner is removed and the carburettor intake lengthened. The An-2 has also been built under licence by China's State Aircraft Factory, where the first locally-built one was finished in December 1957, and in Poland by the WSK factory at Mielec, which is now the only producer of An-2s.

Polish production started in 1960, and by the beginning of 1976 more than 6,900 An-2s of all versions had been built at Mielec, over 90% of them for export. The Polish versions have their own designations, sometimes differing from the Russian ones: the An-2T is the basic Polish general purpose version, and the An-2P the passenger version, seating 12 adult passengers and two children, with various improvements over the Russian An-2. The An-2R agricultural (similar to the Russian-built An-2S) and An-2S ambulance versions are supplemented by the An-2PK, a five-seat executive variant, the An-2P-Photo for photogrammetric surveys, the An-2 Geofiz for geophysical surveys, the An-2TD paratroop transport and trainer, the An-2TP cargo passenger variant and the An-2M twin-float version of the An-2T.

Antonov An-10 and An-12   USSR

Photo: Indonesian An-12
Data: An-12V

Engines: Four 4,000ehp Ivchenko AI-20K turboprops
Span: 124ft 8in
Length: 121ft 4$\frac{1}{2}$in

Height: 32ft 3in
Wing area: 1,286sq ft
Weight: 61,730lb (empty)
121,475lb (loaded)
Max payload: 44,090lb
Speed: 444mph (max)
342mph at 25,000ft (normal cruising)
Range: 2,110 miles with 22,050lb payload

Russia's equivalent of the Lockheed C-130 Hercules is the Antonov An-10, also known as the Ukraina (the name given to the prototype) and by the NATO codename Cat. But, whereas the C-130 was designed from the start as a military transport and later developed into commercial versions, the opposite is true of the An-10, design work on which began in November 1955 to Aeroflot's requirements for a large-capacity transport for its extensive domestic network, with many small rough airfields as well as larger well equipped ones. The prototype An-10 first flew in March 1957 powered by Kuznetsov NK-4 turboprops and there were some stability problems during the development period, small auxiliary fins being added to the tailplane, a ventral fin to the rear fuselage and anhedral being applied to the outer wing panels to overcome these problems. On later aircraft the endplate fins were replaced by two additional ventral fins. The production An-10 was powered by 4,015ehp Ivchenko AI-20 turboprops driving four-blade reversible airscrews. Aeroflot began services with the An-10 in an 85-passenger configuration on 22 July 1959 on routes from Simferopol in the Crimea to Moscow and Kiev, and the type also underwent a period of experimental services during 1958-59 carrying freight and mail. Only a small batch of An-10s was produced before being succeeded by the An-10A, which had a 6ft 7in longer fuselage and normal accommodation for 100 passengers, or seating for 120-130 in higher density layouts. The An-10A entered service with Aeroflot in February 1960 and later, after two months of trials on skis, it began operating in the Arctic regions; wheels are interchangeable with ski landing gear for Arctic operation.

The An-10 is now retired from Aeroflot service, and it was succeeded by the An-12 military freighter, codenamed Cub by NATO, which has an entirely redesigned, upswept rear fuselage with a loading ramp in the underside, a new tail unit with no endplate fins and a tail gun position with two 23mm NR-23 cannon; there is a built-in gantry of 5,070lb capacity for handling loads. The rear ramp door is in right and left halves which fold upwards inside the fuselage for loading or unloading or the dropping of 100 paratroops in less than a minute. Like the An-10, the An-12 is fully pressurised and can operate from unpaved surfaces, yet has an outstanding performance. There is a weather and mapping radar under the nose, and in most of the Soviet Air Force's 800 An-12s this has been changed to a more powerful and modern set. An-12s have also been supplied to the air forces of Algeria, Bangladesh, Egypt, India, Indonesia, Iraq and Poland; Egyptian AF An-12s have also been used by UAA (now Egyptair). The An-12V is the commercial freighter used by Aeroflot, which has some 250, and An-12Vs have been supplied in ones and twos to Balkan Bulgarian Air Transport, LOT of Poland, Air Guinee, Ghana Airways, Iraqi Airways (which has six) and CAAC of China. Early commercial An-12s retained the tail turret position with the guns removed, but later An-12Vs, and some military ones, have the turret removed and replaced by a fairing. One of Aeroflot's An-12Vs was tested with large skis with shallow curved-vee planing surfaces which had heating and braking devices to operate off snow-covered terrain.

Antonov An-14 Pchelka   USSR

Engines: Two 300hp Ivchenko AI-14RF 9-cylinder radials
Span: 72ft 2in
Length: 37ft 6in
Height: 15ft 2½in
Wing area: 427.5sq ft
Weight: 4,409lb (empty)
Max payload: 1,590lb
Max take-off weight: 7,935lb
Speed: 138mph (max) at 3,280ft
112mph (normal cruising)
Range: 404 miles with max payload
497 miles with max fuel

In the same class as the Britten-Norman Islander but seating fewer passengers, the Antonov An-14 Pchelka ('Little Bee') was intended to meet an Aeroflot requirement for a small utility transport with a similar STOL performance to the widely-used An-2 and better standards of passenger comfort. The prototype made its first flight on 15 March 1958 and was followed by a second, both powered by 260hp Ivchenko AI-14R radials and seating six passengers. At first the tailplane had no dihedral and the twin fins had V-shaped leading edges, but later a dihedral tailplane and rectangular fins and rudders with greater area were substituted and 300hp AI-14RF radials fitted; this enabled an extra passenger to be carried. But performance was still unsatisfactory, and the wing was completely redesigned, span being increased from 64ft 11½in to 72ft 2in and the trailing edges outboard of the nacelles being tapered. The wing has full-span leading edge slats and double-slotted flaps. The fuselage contours were also modified, and this protracted development meant that it was not until 1965 that first production deliveries to Aeroflot were able to begin as the An-14A (NATO codename Clod).

Six or seven passengers could be carried in the cabin plus one beside the pilot, and alternative versions were an executive variant seating five passengers, an all-cargo variant, an air ambulance with accommodation for six stretcher cases and a medical attendant, an aerial photography variant and a similar one for geological survey. An aerial agriculture version has a 220 Imp gallon chemical tank in the cabin and spraying bars under the wings and running down the wing bracing struts. An unusual feature is that passengers enter the cabin through clam-shell type rear doors forming the underside of the upswept rear fuselage. Several hundred An-14s have been built, mainly for Aeroflot use, and the type can also be operated on skis or floats.

Antonov An-22   USSR

Engines: Four 15,000shp Kuznetsov NK-12MA turboprops each driving two 4-blade contra-rotating propellers of 20ft 4in diameter
Span: 211ft 3½in
Length: 189ft 8in
Height: 41ft 1in
Wing area: 3,713.6sq ft
Weight: 251,327lb (empty equipped)
Max payload: 176,350lb
Max take-off weight: 551,156lb
Speed: 460mph (max)
422mph (max cruising)
Range: 3,107 miles with max payload
6,800 miles with max fuel

Completely unknown in the west when it first appeared at the Paris Salon Aeronautique on 16 June 1965, the Antonov An-22 Antei (or Antheus), also known by the NATO codename Cock, is one of the world's largest aircraft and Russia's nearest equivalent of the Lockheed C-5A Galaxy. The first of five prototypes of this heavy military and commercial freighter made its first flight on 27 February 1965. Two of these aircraft entered service with Aeroflot in 1967 on experimental cargo flights, and about 50 production An-22s have since gone into service with the Soviet state airline, primarily being used for special supply flights in remote and undeveloped parts of the country, especially ones involving the carriage of outsize loads such as large items of civil engineering equipment into short rough airfields. An-22s also serve as strategic freighters with units of the Air Transport Aviation (Voenno-transportnaya Aviatsiya) element of the Soviet Air Force; about 30 are believed to be in service. In October 1967 an An-22 set up 14 payload-to-height records, including reaching a height of 25,748ft with a load of 220,500lb; the take-off run for this record flight was reported to have been only just over 3,000ft.

The An-22 has a crew of five or six with a navigator's station in the nose, and just aft of the flight deck there is a cabin seating 28-29 passengers and separated from the main hold by a bulkhead. Rails in the roof of the hold carry four travelling gantries and there are two winches, used in conjunction with the gantries, each of which has a capacity of 5,500lb. There is a rear loading ramp, and when this is lowered, the large door forming the underside of the rear fuselage retracts upwards to permit the loading of large vehicles; the four gantries continue rearwards on the underside of this door. Loads such as bulldozers, snowploughs, missile-carrying tracked vehicles and missiles themselves can be accommodated. The main landing gear consists of three twin-wheel levered-suspension units in tandem retracting upwards into long fuselage side fairings to leave the hold clear. Twin fins and rudders are featured to keep the height to a reasonable level, and there is also the characteristic Antonov outer wing anhedral.

A projected 724-passenger version with a 45ft longer fuselage and twin decks was announced in 1966; the upper deck was to carry 423 passengers in six cabins and the lower deck 301 people in four cabins. The two decks, each of which was to have a bar and buffet, would have been linked by six

stairways; other features included a special saloon for mothers and children, TV and film shows in flight and no less than 12 cabin entrance doors. This version was not developed, but a mixed-traffic version carrying 66,000lb of freight and 350 passengers has been studied, and doubtless other possible civil variants have been considered. The An-22 has obvious possibilities as a troop carrier and for the air dropping of outsize military loads.

Antonov An-24   USSR

Photo: Somali Air Force An-26
Data: An-24V Series 2

Engines: Two 2,550ehp Ivchenko AI-24 Series 2 turboprops
Span: 95ft 9$\frac{1}{2}$in
Length: 77ft 2$\frac{1}{2}$in
Height: 27ft 3$\frac{1}{2}$in
Wing area: 807.1sq ft
Weight: 29,320lb (empty)
Max take-off weight: 46,300lb
Speed: 310mph at 19,700ft (max cruising)
280mph at 19,700ft (best range cruising)
Range: 341 miles with max payload
1,490 miles with max fuel

In the same category as the Fokker Friendship and Handley Page Herald, the Antonov An-24 was designed to replace piston-engined types, in particular the II-14, on Aeroflot's shorter haul domestic routes. Development started in 1958 and the An-24 (NATO codename Coke) was originally intended to carry 32-40 passengers, but when the prototype first flew in April 1960 it had been developed into a 44-seater. A second prototype and five pre-production aircraft followed, two of the latter being for static and fatigue testing, production aircraft differing externally from the prototype in having a ventral tail fin and lengthened engine nacelles with conical rear fairings, whereas on the prototype these extended only a little way past the wing trailing edge. Aeroflot began services with the An-24 between Moscow, Voronezh and Saratov in September 1963, and the type was soon deployed on a number of other domestic routes. The initial production 44-passenger An-24 was powered by two 2,550ehp Ivchenko AI-24 turboprops, and featured double-slotted Fowler flaps for operating into short, semi-prepared runways; it brought the

benefits of weather radar and pressurisation to many remoter parts of the Soviet Union served only by II-14s or Li-2s. Aeroflot's Ukrainian Territorial Directorate increased to 48 the number of seats in its early production An-24s in 1964, this variant leading to the 50-passenger An-24V as the next production version; in mixed passenger/cargo form this could carry 30 passengers in tip-up wall-mounted seats with freight and mail in a 494cu ft capacity forward hold additional to the rear baggage hold, while the all-cargo version had 1,391cu ft of cargo space. De Luxe and Saloon versions for VIP use were also produced.

In 1968 the An-24V was succeeded by the An-24V *Seriiny II* (Series II) which had an extended centre section chord with enlarged flaps, increasing the wing area from 779.9 to 807.1sq ft, and AI-24 *Seriiny II* (Series 2) turboprops with water injection. These could be replaced by the uprated 2,820ehp AI-24T engines for operations in adverse temperature/altitude conditions. The An-24T freighter is a version of the An-24V Series 2 with the rear passenger door deleted and replaced, not by the usual large cargo door in the fuselage side, but by an upward-hinging ventral freight door under the rear fuselage. Cargo is loaded by means of a 3,300lb capacity electric winch and moved along by a 9,920lb capacity electrically- or manually-operated conveyor in the cabin floor. The An-24RT is the same as the T but with a 1,984lb st Tumansky RU-19-300 auxiliary turbojet in the rear of the starboard nacelle for emergency thrust in the event of starboard engine failure and to provide compressed air for starting the main engines. The booster jet enables a full payload to be lifted out of limiting airfields up to 9,840ft above sea level and in temperatures up to ISA+30°C. The An-24RV is the same as the passenger An-24V, but with the same booster jet as in the RT. The An-24P is a special forest fire-fighting version able to

carry parachutists and fire-fighting equipment to a major fire; it was test flown in October 1971.

A development of the An-24RT for military and civil use, the An-26, production deliveries of which commenced in 1969, has a redesigned rear fuselage with a two-position loading door which can be lowered to form a conventional ramp for loading of vehicles, or swung down and forward under the fuselage to allow straight-in loading of freight at truck-bed height. The An-26 has 2,820ehp AI-24T turboprops and increased operating weights. Eight have been supplied to the Peruvian Air Force. Another specialist variant is the photo survey An-30 developed from the An-24RT for use by Aeroflot for mapping the remoter parts of the Soviet Union; flight tests began in the summer of 1973. The forward fuselage has been redesigned, with an extensively glazed nose with a navigator's position, and a raised flight deck giving an improved pilots' view and a larger navigator's compartment. There are four survey cameras mounted in the cabin, with five camera hatches provided, and the crew of seven operates a variety of specialist equipment.

Latest version is the An-32, similar to the An-26 but with almost twice the power, being fitted with two 5,180shp Ivchenko AI-20M turboprops for operation under extreme 'hot and high' conditions, such as 15,000ft high airfields in ISA+10°C conditions; the take-off weight is raised to 57,300lb. The engines are mounted overwing, and a TG-16M auxiliary power unit replaces the RU-19-300 booster jet, while the ventral fins are enlarged. Over 1,800 of the An-24 family have been built, more than 800 for Aeroflot, and the An-24 has become one of the most widely exported Russian airliners, having been supplied to Air Guinee, Air Mali, Balkan Bulgarian, CAAC of China, Cubana, CAAV of Vietnam, Civil Aviation Co (Laos), Egyptair and Misrair, Interflug, Syrian Arab Airlines, TAROM, Iraqi Airways, Lebanese Air Transport, LOT, Lina Congo and Mongolian Airlines.

Aviation Traders ATL-98 Carvair UK

Engines: Four 1,450bhp Pratt & Whitney R-2000-7M2 Twin Wasp 14-cylinder 2-row radials
Span: 117ft 6in
Length: 102ft 7in
Height: 29ft 10in
Wing area: 1,462sq ft
Weight: 41,365lb (empty equipped)
Capacity payload: 18,500lb (car ferry)
Max take-off weight: 73,800lb
Speed: 250mph (max)
207mph at 10,000ft (best economy cruising)
Range: 2,300 miles with max payload

Conceived by Mr Freddie Laker when he was managing director of Channel Air Bridge Ltd, the Carvair is a modification of the basic Douglas DC-4 airframe for vehicle ferry work aimed at meeting Mr Laker's requirements for an aircraft carrying five cars and 25 passengers; cheap to buy and cheaper to operate than the Bristol 170 Freighter, with a longer range. To achieve nose loading capability an entirely new forward fuselage 12ft longer than the original is built on to the existing DC-4, with a raised flight deck; a sideways-opening hydraulically-operated nose door 6ft 9in square gives access to a hold of 80ft 2in unobstructed length in an all-freight version, although with five cars on board 22 passengers are accommodated in the rear with a galley and toilet and up to 84 could be seated in an all-passenger interior. A DC-7 type fin and rudder is featured, but the rest of the airframe is a standard DC-4 with the same engines and systems. Design and conversion of the Carvair was undertaken by Aviation Traders (Engineering) of Southend-on-Sea, and the prototype made its first flight on 21 June 1961; the type began services with British United Air Ferries (as Channel Air Bridge had become) in 1962, and BUAF ordered 10.

The Carvair's combination of low first cost and large payload interested other airlines, and the type was supplied to Interocean Airways SA of Luxembourg (3), Aer Lingus (3), Aviaco of Spain (3), Ansett-ANA (2) and Compania Dominicana de Aviacion (2). Two of Interocean's Carvairs were sold to the French operator Cie Air Transport, which also acquired a third, while the three ex-Aer Lingus

aircraft, which had been used for vehicle ferry services and were later modified to carry up to eight racehorses, were sold to Eastern Provincial Airways of Canada in 1968. One was leased by BUAF to the Italian operator Alisud-Compagnia Aerea Meridionale — for four months in 1963 for a Naples-Palermo car ferry service. The Ansett Carvairs featured a new palletised loading system and a specially designed freight floor with four roller tracks along which up to seven 88in × 108in pallets could be slid. Aviation Traders also did design studies of Carvair-type conversions of the Douglas DC-6, DC-6A and DC-6B (the latter with Rolls-Royce Darts as well as piston engines) and the DC-7B; the latter was studied with the existing piston engines, with Allison 501 turboprops and with RDa14 Darts.

Avro 652A Anson

UK

Photo: Anson 1
Data: Anson 19 Series 2

Engines: Two 420hp (max take-off) Armstrong-Siddeley Cheetah 15 7-cylinder radials
Span: 57ft 6in
Length: 42ft 3in
Height: 13ft 10in
Wing area: 440sq ft
Weight: 7,525lb (empty)
10,400lb (loaded)
Speed: 182mph (max) at 5,000ft
168mph at 5,800ft (max cruising)
Range: 820 miles

The Anson trainer and light transport was a military version of the Avro 652 six-passenger monoplane, two of which were ordered by Imperial Airways in 1933, primarily for charter work and mail carrying. The Avro 652A Anson made its first flight on 23 March 1935, and the Avro 652 differed from the Anson in having a shorter undercarriage, smooth instead of 'helmeted' cowlings and three circular cabin windows. Powerplants were two Armstrong-Siddeley Cheetah VI radials, and construction was mixed, with a welded steel tube fuselage and wooden wings with fabric covering. Both Avro 652s were impressed into RAF service in 1941. In 1935 the initial order for the Anson 1 coastal reconnaissance version was placed, this featuring a dorsal turret, taller undercarriage, more powerful Cheetah IXs, modified fin and rudder and long 'glasshouse' cabin windows. When war came, the

Anson 1 went into large-scale production as a navigational, radio and armament trainer and was widely used on communications work. Many surplus Mk 1s were acquired after the war in Britain and other countries, especially by the small independents, air taxi and charter firms. They usually seated 6-8 passengers and a wide variety of cabin window arrangements appeared, ranging from the 'glasshouse' type to the windowless layout of Anson 1s used by the British independent Transair for newspaper delivery flights to the Continent. In Canada, too, and also in Mexico numbers of surplus Ansons went into service with airline and other operators, these being mostly Mk 5s, the version built by Federal Aircraft Ltd at Montreal with a new fuselage made by the Vidal process of moulded plastic parts and with 450hp Pratt & Whitney R-985-AN12B or -AN14B Wasp Juniors.

The Avro 19 postwar civil version was developed through the Ansons 10, 11 and 12, the Mk 11 being the first version to feature a raised cabin roof. One Anson 11 was used by Ekco Electronics to flight test and demonstrate a weather radar set fitted in the nose. The Avro 19 had Cheetah 15 engines driving Rotol variable-pitch airscrews, five oval cabin windows in place of the three square ones of the Mks 11 and 12, a new entrance door to a cabin usually seating nine passenters, and a 24-volt electrical system. The Avro 19 Series 1 and its RAF version, the Anson C19 Series 1, had the wooden wings and tailplane of earlier Ansons, but the Series 2 introduced in 1946 had a new metal wing and tailplane, the span being increased and the wing

outer panels more tapered; some civil and most of the RAF Series 1s were later converted to Series 2 standard. Avro 19s were also used for executive transport and navaid calibration as well as scheduled

and charter services. Anson production did not end until May 1952 when the 11,020th and last, a T21 navigational trainer, was delivered; of this total, 2,882 were built in Canada.

Avro 685 York

Photo: York I

Engines: Four 1,610hp (max take-off) Rolls-Royce Merlin 502 12-cylinder in-line engines
Span: 102ft 0in
Length: 78ft 6in
Height: 20ft 0in (tail down)
Wing area: 1,297sq ft
Weight: 39,460lb (empty)
Capacity payload: 20,000lb
Max take-off weight: 70,000lb
Speed: 210mph at 10,000ft (continuous cruising)
Range: 1,400 miles with max payload
2,700 miles with max fuel

Originally intended as an interim type to fill the gap until such time as postwar designs like the Avro Tudor would be ready for airline service, the Avro 685 York long outlived the type intended to replace it. Designed to Spec C1/42, the York featured the same wings, engines, undercarriage and tail unit of the Lancaster bomber married to a square-section fuselage of 8ft maximum internal width × 8ft maximum height on which the wings were mounted high. The prototype LV626, which first flew on 5 July 1942, at first had twin fins and rudders, as did the second prototype, the third, central fin being fitted to both later and being standard on the third prototype and production aircraft. The first prototype was later fitted with four Bristol Hercules radials to become the only York II. During the war York production for the RAF had to take second place to that of the Lancaster, and most of the few built before hostilities ended were VIP aircraft for Winston Churchill, Lord Mountbatten (C-in-C South-East Asia), Field Marshal Smuts and the Duke of Gloucester, who was Governor-General of Australia. The first Transport Command York squadron, No 511, was not fully equipped until 1945, but with the war's end production quickened and six RAF York squadrons took part in the Berlin airlift, as well as flying regular

services to the Far East and elsewhere. Five RAF Yorks had been diverted to BOAC in 1944 and were followed by 25 more in 1945-46 for use on BOAC's longer haul routes. Twelve more Yorks went to British South American Airways for its services to Brazil and Argentina and for certain routes in the Caribbean; the nine survivors were passed to BOAC when the latter took over BSAA on 30 July 1949. BOAC's Yorks were soon replaced as first-line equipment by Argonauts and Constellations, the last York scheduled service, between Nassau (Bahamas) and Santiago in Chile, being flown on 7 October 1950; the type remained in BOAC service for charter work for some years after.

Five Yorks were delivered to the Argentine airline FAMA — Flota Aerea Mercante Argentina — for its services from Buenos Aires and Rio to London, which they operated together with DC-4s, but after FAMA was taken over by Aerolineas Argentinas in May 1949 the Yorks were replaced by DC-6s. Three Yorks were delivered to the British independent Skyways Ltd and South African Airways used seven Yorks leased from BOAC for its 'Springbok' route from Johannesburg to London until they were replaced by DC-4s. BOAC and RAF Yorks were sold off mostly to the British independents such as Dan-Air, Eagle Aviation (later British Eagle), Scottish Aviation, Hunting Clan and Skyways, the latter being the largest operator, with 14 Yorks in its fleet in 1959; these were used for trooping and freight flights, freight doors being fitted in the rear fuselage. Yorks were also used by the Lebanese operators Air Liban, Middle East Airlines and Trans-Mediterranean Airways, by Persian Air Services, by Tropic Airways of South Africa, by the French Navy, which had two, and by the Canadian operators Pacific Western Airlines and Trans-Air. Avro had built 253 Yorks when production ended in 1948, and one more, serial FM400, was built by Victory Aircraft Ltd at Toronto, this differing from standard in not having a sloping cabin floor.

BAC One-Eleven

Photo: One-Eleven 475
Data: One-Eleven 500

Engines: Two 12,550lb st (max take-off) Rolls-Royce RSp4 Spey 512-14DW turbofans
Span: 93ft 6in
Length: 107ft 0in
Height: 24ft 6in
Wing area: 1,031sq ft
Basic operating weight: 54,582lb
Max payload: 26,418lb
Max take-off weight: 104,500lb
Speed: 541mph at 21,000ft (max cruising)
461mph at 25,000ft (best economy cruising)
Range: 1,480 miles with capacity payload
2,149 miles with max fuel

First of the short haul jets to fly, the One-Eleven was the first major civil programme undertaken by BAC — British Aircraft Corporation as a unified company — and was intended as a jet successor to the turboprop Viscount, similar in seating capacity and range, but cruising some 180mph faster than the Viscount 810. The One-Eleven had its origins in the Hunting H-107 small jet airliner project of 1956, a 48-seater with two rear-mounted engines and a T-tail, having a range of up to 1,000 miles. At first two Bristol Orpheus turbojets were the powerplants, but later Bristol Siddeley BS61 or BS75 turbofans were chosen, and in September 1958 the H-107 design was revised around these engines. With 7,000lb st BS61s, the H-107 would have had a span of 80ft, accommodation for 48-56 passengers and a take-off weight of 42,400lb. A mock-up of the project was built and during 1960, when Hunting Aircraft Ltd was acquired by BAC, which had been set up to merge Vickers, Bristol and English Electric, the H-107 became a joint effort between the Hunting and Vickers-Weybridge design teams. After initial airline reactions to the project had been obtained, it was enlarged somewhat to seat up to about 65 passengers five-abreast; the engines were changed to two Rolls-Royce Spey turbofans and the optimum range was about 600 miles. In this form the project became known as the BAC-111, or the One-Eleven, although the BAC-107 (formerly H-107) remained on offer to the airlines for a time after the go-ahead

had been given to the One-Eleven. This was made on the strength of an initial order by British United Airways for 10, announced on 9 May 1961, and the month before it had been decided to lay down a batch of 20 aircraft to enable the first deliveries to be made in the autumn of 1964.

The BUA order was followed in October 1961 by an important US order, from Braniff International Airways for six, plus six on option, and later by the local service carrier Mohawk Airlines; Braniff finally ordered 14 and Mohawk 17 of the initial production 200 series, while an even more important customer was American Airlines, one of the 'Big Four' US domestic trunk carriers, which in July 1963 ordered 15 plus 15 on option (later taken up) of the Series 400. By the time the prototype One-Eleven 200 first flew on 20 August 1963 a total of 60 had been ordered; the Series 200 now seated up to 79 passengers in an all-coach or economy interior, or 16 first-class or 49 tourist in a typical mixed layout. Gross weight was initially 73,500lb, later 78,500lb, and engines were 10,410lb st RSp3 Spey 506-14 turbofans. On 22 October 1963 the One-Eleven prototype crashed as the result of getting into a deep stall, and the resulting investigation and corrective action, which included the fitting of a stick-pusher, set the flight test programme back a little, although the lessons learnt were made available to other, rival manufacturers such as Douglas with the DC-9. British certification was finally achieved on 6 April 1965, and FAA Type Approval followed on 15 April; BUA inaugurated One-Eleven services on 9 April and Braniff began its first One-Eleven services on 25 April over a multi-stop route from Corpus Christi in Texas to Minneapolis/St Paul. Altogether 56 Series 200s were built, of which five went to government, executive and military customers. The Series 300 had uprated 11,400lb st RSp4 Spey 511-14 engines in 4in longer nacelles, extra fuel in a centre-section tank, a strengthened wing structure and undercarriage to cater for the higher gross weight of 87,000lb, and stronger wheel brakes. The Series 400 incorporated a number of features to meet FAA certification requirements but was otherwise the same as the 300, with identical engines and structural strengthening; it was at first restricted to a gross weight of 79,000lb to comply with the then

Above: *One-Eleven 521*

American upper weight limit of 80,000lb for two-crew operation, but when this limit was abolished it was re-certificated at the 300's higher gross weight of 87,000lb; as a result, the Series 300 was no longer separately identified as such. The first One-Eleven 401 flew on 13 July 1965 and this variant began services on American's short haul routes on 6 March 1966. Nine Series 300s and 69 Series 400s were built, several of the latter being supplied new to governments and corporations, while more ex-airline Series 400s have since been converted to executive transports. Stretched versions had been studied by BAC since before the type first flew, but it was not until BEA decided to order the Series 500 — its order for 18, with six on option, was announced on 27 January 1967 — that the go-ahead for this, the first stretched version, was given, and by this time the DC-9 Series 30 and Boeing 737 were competing powerfully for the available customers.

The Series 500 has a 13ft 6in longer fuselage seating up to 97 passengers initially, or 119 when higher weights were certificated, a 5ft increase in wing span, and uprated 12,000lb st RSp4 Spey 512-14 engines. BAC's own Series 400 demonstrator was converted to Series 500 standard and first flew in this form on 30 June 1967, initially with Spey 511-14 engines. BEA began One-Eleven 510 services on 18 November 1968, initially from Manchester, the 510s later being put on to the German internal routes serving Berlin. Gross weight was 92,483lb at first, but went up to 99,650lb when 12,550lb st RSp4 Spey 512-14DW engines with water injection were fitted, or up to 104,500lb when extra tankage was installed in the rear freight hold. Eighty Series 500s had been ordered by the end of 1977, this version being widely used for charter and IT flights.

The One-Eleven 475 is a 'hot and high' version with the Series 500's long-span wings and Spey 512-14DW engines with the original fuselage length; low pressure tyres are featured. The Series 400/500 development aircraft was converted back to have the short fuselage and first flew as the 475 prototype on 27 August 1970. The first 475 delivery, to Faucett of Peru, was made in July 1971 and only nine of this version have so far been ordered, by Faucett, Air Pacific, Air Malawi and the Sultan of Oman's Air Force. The latter has three with a 10ft 0in × 6ft 1in upward-opening forward freight door, one of a number of new features currently offered to One-Eleven operators. These include 'hush kits' to reduce engine noise, a 'wide body look' for cabin interiors, and auxiliary fuel systems for longer range executive and other operations. About 80 One-Elevens are eventually to be built in Rumania, and new versions are the Series 670 for Japanese domestic operators and the Series 700 120/130-seaters.

Beechcraft Super H18   USA

Photo: G-18S
Data: Super H18

Engines: Two 450hp Pratt & Whitney R-985-AN14B Wasp Junior 9-cylinder radials
Span: 49ft 8in
Length: 35ft 2½in
Height: 9ft 4in
Wing area: 360.7sq ft
Weight: 5,680lb (empty)
Max take-off weight: 9,900lb
Speed: 236mph (max) at 4,500ft
220mph at 10,000ft (max cruising)
Range: 1,530 miles with max fuel

The Beech Model 18 7-9 passenger light transport and trainer had one of the longest production runs of any aircraft, spanning 32 years from 1937, US Type Approval being received on 4 March that year, to 1969; more than 9,000 were built of which nearly 2,000 were postwar commercial models and 5,204 military versions delivered during the war. The prototype Model 18 made its first flight on 20 January 1937, prewar Models being the 18, A18 and B18. Early in 1940 the first C-45 for the US Army Air Corps was delivered, and C-45/UC-45 variants up to TC-45J were produced, the C-45G and H being converted from T-7 and T-11 Kansan trainers, the RC-45H and TC-45H being

photographic and training versions while the RC-45J and TC-45J were similar models for the US Navy. The latter's JRB-1s to -4s were utility transports; the SNB-1 trainer corresponded to the T-11 Kansan while the SNB-2 was a version of the AT-7 navigational trainer. The AT-7/T-7 was based on the commercial B-18S, whereas the AT-11/T-11 featured an extended transparent nose with a bombaimer's position, and a small weapons bay. The F-2 was a photo survey version for the USAAF. Model 18s were supplied to many foreign air forces during and after the war, being used by the RAF and Royal Navy as the Expediter I and II, and by the mid-1960s about 30 foreign air forces were using the basic C-45. Postwar civil versions were the C18 and D18, of which 1,030 were built, the refined E18 Super 18 introduced in 1954, the G18 which appeared late in 1959 and the last production version, the Super H18, which has a new main undercarriage with 'half fork' instead of 'full fork' legs, a redesigned exhaust system and lightweight propellers. The Super-Liner is a high density 10-passenger version of the Super-H18.

From 1963 a Volpar-designed nosewheel undercarriage has been an optional feature, and other 'extras' include Bendix or RCA weather radar and a standby ATO rocket installation. A few Beech 18s have also been fitted with twin floats. Several modernised versions of the basic Model 18 airframe, sometimes extensively remanufactured, have been produced. The Dumod I (formerly Infinité I) is a 9-passenger version with Volpar nosewheel undercarriage, high performance wing tips and glass-fibre control surfaces, larger windows, airstairs and an enlarged flight deck. The Dumod Liner (formerly Infinité II) is similar, but has a 6ft 3in longer forward fuselage seating up to 15 people and an additional central fin with dorsal and ventral fins. The Volpar/Beech 18 has a nosewheel undercarriage in which the main wheels completely retract, and a longer nose. The Volpar Super Turbo 18 is similar, but with 575shp Garrett AiResearch TPE331-25 turboprops driving Hartzell 3-blade reversible props, a new wing leading edge giving greater sweep-back and smaller wing tips. The Volpar Turboliner has a lengthened fuselage seating up to 15 passengers and is otherwise similar to the Turbo 18. The Pacific Airmotive Tradewind is a version with nosewheel undercarriage, picture windows and a single fin and rudder, the Turbo Tradewind being similar but with PT6A-6 turboprops, while the Hamilton Westwind II and Westwind III are versions with Pratt & Whitney PT6A turboprops. The Rausch Star 250 is yet another version of the Model 18, with a backwards-retracting nosewheel and raised cabin roof.

Beechcraft B55 Baron   USA

Data: Baron 58

Engines: Two 285hp Continental IO-520-C
6-cylinder horizontally-opposed air-cooled engines
Span: 37ft 10in
Length: 29ft 10in
Height: 9ft 6in
Wing area: 199.2sq ft
Weight: 3,268lb (empty equipped)
5,400lb (max gross)
Speed: 230mph (max cruising)
Range: 1,212 miles (max)

Widely used as a private and executive aircraft, the Baron also serves with third-level airlines and air taxi operators. Basically a more powerful version of the Beech Model 95 Travel Air, the Baron prototype first flew on 29 February 1960 with first production deliveries of the Model 55 beginning in November that year. This version was a 4-5 seater, but the improved Model A55, deliveries of which began in January 1962, could feature an optional six-seat cabin arrangement. The Model B55, introduced at the begining of 1964, featured a longer nose to increase baggage compartment size and space for

radio equipment; gross weight was increased from 4,880lb to 5,100lb. The Baron 58 features an enlarged cabin with a fourth window on each side and seating six people, four of them in club-type seats, a gross weight raised to 5,400lb and 285hp. Continental 10-520-C engines replacing the 260hp Continental 10-470-L powerplants of earlier models; the nose is further lengthened to provide more baggage space and the nosewheel is moved forward. The airscrew spinners are extended and the cowlings redesigned.

Meanwhile, the development of a turboprop version of the Baron was undertaken in France by SFERMA, who fitted a Beech Travel Air with Turboméca Astazous as the Turbo Travel Air, this aircraft first flying on 12 July 1960. It was later fitted with new and enlarged tail surfaces similar to the Baron's, and was then renamed Marquis. Beech supplied a number of A55 Baron airframes to SFERMA for conversion to Marquis standard, these being re-engined with two 450shp Turboméca Astazou IIJ turboprops and fitted with the enlarged vertical tail surfaces of higher aspect ratio, and other changes; the cabin seated 5-6 people. The first

Marquis conversion from an A55 Baron was completed in May 1961 and the first production delivery, to the German operator Travelair GmbH, followed on 10 July 1962. Altogether 33 Marquis conversions were produced, and the second production Marquis was fitted for a time with 600shp Astazou Xs. The C55 Baron introduced in August 1965 had Continental 10-520-C engines, increased tailplane span and an extended nose baggage compartment, the D55 was similar with minor improvements and the Model E55, introduced late in 1969, has an improved interior and systems accessory refinements. The US Army ordered 65 of an instrument trainer version of the B55 which became the T-42A Cochise, and five more T-42As were supplied to the Turkish Army. The Baron 58P is a pressurised version of the Model 58 that first flew in August 1973 and has 310hp Continental TSIO-520-L engines; deliveries began late in 1974. The Model 58TC is similar to the 58P with the same turbocharged engines but unpressurised, and with various detail differences; deliveries began in June 1976. Some 3,800 Barons of all versions had been delivered by mid-1976.

Beechcraft Queen Air

USA

Data: B80 Queen Airliner

Engines: Two 380hp Lycoming IGSO-540-AID 6-cylinder horizontally-opposed air-cooled engines
Span: 50ft 3in
Length: 35ft 6in
Height: 14ft $2\frac{1}{2}$in
Wing area: 293.9sq ft
Weight: 5,277lb (empty equipped)
Max take-off weight: 8,800lb
Speed: 248mph (max) at 11,500ft
225mph at 15,000ft (cruising 70% power)
Range: 1,517 miles with max fuel (45% power)

The Queen Air 65 was developed as a commercial version of the US Army's U-8F Seminole

6-passenger utility transport, itself a development of the U-8D, equivalent to the Model F50 Twin Bonanza, with a larger, redesigned fuselage giving more cabin space. The US Army ordered 68 U-8Fs and Japan's Maritime Self-Defence Force used the Queen Air 65 as a command transport and navigational trainer. The Queen Air 65 prototype first flew on 28 August 1958 and the initial production version with 340hp Lycoming IGSO-480-A1B6 engines seated seven passengers The type proved to be more popular at first for company and executive use, later being used by commuter airlines and air taxi operators. Its first use in the third-level/commuter role was in 1964 when four Queen Air 80s were delivered to Trans-Australia Airlines for routes in Tasmania. The Queen Air 65 had the

straight fin and rudder of the U-8F and Twin Bonanza, but the 6-9 seat Model 65-80, or Queen Air 80, which first flew on 22 June 1961, had swept vertical tail surfaces and more powerful Lycoming IGSO-540-A1A engines. This was followed in January 1964 by the Queen Air A80 with wing span increased by 5ft to 50ft 10½in, the gross weight increased to 8,500lb, new interior styling, increased fuel capacity and a redesigned nose compartment with more radio space. This was followed by the Queen Air 70, the improved Model B80 and the Queen Airliner B80, a version for commuter and third-level airlines with high-density seating for up to nine passengers. The B80 usually seats up to seven passengers for airline use, or fewer in the executive version. Over 900 Queen Airs and Queen Airliners had been built by 1977 and Queen Airs had been supplied to the air forces of Venezuela and Uruguay.

Beechcraft B99 USA

Photo and Data: B99A

Engines: Two 715eshp Pratt & Whitney PT6A-27 turboprops
Span: 45ft 10½in
Length: 44ft 6¾in
Height: 14ft 4in
Wing area: 279.9sq ft
Weight: 5,872lb (empty equipped)
Max take-off weight: 10,900lb
Speed: 283mph at 8,000ft (max cruising)
Range: 530 miles with max payload
838 miles with max fuel

The Beech 99 was developed from the Queen Air during 1965 for the commuter and third-level airlines, who needed an aircraft with more seating capacity than the executive light twins they were then using extensively. The 99 had the same wings as the Queen Air but the fuselage was lengthened to provide seating for up to 15 passengers in single seats each side of a single aisle, airstairs being fitted in the main cabin door. A long-fuselage prototype of the Queen Air was flown in December 1965 and, with 550shp Pratt & Whitney PT6A-20 turboprops fitted the following July, this became the prototype of the Beech 99, FAA Type Approval being obtained

on 2 May 1968. First delivery of a fully certificated aircraft was made the same day to Commuter Airlines of Chicago, and initial production aircraft had the PT6A-20 engines, while the Model 99A featured two 680shp PT6A-27s.

A wide cargo door adjacent to the cabin entrance door could be fitted for use in the mixed traffic or all-freight role. The lack of baggage space in the 99 and 99A, of which 148 were built, was overcome in the Model B99 which introduced an external baggage pannier under the fuselage, with a capacity of 44cu ft, supplementing the forward and rear baggage compartments; the B99 features various other minor changes. Beech 99s are widely used by commuter airlines in the United States, and small numbers are used by similar operators in France, Belgium and South Africa.

Boeing 307 Stratoliner

USA

Photo and Data: Model SA-307B-1

Engines: Four 1,200bhp Wright GR-1820-97 Cyclone radials
Span: 107ft 3in
Length: 74ft 4in
Height: 20ft 9½in
Wing area: 1,420sq ft
Weight: 34,156lb (empty)
54,000lb (max gross)
Speed: 228mph (max)
200mph at 10,000ft (cruising)
Range: 1,100 miles

Only 10 Boeing Model 307 Stratoliners were built because of the war and the demands of B-17 production, and although it earned its place in history as the first airliner to feature cabin pressurisation most of its active service life was spent operating in unpressurised form. In mid-1936 Pan American and TWA started discussions with Boeing about a possible airliner development of the B-17 Flying Fortress, which had flown the previous year, and the resulting Boeing 307 married a large-diameter circular section fuselage to the wings, engines, undercarriage and tail of the B-17C; cabin pressure differential was a modest 2½lb/sq in to give a cabin altitude of 8,000ft when flying at 14,700ft. Pan Am ordered four Boeing 307s and TWA five 307Bs, which differed from the earlier model in having slotted instead of split flaps, a maximum take-off weight raised by 3,000lb to 45,000lb and more powerful Wright R-1820-G105A Cyclones. The S-307 prototype first flew on 31 December 1938; it got into a spin and crashed on 18 March 1939, and addition of a dorsal

fin was one of several modifications made as a result. The third production Stratoliner was built for Howard Hughes, who planned a round-the-world flight in it; it was a Model SB-307B with four 1,600bhp Wright R-2600 Cyclones, but the war put an end to the projected globe-girdling flight and the standard powerplants were later fitted to this 307. Pan Am began Stratoliner services in the summer of 1940 from Miami down through the Caribbean to Belem in Brazil, but it was on US domestic routes with TWA that the 307 made its greatest impact. TWA began Stratoliner services on 8 July 1940 on the New York-Los Angeles route via Chicago, Kansas City and Albuquerque, and the 307s gave TWA an immediate competitive lead on this plum route over American Airlines.

In December 1941 TWA sold its 307s to the US government, and they operated overseas services for USAAF Air Transport Command under the designation C-75, flying over 7½ million miles and more than 3,000 ocean crossings in USAAF service and carrying many Allied VIPs. In July 1944 the C-75s were released from military service and underwent complete refurbishing by Boeing before returning to TWA. They were refitted with B-17G wings, undercarriages, engines and the larger span B-17G tailplanes, the gross weight went up to 54,000lb, passenger seating was increased from 33 to 38 and the cabin pressurisation was removed; in this form they were redesignated Model SA-307B-1. They concentrated largely on TWA's shorter routes between New York and the midwest, and in April 1951 all five were sold to the French independent Aigle Azur. The latter used them for its routes from Paris to French West and Equatorial Africa, to

Madagascar and to Saigon and Hanoi until it was taken over by UAT in 1955. Its Saigon-based affiliate Aigle Azur Extrême Orient continued as a seperate entity, operating the 307s for its own charters and, from 1964, for a quasi-military airline known as CIC — Cie Internationale de Transports Civils Aériens. This was set up to fly regular services between

Saigon and Hanoi for the International Control Commission and to provide diplomatic and government passengers with air transport between the two warring halves of Vietnam, and also to Laos and Cambodia; the 307s kept on flying these services, sometimes in decidedly hazardous conditions, until CIC closed down in mid-1974.

Boeing 377 Stratocruiser

Photo: Model 377-10-30

Engines: Four 3,500bhp (max take-off) Pratt & Whitney R-4360-TSB3-G Wasp Major 28-cylinder 4-row radials
Span: 141ft 3in
Length: 110ft 4in
Height: 38ft 3in
Wing area: 1,769sq ft
Weight: 83,500lb (empty)
Capacity payload: 23,640lb
Max take-off weight: 145,800lb
Speed: 375mph (max) at 25,000ft
340mph at 25,000ft (max cruising)
Range: 2,600 miles with 23,000lb payload
4,400 miles with max fuel

The Stratocruiser had its genesis in a suggestion made by Boeing for a transport version of the B-29 Superfortress bomber, the C-97, featuring B-29 wings, engines, undercarriage and tail unit married to a new 'double bubble' fuselage in which the lower half was the same width as the B-29's and the upper half of 11ft maximum diameter, resulting in twice the volume of the B-29 fuselage. The resulting two-deck layout enabled large doors and a ramp to be fitted under the rear fuselage for loading vehicles or, in the Stratocruiser, a lounge and cocktail bar installed aft with a spiral staircase leading to the upper deck, which made the aircraft a great favourite with passengers. The USAAF ordered three XC-97s

in January 1942 and one of these, on 9 January 1945, set a new transcontinental record by flying from Seattle to Washington, DC, in 6hr 3min at an average speed of 383mph and carrying a payload of 10 tons. The XC-97s and YC-97 freighters had the Wright R-3350-23 Duplex Cyclones of the B-29, whereas the C-97A Stratofreighter, of which 50 were built, had the wings, undercarriage, tail unit with folding fin and rudder and engines — Pratt & Whitney R-4360-27 Wasp Majors — of the B-50 Superfortress. The Stratocruiser was the airliner version of the C-97A, and its initial trials were conducted with the military XC-97. In all, 56 were built: for Pan American, American Overseas Airlines (AOA), Northwest Orient Airlines, United Airlines, SAS and BOAC, the different Model numbers indicating the various cabin interiors. Pan Am's 22 Model 377-10-26s seated 61 passengers on the main deck by day or 27 by night in single and double berths plus 25 more in seats. Pan Am began first class 'President' services with the Stratocruiser over the North Atlantic on 3 June 1949. AOA's Model 377-10-29s seated 60 by day or 45 in double and single berths plus 25 more in seats; the eight AOA aircraft joined the Pan Am fleet after the airline was acquired by Pan Am in September 1950. Northwest Orient's 10 377-10-30s seated 61 passengers by day or 29 by night on routes to Tokyo, Manila and Honolulu while United's six 377-10-34s seated 55 people and entered service on the Hawaii vacation route. The four 377-10-28s ordered by SAS were

taken over by BOAC before delivery to join the six 377-10-32s ordered by the Corporation, which also acquired the six United Stratocruisers and one from Pan Am in 1954 when more aircraft were needed after the Comet 1 accidents. BOAC's 377s operated services to London for West African Airways Corporation, and also for Ghana Airways and Nigeria Airways when these airlines started. Fourteen of BOAC's 377s were sold through Boeing to the US supplemental Transocean Airlines, which went out of business in 1960 before it could start operating them. Pan Am later had 10 of its 377s modified to Super Stratocruiser standard for the North Atlantic routes with extra wing tankage and redesigned turbo-superchargers giving an extra 50hp for each

engine; weather radar in a KC-97G type nose radome was also fitted to all Pan Am 377s. One ex-Pan Am Stratocruiser was used by the Ecuadorean operator Linea Internacional Aerea SA during 1961 for services between Guayaquil and Quito, while the Venezuelan carrier RANSA used six Stratocruisers for freighting from 1961. Five more were acquired by Israel Aircraft Industries for conversion into paratroop transports, with rear loading cargo doors and twin aft jump doors, the first of these conversions being completed in 1964. Five more were later acquired for the Israeli Air Force (Heyl Ha'Avir) two of them being fitted as tankers for in-flight refuelling.

Boeing 707   USA

Photo: 707-344
Data: 707-320C

Engines: Four 17,000lb st (max take-off) Pratt & Whitney JT3D-1 or 18,000lb st JT3D-3 or -3B or 19,000lb st JT3D-7 turbofans
Span: 145ft 8$\frac{1}{2}$in
Length: 152ft 11in
Height: 42ft 5$\frac{1}{2}$in
Wing area: 3,050sq ft
Basic operating weight: up to 146,000lb
Max payload: 84,000lb (passengers)
91,390lb (cargo)
Max take-off weight: 333,600lb
Speed: 600mph at 25,000ft (max cruising)
550mph (best economy cruising)
Range: 4,300 miles with max payload
7,475 miles with max fuel

The first US commercial jet airliner, the Boeing 707 has now been in production for just over 20 years, longer than any other jet in this class, and continues to sell slowly but steadily, nearly 800 having been ordered by the end of 1978. Boeing had been studying future turboprop and turbojet-powered transports to succeed the KC-97 and Stratocruiser eventually since before 1950, various studies being made under the designations Model 367 and 473, and by the beginning of 1952 one of these, the Model 367-80, had been chosen for further development, this having the now familiar

configuration of swept-back wings and tail surfaces and four turbojet engines in individual underwing pods. On 20 May 1952 Boeing decided to build a prototype of the Model 367-80 as a private venture, and this made its first flight at Renton, near Seattle, on 15 July 1954. Also known as the Model 707-80, the Dash Eighty, as it was to become popularly known, served as the 707 prototype and was used to demonstrate both the civil and military potentialities of the basic design to airlines and the USAF. The Dash Eighty was slightly smaller and considerably lighter than the production 707-120, with a gross weight of 160,000lb initially, four 9,500lb st Pratt & Whitney JT3P turbojets and a fuselage length of 119ft 6in. It was later fitted with several different types of engine that powered forthcoming versions of the 707, such as the JT3C-1, JT3C-4 and JT4 turbojets, JT3D-1 turbofans (with which it was designated 367-80B) and an aft-mounted JT8D-1 for the 727. It was also used to test various technical features that Boeing was investigating for the 707 and other transport projects: these included boundary layer control systems, blown flaps, the 727's leading edge flaps and slats and a soft-field landing gear. But first of all it had a flight refuelling boom for demonstration to the USAF, and the latter placed an initial order for for 88 tanker/transport versions, known as the KC-135A (Boeing Model 717), on 1 September 1954. The KC-135A Stratotanker was similar to the 707-120 but had a smaller diameter fuselage in which 80 passengers or

Above: *B707-320C of Pelican Air Cargo.*

some 50,000lb of cargo could be carried. No less than 732 KC-135As were eventually built, the last one coming off the line in December 1964, and from these a prolific family of C-135 variants was developed, some turbofan-powered, including EC-135 command posts, RC-135s for photo mapping, electronic intelligence gathering and countermeasures, WC-135s for weather reconnaissance and others used for such special jobs as nuclear blast detection.

Without the big military orders, a civil 707 programme would not have been possible, for Boeing lost money on 707s ordered in the early years, and did not break even on its jet transports until 1964, when about 1,000 707s, KC-135s and 720s had been built. Pan American had placed its historic order for 20 Boeing 707s and 20 DC-8s on 13 October 1955, and this set off what came to be known as the big jet buying spree by leading airlines. Boeing offered the initial production 707-120 in alternative long-body and short-body versions, with fuselage lengths of 144ft 6in or 134ft 6in, only one airline, Qantas, choosing the latter (the 707-138). The 707-120's fuselage width had been increased by 4in over the Dash Eighty's to allow six-abreast seating, and up to 181 passengers could be accommodated in a one-class high density layout. Engines were 13,500lb st Pratt & Whitney JT3C-6 turbojets, fuel capacity was up to 13,478 US gallons, and gross weight was 257,000lb. The first production aircraft, a 707-121 for Pan Am, flew on 20 December 1957 and FAA Type Approval was received on 23 September 1958. Pan Am inaugurated 707 services over the North Atlantic on 26 October between New York and London, although the -120 did not have the range for non-stop operation over this route at all times. First US domestic operator of the 707 was National Airlines, which opened New York-Miami services with 707-121s leased from Pan Am on 10 December 1958, and the first transcontinental services, from New York to Los Angeles by American Airlines, started on 25 January 1959. Altogether 60 707-120s were built. To provide improved take-off performance, the

basic -120 was fitted with 15,800lb st Pratt & Whitney JT4A-3 or JT4A-5 engines to produce the 707-220, which had a gross weight of 247,000lb. Only five of these were built, for Braniff International (707-227), the first one flying on 11 June 1959; Braniff began domestic jet services with these on 20 December and flights to South America on 1 April 1960.

The first true long range version was the 707-320 Intercontinental, which featured an increase in wing span by 11ft 7in to 142ft 5in and more wing area, an 8ft longer fuselage seating up to 189 passengers, fuel capacity increased to 23,855 US gallons and higher weights, the gross weight going up to 312,000lb and finally to 316,000lb. Engines were JT4A-3 or -5 turbojets, with the 16,800lb st JT4A-9 and -10 and 17,500lb st JT4A-11 and -12 later becoming available. The first 707-320, which was the 16th production 707, first flew on 11 January 1959 and FAA Type Approval was received on 15 July, Pan Am beginning -320 services on 26 August. Altogether 69 707-320s were built and the next version, the 707-420, first ordered by BOAC, was the same as the -320 but with 16,500lb st Rolls-Royce RCo10 Conway 505 by-pass engines. First flown on 20 May 1959, the -420 in the process of gaining British certification introduced the 35in taller fin and, the ventral underfin which were soon applied to all 707 variants, as well as improvements to the flying controls for better handling qualities. The -420 did not receive British certification until 27 April 1960, BOAC inaugurating services in May. The 17,500lb st RCo12 Conway 508 was later fitted, and gross weight went up to 316,000lb. Air-India, Lufthansa, El Al and Varig also ordered -420s, a total of 37 being built. It was with the turbofan that the 707 really came into its own, since this engine promised greater power and lower specific fuel consumption, enabling very long stage lengths to be flown; a front fan version of the JT3C was developed as the 17,000lb st JT3D-1, this being fitted to the

707-320 and -120 to produce the 707-320B and - 120B. The first 707-120B flew on 22 June 1960, and this variant also featured, as well as the new engines, the inner wing leading edge 'glove' and leading edge flaps of the Boeing 720 for higher cruising speeds, and the taller fin and ventral underfin first flown on the 707-420. American Airlines began -120B services on 12 March 1961, and 78 of this version were built in all; several other airlines, such as Qantas and Pan Am, had their -120s converted to -120B standard, and the 18,000lb st JT3D-3 or -3B turbofans were later fitted. The 707-320B had new low drag wing tips which increased the span by 3ft $3\frac{1}{2}$in, slotted leading edge flaps and improved trailing edge flaps, but the -120B's inner wing 'glove' and ventral underfin were not featured. JT3D-3, -3B or -7 engines could also be fitted in place of the earlier JT3D-1s, and the gross weight went up to 327,000lb, with later structural provision for operating at up to 335,000lb. The first -320B flew on 31 January 1962, FAA Type Approval was received on 31 May and Pan Am operated the first -320B services in June.

Altogether 182 -320Bs were built, and the 707-320C is now the only version in production. This has a 7ft 7in × 11ft 2in cargo door forward, a strengthened freight floor and a Boeing-developed cargo loading system using pallets or containers. Up to 202 passengers can be carried, or 91,390lb of cargo or varying amounts of cargo and passengers together. The -320C first flew on 19 February 1963, received FAA Type Approval on 30 April and began services with Pan Am that June. The same choice of JT3D variants as for the -320B is available. Some -320Cs, like those of American Airlines, operate as pure freighters with the cabin windows blanked off, 707-323CF being the unofficial designation for American's all-freight versions and 707-323CC denotes the convertible ones. By late 1978 a total of 335 707-320Cs had been ordered, and over 900 of all 707 and 720 variants had been sold, while production of KC-135A and C-135 military variants and the four VC-137 Presidential and VIP transports totals 836. Next version of the civil 707 is to be the 707-700, similar to the -320B but with 22,000lb st CFM56-1B turbofans.

Boeing 720   USA

Data: 720B

Engines: Four 17,000lb st (max take-off) Pratt & Whitney JT3D-1 or 18,000lb st (max take-off) JT3D-3 turbofans
Span: 130ft 10in
Length: 136ft 9in
Height: 41ft 7in
Wing area: 2,521sq ft
Basic operating weight: 115,000lb
Max payload: 41,000lb
Max take-off weight: 234,000lb
Speed: 627mph (max)
608mph at 25,000ft (max cruising)
Range: 4,110 miles with max payload
6,450 miles with max fuel

To complement the 707 series on long haul routes, and in particular to meet a possible order from United, which had been considering buying a

developed Convair 880, Boeing developed a short-to-medium range version of the 707-120 designed to operate over stage lengths of up to 1,500 miles. Announced in July 1957 as the Model 717 (the type number used for the military KC-135), and before that designated 707-020, the Boeing 720, as it came to be known, was very similar in external dimensions to the short-body 707-120, with a fuselage length 1ft 8in longer than the latter. Major weight saving was made possible by reducing the fuel capacity initially to 11,835 US gallons (about half the tankage of a 707-320), this giving improved runway performance; the structure was lightened by using thinner skin gauges in many areas and lighter-weight undercarriage forgings. The engines, 12,000lb st Pratt & Whitney JT3C-7s, were also lighter than those in the 707-120 and JT3C-12s of the same thrust could also be fitted. Maximum take-off weight was initially 202,000lb, and was eventually approved at up to 229,000lb. To meet

competition from the Convair 990 and raise the cruise Mach number from 0.88 to 0.90 an inner wing 'glove' extending the leading edge forward between the fuselage and inner engine pylons was featured, this reducing the thickness/chord ratio of the inner wing. At the same time three 'lift booster' wing leading edge flaps were added on each side to improve take-off and landing performance. The first 720, built on production jigs, made its first flight on 23 November 1959 and FAA Type Approval was received on 30 June 1960.

The first 720 services were flown by United on 5 July between Chicago, Denver and Los Angeles and altogether 65 Boeing 720s were built, other customers being American (which called its 720s 707-023s), Aerlinte Eireann, Braniff International and Pacific Northern; the FAA also bought one. Many 720s were later converted to 720B standards with turbofans, and up to 149 passengers could be carried initially, approval being given later for the carriage of up to 165. The 720 and 720B both featured the taller fin and rudder and ventral fin first introduced on the 707-420. The 720B had 17,000lb st JT3D-1 turbofans, increased fuel capacity and a maximum gross weight of 234,000lb. More powerful JT3D-3s or JT3D-7s could also be fitted. The first 720B flew on 6 October 1960 and received FAA certification on 3 March 1961. Altogether 89 720Bs were built in addition to the 720s converted to Bs, and this version was popular with overseas airlines such as Pakistan International, Ethiopian, Avianca and Lufthansa who were just starting jet operations or who needed a jet for routes where traffic was not heavy enough for the bigger 707s. Its seating capacity, fuel economy and excellent reserves of power also made used examples of the 720B popular with charter and inclusive tour operators such as Maersk Air, Monarch Airlines and Trans European Airways. About 100 720s and 720Bs are in service in late 1978 with 31 airlines; a few are used by US travel clubs and one was refurbished as a VIP transport for the late General Chiang Kai-Shek.

USA

Boeing 727

Photo: 727-251
Data: Advanced 727-200

Engines: Three 15,500lb st Pratt & Whitney JT8D-15 or 16,000lb st JT8D-17 or 16,400lb st JT8D-17R turbofans
Span: 108ft 0in
Length: 153ft 2in
Height: 34ft 0in
Wing area: 1,700sq ft
Operating Weight: 100,000lb (empty)
Max payload: 42,800lb
Max take-off weight: 207,500lb
Speed: 599mph at 24,700ft (max cruising) 570mph at 30,000ft (best economy cruising)
Range: over 2,800 miles with max payload

With over 1,600 ordered to date, the Boeing 727 retains its position as the world's best-selling turbine-powered airliner, and a few years ago overtook the Douglas DC-3 as the world's most widely used airliner; it was the first transport aircraft ever to reach 1,000 orders in commercial form alone, without the benefit of military orders, the 1,000th 727 delivered to Delta Air Lines on 4 January 1974 — just four weeks short of 10 years after Eastern operated the first 727 scheduled services. Design studies of the medium-to-short haul jet that eventually was to materialise as the 727 had begun as early as February 1956, more than two years before the 707 entered service, and from the start the 727 was intended to be a real short-field aeroplane, capable of operating into the smaller US airports like New York's La Guardia and Chicago's Midway. A second major design objective was the achievement of maximum commonality with the 707, and to this end the 727 was given the same upper fuselage cross-section as the 707 and 720, and a cabin floor of identical width; thereby permitting the same six-abreast seating and a similar flight deck, as well as the use of many parts and systems of the bigger Boeings. Altogether no fewer than 150 design studies were analysed in detail and 68 of these were put through wind-tunnel testing before the final 727 layout was selected, the balance of customer preference favouring a tri-jet configuration similar to that of the de Havilland DH121. The design was finalised by 18 September 1959 except for the final choice of powerplant; for almost another year the favoured engine was the 12,750lb st Allison ARB963, a proposed Allison-built version of the RB163 Spey, but the final choice

was the new 14,000lb st Pratt & Whitney JT8D-1 turbofan, a derivative of the military J52.

The go-ahead for the 727 programme was announced on 5 December 1960 when Eastern and United revealed the first orders, for 40 aircraft each. To achieve an exceptional short-field performance and to operate from 5,000ft runways, a high-lift system of some complexity was necessary, this consisting of three Krueger leading edge flaps on the inner wing and four leading edge slats on the middle and outer portions plus triple-slotted trailing edge flaps, with inboard (high-speed) and outboard (low-speed) ailerons operating in conjunction with flight and ground spoilers. The basic 727-100, as it was now known, could accommodate up to 131 passengers and operate over stage lengths of up to 1,700 miles, and Boeing was able to offer this version with three different gross weights, of 142,000lb, 152,000lb and 160,000lb. The first 727, for United, made its first flight on 9 February 1963 and was followed by a second, a Boeing-owned demonstrator, on 12 March and two static test airframes. FAA Type Approval was obtained on 24 December 1963 and Eastern flew the first 727 scheduled service, from Miami to Washington and Philadelphia, on 1 February 1964. United began 727 services five days later and Lufthansa, the first non-US customer, on 16 April. From 1967 the 14,000lb st JT8D-7 engine could be fitted to 727-100s, and later the 14,500lb st JT8D-9 became available. In July 1964 the 727-100C convertible passenger/cargo version was revealed, this having the same large cargo door in the port side (measuring 11ft 2in × 7ft 2in) as the 707-320C, enabling the same cargo pallets and handling system as in the -320C to be used. The floor was strengthened and the undercarriage 'beefed up' to cater for a gross weight up to 169,000lb. Northwest Orient was the first customer for this version, which first flew on 30 December 1965, and Northwest began 727-100C services on 23 April 1966. A typical mixed load would be 52 passengers and baggage, plus 22,700lb of cargo on four pallets. The convertibility of the -100C was taken a stage further by the 'Quick Change' concept originated by United, which resulted in the 727-100QC, a version of the -100C in which the passenger seats are mounted on pallets and the galleys on floor-mounted rollers. This enables a complete conversion from an all-passenger to an all-freight interior to be made in less than 30 minutes, thus enabling utilisations to be increased by rapid changes from passengers to freight, although there is a weight penalty of about 3,000lb over the

-100C. United began limited 727-100QC services in May 1966. The Model 727M was a proposed multi-role military version of 1965 that was not built. In August that year the first stretched version, the 727-200, was revealed; this has a 20ft longer fuselage, the stretch being in two equal sections fore and aft of the wing, and maximum seating capacity now went up to 189 in a high-density interior, or 163 seats at 34in pitch. Gross weight was now 169,000lb with JT8D-7 or JT8D-9 engines, but from 1972 uprated 15,000lb st JT8D-11s could be fitted. Northeast Airlines was the first 727-200 customer, and the prototype -200 first flew on 27 July 1967, this version beginning services on 14 December that year with Northeast between Montreal, New York and Miami.

Pursuing their favourite theme of product improvement, Boeing introduced the Advanced 727-200 in 1970 with extra centre section fuel tanks, more powerful JT8D-15 engines with improved sound suppression, structural strengthening for higher gross weights, the 'Superjet look' wide-body cabin interior and improvements in the aircraft systems. Gross weight, initially set at 183,000lb, was raised to 185,200lb in 1972 for Iberia's Advanced -200s and this was soon succeeded by the new gross weight of 191,000lb, with wing and undercarriage strengthening, and an increased fuel capacity of 9,780 US gallons. The first Advanced 727-200, for All Nippon Airways, made its initial flight at this weight on 3 March 1972, entering service with All Nippon in July. In May that year an even higher gross weight of 207,500lb was specified for three Advanced -200s ordered by Sterling Airways, this enabling a full load of 189 passengers to be flown on charter flights from Scandinavia to the Canary Islands; this variant first flew on 26 July 1973. Other optional 'extras' for the Advanced version include a modification kit for gravel runway operations, a Mk III brake anti-skid system and — from 1974 — the 16,000lb st JT8D-17 engine. In 1976 the so-called 'contingency rated' JT8D-17R of 16,400lb st became available, this having an automatic performance reserve system enabling power to be increased to 17,400lb st in the event of an engine failure. The projected 727-300 with 18ft 4in fuselage stretch was shelved in 1975, but Boeing continues to study a number of lesser improvements to the 727, of which over 1,300 are now in airline service.

Boeing 737

Photo: 737-2M2C
Data: Advanced 737-200

Engines: Two 14,500lb st Pratt & Whitney JT8D-9
or 15,500lb st JT8D-15 or 16,000lb st JT8D-17
turbofans
Span: 93ft 0in
Length: 100ft 0in
Height: 37ft 0in
Wing area: 980sq ft
Operating weight: 60,980lb (empty)
Max payload: 34,000lb
Max take-off weight: 117,000lb
Speed: 564mph at 25,000ft (max cruising)
Range: 1,850 miles with max payload
3,085 miles with max fuel

Boeing was the last of three major manufacturers to
go ahead with a short haul jet, the 737 being
announced in the same month, February 1965, that
the DC-9 first flew and when the One-Eleven was
about to start commercial operations. In two
important respects the 737 differed from its earlier
rivals; it broke away from the fashion for rear-
mounted engines set by the Caravelle and it was the
only small jet with six-abreast seating, the fuselage
having the same overall width as the 707 and 727,
enabling operators of these types to standardise on
such things as seats and galleys, and a high degree
of commonality with the 707 and 727 to be
attained. Boeing claimed that the underwing engine
position gave a lower structure weight, more cabin
volume for the overall size and minimum drag with a
wider body. The 737 was unique for a US airliner in
that the initial launching order came not from a US
airline but from Lufthansa, who signed for 21 of
what was to be the 737-100, the first US order, from
United Air Lines for 40 737-200s, being announced
on 5 April 1965. Although in the original design
studies the 737 seated from 60 to 85 passengers, at
Lufthansa's request the capacity was increased to
100 seats, which was more than either the DC-9
Series 10 or One-Eleven 200. Powerplants were
14,000lb st Pratt & Whitney JT8D-7 turbofans —
the same engines as the 727 — and the 737-100

had an initial gross weight of 97,800lb, later raised
to 100,000lb and, in a variant first produced for
Malaysian Airlines System, to 110,000lb. The
14,500lb st JT8D-9 became available for later
production 737-100s, and passenger capacity was
88-107. The prototype 737 first flew on 9 April
1967 and the fifth, the first for United, was the first
737-200 to fly, on 8 August.

The -200 has a 6ft longer fuselage to provide for
two more seat rows giving accommodation for up to
119 passengers, or up to 130 in some later high-
density layouts. The gross weight was initially
97,000lb with JT8D-7 engines and the two optional
centre-section fuel tanks fitted, and was later raised
to 109,000lb and ultimately to 115,500lb; operators
could later specify the uprated JT8D-9s or 15,500lb
st JT8D-15 turbofans. FAA Type Approval for both
the -100 and -200 was granted in December 1967,
and Lufthansa began 737-100 services over
European routes on 10 February 1968, followed by
United with the -200 on 28 April. Only 30 737-100s
were built (including one for NASA), and two
projected versions were the 737-100E executive
transport seating up to 25 passengers and the multi-
role 737-100M military variant, which could take up
to 44 stretcher cases. The 737-200C was a
convertible passenger/cargo version with a 7ft 2in ×
11ft 2in forward cargo door, strengthened freight
floor and the ability to carry the same size cargo
pallets as the 727 and 707; the -200C first flew in
August 1968 and the first operator of this variant
was Wien Consolidated Airlines. The 737-200QC
was the same as the -200C but employed palletised
passenger seats and galleys and advanced loading
techniques for 'quick change' from passenger to
cargo. From March 1969, beginning with the 135th
737, Boeing introduced some modifications and
offered airlines conversion kits for correcting certain
deficiencies in the 737's specific range and thrust
reversers; the latter were changed from clamshell
type to target-type, and some drag reducing
modifications made to the wing and changes to the
flaps and their settings.

Later that year the Advanced 737-200 was
offered, with improvements to the flaps and leading

edge slats for better landing and take-off performance, optional use of the 15,500lb st JT8D-15 engine, fully automatic brakes and an improved anti-skid system. The first Advanced -200 flew on 15 April 1971, and All Nippon Airways was the first operator of this variant. Continuing the theme of product improvement, a 'wide body look' cabin interior was offered later in 1971, and a 'quiet nacelle' modification followed in 1973 to enable airlines to comply with the latest FAA noise regulations; low pressure tyres can also be fitted for operating from unpaved runways. Chiefly to meet the needs of some Canadian regional airlines for operating from gravel and dirt runways, the 737 was modified to feature gravel deflection shields on the

Above: *737-268*

main and nosewheel gears, blow-away jets beneath the engine intakes to prevent the ingestion of debris, and protection for the fuselage and flaps from gravel, stones etc thrown up while taxying. Latest 737 improvement is a 2,500lb increase in maximum taxi weight giving 200 nautical miles more range with a full passenger load. The T-43A, of which 19 have been supplied to the USAF, is a navigational trainer version replacing the Convair T-29, carrying 12 trainee navigators with very advanced equipment, and having fewer cabin windows and extra fuel tankage. By the end of 1978 just over 600 737s had been sold for airline use.

Breguet 763 Deux Ponts

France

Photo: Breguet 765 Sahara
Data: Type 763

Engines: Four 2,400bhp (max take-off) Pratt & Whitney R-2800-CA18 Double Wasp radials
Span: 141ft 0in
Length: 94ft 11in
Height: 31ft 8in
Wing area: 2,350sq ft
Weight: 71,080lb (empty)

Capacity payload: 32,400lb
Max take-off weight: 113,800lb
Speed: 231mph at 10,000ft (max cruising)
Range: 870 miles with 24,250lb payload
2,740 miles with max fuel

This big Breguet design was an early postwar attempt at a genuinely two-deck aeroplane with approximately equal volumes on both upper and lower decks; the name Deux Ponts means 'two

decks', and the maximum depth was no less than 16ft 5in, the maximum width being 10ft 9½in. Rather than pressurise such a large volume fuselage, Breguet streamlined it to give a reasonable cruising speed at moderate height, and the Deux Ponts was intended for stage lengths of about 1,240 miles. Design work on the Type 761 began in 1944 and the prototype, powered by four 1,600bhp SNECMA (Gnôme-Rhône) 14R radials, made its first flight on 15 February 1949; it did not have a dorsal fin and the vertical tail surfaces were of narrower chord than on production aircraft. It was awarded a C of A at a maximum gross weight of 88,000lb, and the second prototype flew 600 hours with Air Algérie in 1952 on operational trials between Toulouse and Algiers. In 1953 it was used for a time by Silver City Airways on the Berlin-Hamburg airlift. A pre-series of three Type 761S Deux Ponts followed, these being powered by four 2,000bhp Pratt & Whitney R-2800-B31 Double Wasps, which permitted a maximum gross weight of 99,000lb. These three aircraft underwent military trials in 1954, dropping loads such as a 'stick' of 150 paratroops, a field gun or a tank, the rear loading doors being removed. They were also used by Air Algérie for a time as 120-passenger aircraft and later went via Air Outremer, to the French Air Force in 1957. Twelve Type 763s were ordered by Air France as a production development of the 761, and the 763 made its first flight on 20 July 1951; Air France used its 763s under the name Provence. The 763 was powered by four 2,400bhp R-2800-CA18 Double Wasps driving Hamilton Standard 43E60 reversing airscrews

instead of the Ratier reversible props of the 761S; the more powerful engines made possible a take-off weight of 105,600lb, later increased to 113,800lb. Wing span was increased and the wings strengthened.

Up to 59 tourist passengers could be accommodated on the upper deck and 48 second-class passengers on the lower deck in folding seats, or varying amounts of passengers and freight on the two decks; in the freighter version mechanical hoists and overhead rail carriers served both decks. Air France used its 763s mainly on routes to North Africa, and occasionally on the Paris-London run; it was on the latter route that the type made its last flight with the French airline on 31 March 1971. The Type 764 was a proposed anti-submarine warfare version with a war load of five tonnes, and the 761 prototype was fitted with dummy turrets, radomes and other features of the 764. The Type 765 Sahara was a military heavy-duty transport version of the 763 with accommodation for up to 146 fully-equipped troops or 85 stretcher cases; it could also carry a 15ton AMX medium tank, two dismantled fighters or 17 tons of freight. Of 15 Saharas ordered, only four were completed; the 765 had 2,400bhp R-2800-CB16 engines and wing tip tanks. Six Air France Type 763s were transferred to the French Air Force in 1964 for use in the Pacific, while the other six were converted to a cargo/vehicle/passenger-carrying configuration known as the Universel which could take up to seven vehicles on the two decks and had an electric lift to transfer cars to the upper deck.

Bristol 170 Freighter

Photo and Data: Mk 31

Engines: Two 1,980hp (max take-off) Bristol Hercules 734 14-cylinder 2-row radials
Span: 108ft 0in
Length: 68ft 4in
Height: 21ft 6in
Wing area: 1,487sq ft
Weight: 27,229lb (basic operating)
44,000lb (max gross)
Max payload: 12,500lb
Speed: 229mph (max) at 3,000ft
193mph at 10,000ft (max cruising)
Range: 820 miles with max payload
1,730 miles with max fuel

Although designed in 1944 from the outset for use as a military transport the Bristol Type 170 was never to be used by the RAF although it was exported to a number of foreign air forces. Instead, it was to go down into history as the aeroplane whose nose-loading capability made possible the development of car ferry services to the Continent by Silver City Airways and Air Charter Ltd, as well as the carriage of conventional passengers and freight and such loads as racehorses or livestock. The nose doors opened to a capacious hold measuring (in the Freighter 31) 49ft long × 8ft max width × 6ft 7½in

max height, and giving a volume of 2,360cu ft. The Bristol 170 was originally offered in two main versions, the Freighter with nose doors and the Wayfarer all-passenger version without. The prototype, a Freighter 1, first flew on 2 December 1945 with a high-set tailplane which was later lowered and increased in span; some years later this 170 was fitted with a thimble nose radome for use by the TRE. The second prototype, which first flew on 30 April 1946, was a Wayfarer 2A and was followed by two more prototypes, a Freighter 1 and a Wayfarer 2A. The first production aircraft included 15 Wayfarers, but almost all of these were later converted to Freighter 1s and/or 21s; one of them was used to test a half-scale model of the Britannia tail unit. The Freighter XI was soon succeeded in 1948 by the New Freighter, as it was at first called, which featured a 10ft increase in wing span to 108ft with rounded instead of square tips, and a maximum gross weight increased to 40,000lb; the Bristol Hercules 631s and 632s of the Mks 1 and 2A were replaced by 1,700bhp Hercules 672s. There were several variants: the Mk 21 all freighter, with only the flight deck soundproofed; the Mk 21A mixed traffic version seating 16-20 passengers plus freight; the Mk 21E mixed traffic version with a movable bulkhead and the entire cabin soundproofed, enabling it be adapted to Mk 21, 21A or all-

passenger Wayfarer 22A standards; and the latter Mk 22A without nose doors and seating 32-36 passengers.

The Mks 21 and 22 were succeeded by the Freighter 31 and 31E with more powerful Hercules 734 engines, a dorsal fin and maximum gross weight increased to 44,000lb; the Mk 31E had the same interior as the Mk 21E. The Freighter 31M was a military version with accommodation for 30 fully-equipped troops, or 28 stretcher cases plus medical attendants, or 20 paratroops or freight. Not only this version but examples of the Freighter 1A, 21, 21E and 31 were supplied to the air forces of Argentina (1As), Australia (21Es), Burma (31), Canada (31M), Iraq (31M), New Zealand (31M) and Pakistan (21

and 31M). The Freighter 32, also known as the Super Freighter, was designed for Silver City Airways and had a 5ft 4in longer nose to accommodate three small cars instead of two, while passenger capacity was increased from 15 to 23. The Mk 32, which first flew on 16 January 1953, also featured a taller fin. Altogether 214 Bristol 170s were built for commercial and military customers. Freighter 31s of the New Zealand airline SAFE Air Ltd, which flies all-cargo services across the Cook Strait between the North and South Islands using a special Cargon loading system, are also fitted with self-contained, soundproofed 20-seat 'passenger capsules' for the Wellington-Chatham Island route to ensure compatibility with the Cargon loading system.

Bristol 175 Britannia

UK

Photo: Britannia 253
Data: Series 320

Engines: Four 4,450ehp Bristol Proteus 765 turboprops
Span: 142ft 3½in
Length: 124ft 3in
Height: 37ft 6in
Wing area: 2,075sq ft
Weight: 93,500lb (empty equipped)
Max payload: 34,500lb
Max take-off weight: 185,000lb
Speed: 397mph (max cruising)
357mph (best economy cruising)
Range: 4,160 miles with max payload
5,000 miles with max fuel

The Bristol Britannia had its origins in the requirement of November 1944 for a Medium Range Empire airliner for BOAC, which was the Brabazon Committee's Type III requirement, and as originally submitted the Bristol Type 175 was a 94,000lb aircraft with four Bristol Centaurus 662 or 663 piston engines, a wing span of 120ft and accommodation for only 32-36 passengers. After going through several stages of growth in which the span, fuel tankage, all-up weight and seating

capacity were increased, 25 of the Type 175 were ordered by BOAC in July 1949, and it was then intended that the first six at least would be Centaurus-powered, the rest being powered by Bristol Proteus turboprops. But by the end of 1950 progress on the latter engine had been sufficient to justify the dropping of the Centaurus version, and all 25 were now to be delivered with Bristol BPt3 Proteus 700 turboprops. The prototype first flew on 16 August 1952 with Proteus 625s and an all-up weight of 130,000lb, followed by a second prototype on 23 December 1953 at an all-up weight of 140,000lb and with Proteus 705s. Initial production version was the Britannia 102, of which BOAC had ordered 15, together with 18 Series 312s (superseding the original 1949 order for 25), and the 102 began services on the London-Johannesburg route on 1 February 1957 after a delay of nine months caused by rectification of an engine flame-out problem experienced repeatedly in conditions of dry icing. The 102 could accommodate up to 90 tourist passengers, and had an eventual all-up weight of 155,000lb. Surplus 102s were later sold to BKS Air Transport and Britainnia Airways.

Early in 1953 BOAC and Qantas interest in an all-cargo and passenger/cargo stretched version led to the Series 200 freighter, the 250 passenger/cargo

variant and the 300 all-passenger version, each with a 10ft 3in longer fuselage. The Series 200 freighter in the end was not built, and BOAC later ordered eight Series 300s, one of which, re-allocated as a Ministry of Supply prototype, and known as the Britainnia 301, first flew on 31 July 1956. BOAC's seven 300s were later released for resale to other operators, and instead a similar number of Series 310s ordered to bring its total to 18. This was the non-stop transatlantic version with fuel capacity increased to 8,580 Imperial gallons and all-up weight to 175,000lb; it was powered by 4,120ehp Proteus 755s, which became the standard engines for all the long-fuselage versions. The first Britannia 312 for BOAC first flew on 31 December 1956 and began London-New York services on 19 December 1957, followed only three days later by El Al with Tel Aviv-New York flights; the Series 310 could carry 99 tourist passengers or up to 139 in a high-density interior. Meanwhile, of the seven 300s originally destined for BOAC, two were sold to Aeronaves de Mexico as Series 302s and five were ordered by Northeast Airlines as Series 305s chiefly for the New York-Miami route, but were later cancelled, to be resold to Air Charter Ltd (later part of BUA), Transcontinental of Argentina and Ghana Airways. The designation 305 denoted a 300 modified as nearly as possible to 310 standard, including the extra wing tankage. The two Air Charter/BUA aircraft were later fitted with 10ft 3in × 6ft 7in forward freight doors, and were then known as Series 307Fs. Other export orders for the basic Series 310, in addition to El Al's four 313s, had come from

Canadian Pacific Air Lines (six 314s), Hunting-Clan (later part of BUA) (two 317s), Cubana (four 318s, one leased to Eagle Aviation in 1960-61 and one to CSA of Czechoslovakia) and Ghana Airways (one 319).

The 310 was succeeded by the final production version, the Series 320, with 4,450ehp Proteus 765s and many detailed engineering improvements resulting from 310 operating experience, as well as changes to comply with FAA requirements. Six were produced, two for Canadian Pacific as Series 324s (later sold to British Eagle), and two Cubana 318s, a BOAC 312 and an El Al 313 were later brought up to Series 320 standard. When BOAC and other airlines sold off their 310s these were acquired by British independents such as British Eagle, Caledonian, Donaldson, IAS Cargo, Invicta International, Monarch and also by African Safari Airways, Globe Air and Tellair of Switzerland, and Air Spain. A few ex-BOAC 312s were fitted with freight doors as 312Fs, as were two 308s, and there have been a number of resales of 300s and 310s. Last major variant to make its first flight was the basic Series 250 which, as the Britannia 253 or C1 for RAF Transport Command, flew on 29 December 1958; 20 were built, and three Series 252s originally ordered by the Ministry of Supply also went to the RAF. These had the forward freight door and could take up to 35,000lb of cargo or 117 passengers or 53 stretcher cases. The RAF's Britannias have now been sold off to commerical operators such as Young Cargo of Belgium and Aer Turas. Altogether 85 Britannias were built.

Britten-Norman BN-2 Islander   UK

Data: BN-2A

Engines: Two 260hp Lycoming O-540-E4C5 6-cylinder horizontally-opposed engines
Span: 49ft 0in
Length: 35ft 7¾in
39ft 5¼in with nose extension
Height: 13ft 8¾in
Wing area: 325sq ft
Weight: 3,588lb (empty equipped)
Max take-off weight: 6,600lb

Speed: 170mph (max)
160mph at 7,000ft (max cruising)
Range: 822 miles (75% power)

Designed as a simple light twin-engined transport more suitable to the needs of small airlines, whether feeder airlines in undeveloped countries or commuter operators in developed ones, than the executive light twins such as Aztecs and Cessna 310s widely used by these operators, the Britten-Norman Islander became, in mid-1974, Britain's

best-selling airliner and over 800 have been delivered to operators in 100 countries. The Islander had its origins in the requirements of a Britten-Norman group company, Cameroons Air Transport Ltd, which operated a small network in the British West Cameroons, and detail design work on the BN-2 began in April 1964. The prototype first flew on 13 June 1965 powered by two 210hp Rolls-Royce Continental 10-360-B engines, and had a wing span of 45ft and a gross weight of 4,750lb; it was later modified to have 260hp Lycoming 0-540-E engines, with which it first flew on 17 December 1965, the span being increased to the 49ft of production aircraft and gross weight to 5,700lb. A second prototype, to production standard, flew on 20 August 1966 and the first production BN-2, now named Islander, flew on 24 April 1967. A British C of A was granted on 10 August and the first deliveries, to Glosair and Loganair, followed a few days later; the FAA Type Certificate was granted on 19 December and first deliveries to the USA were in January 1968. The initial production Islanders were BN-2s while those built since 1 June 1969 are BN-2As.

Up to 10 people, including the pilot, are carried on side-by-side front seats and four bench-type seats running right across the cabin; an unusual feature is that there is no central aisle and access to the cabin is by three forward opening doors, two on the port side forward and aft, and one on the starboard side. The Islander can be flown as a freighter, with the seats removed, as an executive aircraft, as an ambulance, carrying up to three stretcher cases and two attendants, or it can be used for photo and geophysical survey, as a transport and trainer for parachutists, or for public health spraying with a 130 Imp gallon tank in the cabin and rotary atomizers on booms under the wings. A version with 300hp Lycoming 10-540-K1B5 engines was first flown on 30 April 1970, this becoming the alternative

powerplant when deliveries started in November that year. A Riley-Rajay turbo supercharging installation can be fitted on the 260hp engines, a supercharged version with 270hp Lycoming T10-540-H engines first flying on 30 April 1971. Wing tip extensions having raked tips and auxiliary internal fuel tanks increasing capacity from 114 to 163 Imp gallons are available, extending the span to 53ft, or two pylon-mounted underwing tanks of 50 Imp gallons each can be fitted. Another version, originally designated BN-2A-8S, has an extended nose with 28cu ft additional baggage space and seats for two more passengers in the cabin space previously used for baggage; this BN-2S model first flew on 22 August 1972 and the extended nose can now be featured if customers desire it. Britten-Norman has introduced a series of modification kits, made available as standard or optional fits on new production aircraft and which can also be supplied for retrofitting by the customer.

A series of dash numbers added to the BN-2A designation serve to distinguish the various optional features, the -1, -3, -7, -9 and -11 having the auxiliary wing tip tanks while the even-numbered variants did not; the -2 and -3 have the 300hp engines and the -10 and -11 have supercharged T10-540-H motors, while the -1, -6, -7, -8 and -9 have the 260hp engines. The BN-2A-6 and -7 featured new camber on the wing leading edges to meet US certification requirements, and the -8 and -9 had drooped flaps as well. The BN-2A-30 is an amphibious version with standard wings (with extended wing tips it is the BN-2A-31) and main wheels retract aft into the twin floats and nose stabilising wheels retract forward. A wheel/ski landing gear can also be fitted to the Islander. In 1967 the Rumanian aircraft firm IRMA signed an agreement with Britten-Norman for the manufacture

Below: Islander of the Zambian Flying Doctor Service

of the Islander under licence by IRMA and the first Rumanian-assembled example flew at Bucharest on 4 August 1969 using British-built components. IRMA-built Islanders, of which over 200 were built initially, are sold through Britten-Norman and its network of distributors. In August 1972 Britten-Norman's whole share capital was acquired by the Fairey Group, and production was later transferred from Britain to the Fairey factory at Gosselies in Belgium, although production is being relocated at Bembridge following Fairey's receivership late in 1977 and B-N's takeover by Pilatus. The Defender is a military version of the Islander for such duties as search and rescue, anti-smuggling patrols or forward air control, and carries a wide variety of weapon loads on four NATO standard underwing pylons. The BN-2A-40 Turbo Islander has two 600shp Lycoming LTP 101 turboprops flat-rated to 400shp.

Britten-Norman Trislander UK

Photo: BN-2 Mk III-2
Data: BN-2 Mk III

Engines: Three 260hp Lycoming 0-540-E4C5 6-cylinder horizontally-opposed engines
Span: 53ft 0in
Length: 47ft 6in with extended nose
Height: 13ft 5$\frac{3}{4}$in
Wing area: 337sq ft
Basic operating weight: 6,178lb
Max payload: 3,550lb
Max take-off weight: 10,000lb
Speed: 183mph (max) at sea level 176mph at 6,500ft (max cruising)
Range: 210 miles with max payload 860 miles with max fuel

The success of the Islander in many countries led naturally to a requirement from some operators for a stretched version to cater for the higher traffic loads they were experiencing. The first step in this direction was a long-fuselage Islander which made its first flight on 14 July 1968, but after some test flying with this it was realised that more power would be needed, and this took the form of a unique configuration in which a third 260hp Lycoming engine was added at the top of a broad chord fin and rudder, the enlarged tailplane being relocated at the rear of the centre engine nacelle fairing instead of on the rear fuselage. The same wing and fuselage cross section were used, the fuselage being lengthened by 8ft 1$\frac{1}{4}$in to 43ft 9in (or 47ft 6in with the extended baggage nose), the longer cabin providing accommodation for a pilot and 17 passengers. There were now two entrance doors on the port side and three to starboard. The prototype Trislander, as the new three-engined version was named, first flew on 11 September 1970 and the first production aircraft, incorporating some changes to the tail unit shape, made its initial flight on 6 March 1971; small-scale production commenced, the first being delivered on 29 June that year. A British C of A and FAA Type Approval were granted on 14 May and 4 August respectively. The lengthened nose with increased baggage space of the BN-2S Islander was later offered as an optional feature, and the all-up weight was increased in 1973 from 9,350lb to 10,000lb. Production was transferred to Gosselies in Belgium when Fairey acquired control of Britten-Norman and over 50 have been ordered so far.

Canadair North Star/Argonaut   Canada

Photo: DC-4M
Data: DC-4M-2

Engines: Four 1,760bhp (max take-off) Rolls-Royce Merlin 626 12-cylinder in-line engines
Span: 117ft 6in
Length: 93ft 7½in
Height: 27ft 6¼in
Wing area: 1,457sq ft
Weight: 46,832lb (empty)
Capacity payload: 17,156lb
Max take-off weight: 82,300lb
Speed: 280mph at 10,000ft (continuous cruising)
Range: 2,385 miles with max payload
3,730 miles with max fuel

The Canadair C-4, or Canadair Four, was known to BOAC as the Argonaut and to its two principal Canadian users, Trans-Canada Airlines and the Royal Canadian Air Force, as the North Star. It was a redesign to TCA's requirements of the basic Douglas DC-4 airframe, incorporating Rolls-Royce Merlins in place of the DC-4's Pratt & Whitney R-2000 Twin Wasps, and also cabin pressurisation, a redesigned flight deck, enlarged cargo compartments and improved integral fuel tanks. Several important features of the Douglas DC-6 were also incorporated, and the prototype made its first flight on 15 July 1946. The initial production version, the DC-4M-1 North Star, known as the C-54-GM to the RCAF and later by the manufacturer's designation CL-2, was unpressurised. Since the development of cabin pressurisation was likely to, and in fact did delay the initial deliveries to TCA of the 20 pressurised DC-4M-2s it had ordered, six C-54-GM North Stars of the RCAF order for 24 were furnished internally to TCA requirements and delivered to the airline as DC-4M-1s, being converted back to C-54-GMs and returned to the RCAF after delivery of TCA's DC-4M-2s was completed. Seventeen more C-54-GMs and the prototype were delivered to the RCAF, the C-54-GM differing from the DC-4M-1 chiefly in such matters as cabin seating and soundproofing;

1,760bhp Merlin 620 engines were fitted. By 1965 North Stars equipped Nos 412, 102, 111 and 121 Squadrons of RCAF Air Transport Command, and could also be used for search and rescue duties.

TCA used its North Stars on routes from Montreal and Toronto to the Caribbean as well as to Europe, and on the domestic transcontinental route, but from 1954-55 they began to be replaced by Super Constellations and Viscounts, being finally disposed of in 1961; five had been converted into freighters. Four DC-4M-2s were also used by Canadian Pacific Air Lines, inaugurating its new Vancouver-Sydney route on 13 July 1949 and the Tokyo and Hong Kong route on 19 September that year. The DC-4M-2 was the pressurised version, 22 of which were ordered by BOAC. These had a lower empty weight and a 9,300lb higher gross weight than the DC-4M-1, and improved payload-range capabilities; engines were 1,760bhp Merlin 626s. BOAC began Argonaut services on 23 August 1949, using the type seating 40 first-class or 54 tourist passengers on routes to Africa, the Middle and Far East until it was retired on 8 April 1960. A high level of cabin noise had been a continuous problem with the Argonaut and North Star, and a number of different exhaust systems were tried out in an effort to minimise it. BOAC Argonauts operated the newly-opened London route of West African Airways Corporation for a time from 1957, and BOAC sold off its Argonauts to Aden Airways (3), East African Airways (3), the Danish charter operator Flying Enterprise AB (5), the Rhodesian Air Force (4) and the British independent Overseas Aviation (4). Subsequent resales went to Derby Aviation, which had five, and Air Links, while Overseas Aviation, also bought most of TCA's DC-4M-2 fleet in 1961, but went bankrupt before it could start operating them. Other TCA aircraft went to International Air Freighters, LAUMSA of Mexico, LEBCA of Venezuela, and World Wide Airways. The very last operator of the type, Turks Air Ltd, retired the last of its two ex-RCAF North Stars in 1976.

Canadair CL-44

Canada

Photo: Conroy CL-44-0
Data: CL-44D-4

Engines: Four 5,730eshp Rolls-Royce RTy12 Tyne 515/10 turboprops
Span: 142ft 3½in
Length: 136ft 10¾in
Height: 38ft 8in
Wing area: 2,075sq ft
Operating weight: 88,952lb (empty)
Max payload: 63,272lb
Max take-off weight: 210,000lb
Speed: 386mph at 20,000ft (cruising)
Range: 3,260 miles with max payload
5,587 miles with max fuel and 35,564lb payload

The Canadair CL-44 arose out of a 1956 Royal Canadian Air Force requirement for a long-haul troop carrying transport and freighter. Canadair had already acquired a licence for the Bristol Britannia, on which it had based the CL-28 Argus maritime reconnaissance aircraft, and several derivatives of the Britannia were proposed with a lengthened fuselage and increased-span wing. The RCAF's choice was a version powered by the Bristol BE25 Orion, but when further work on this engine was discontinued not long afterwards the CL-44 was redesigned with four Rolls-Royce Tyne turboprops, in which form it was designated CL-44D. Twelve were ordered by the RCAF, which called the type the CC-106 Yukon, and the first of these, which served as a prototype, made its first flight from Montreal on 15 November 1959. The Yukons, capable of carrying 60,480lb of freight, equipped No 437 Squadron, and two of them had special convertible interiors to transport VIPs when required; these were operated by No 412 Squadron. From 1973 the Yukons were disposed of as surplus and were acquired mostly by Latin American freight and charter operators such as Aero Transportes Entre Rios, ANDES of Ecuador, Transporte Aereo Rioplatense, Aeronaves del Peru, TACA International and TAISA of Costa Rica, as well as by Air Calypso of Barbados and SGA of Zaire. To meet criticism that the CL-44D's large side-loading doors fore and aft did not enable the fullest advantage to be taken of fuselage capacity, Canadair offered a commercial version, the CL-44D-4, in which the complete tail unit and rear fuselage were hinged to open to starboard, enabling lengthy cargoes such as two complete F-104 fighters to be loaded. The CL-44D-4, which was also known as the CL-44G, was the first transport to feature a swing tail as standard and the prototype first flew on 16 November 1960.

Initial orders for 17 D-4s were placed by the three US all-freight carriers — Flying Tiger, Seaboard World Airlines and Slick Airways. Repeat orders from these plus one for four from the Icelandic airline Loftleidir brought total production to 27; the first delivery, to Flying Tiger, was made on 31 May 1961.

Below: *CL-44*

Loftleidir used its CL-44s as 160 to 178-passenger aircraft for its transatlantic services at sub-IATA fares, and to meet Loftleidir's need for a larger capacity aircraft a new version with a 15ft longer fuselage, the CL-44J (also known as the Rolls-Royce 400 or Canadair 400) was developed, seating up to 214 passengers. This first flew on 8 November 1965, and all four of Loftleidir's D-4s were converted to CL-44J standard by inserting new sections fore and aft of the wing. Three of the CL-44Js were later leased to the Luxembourg operator Cargolux for use on world-wide cargo charters, which has itself now leased one to Aero Uruguay. The CL-44D-4s have all been sold off by their original owners, and are now used by Air Gabon Cargo, SOACO, another Gabonese operator, the British independents IAS Air Cargo, Tradewinds and Transmeridian Air Cargo, and Transvalair of Switzerland. Transmeridian, which leases CL-44s to the German charter operator Express-Flug, has also acquired the only example of the CL-44-O, an outsize, Guppy-style conversion of a D-4 by Conroy Aircraft; this has a new pressurised upper fuselage with a maximum inside diameter of 13ft 11in, the swing tail being retained. The CL-44-O first flew on 26 November 1969. CL-44D-4s are also used by Bab el Mandels Airlines and Tramaco.

Cessna 310 USA

Photo: 310Q
Data: Turbo-System T310

Engines: Two 285hp Continental TS10-520-B 6-cylinder horizontally-opposed engines
Span: 36ft 11in
Length: 31ft 11½in
Height: 10ft 8in
Wing area: 179sq ft
Weight: 3,578lb (empty) (310-11)
Max take-off weight: 5,500lb
Speed: 272mph (max) at 16,000ft
256mph at 20,000ft (max cruising)
202mph at 20,000ft (best economy cruising)
Range: 1,658 miles with 1,218lb usable fuel

One of a family of Cessna light twins widely used by air taxi operators and third-level airlines as well as by private and executive owners, the Model 310 first flew in prototype form on 3 January 1953, entering production the following year as a 4-5 seater. The type soon gained acceptance, and a total of 4,268 of all versions of the 310 had been built by 1 January 1976. The 310 has been in USAF service since 1957, when 80 Model 310As were ordered as 'off-the-shelf' utility transports, being designated U-3A (formerly L-27A); 80 more U-3As were ordered the following year, followed by 36 'all-weather' versions of the Model 310E designated U-3B and delivered from December 1960 to June 1961. Several other air arms have acquired 310s, the Zaire Air Force taking delivery of 15 in 1975. Successive commercial models introduced various refinements and improvements; the Model 310B entered production in 1957 and was succeeded in 1959 by the 310C with 260hp Continental 10-470-D fuel injection engines in place of the earlier 240hp 0-470-M powerplants. All models so far had featured an unswept fin, but the Model 310D of 1960 introduced the swept fin and rudder that appeared on all subsequent versions. The 310F of 1961 featured two additional cabin windows while the 310G had the so-called 'stabila-tip' wings in which the wing tip tanks, previously upright, were canted at 35deg from the horizontal. Another external change, introduced in the Model 310I, was the extension of the rear of each nacelle to form an additional baggage compartment.

Current production models have 285hp Continentals, the standard 5-6 seater 310 having unsupercharged 10-520-M engines and the Turbo-System T310 turbocharged TS10-520-B powerplants and automatic propeller synchronisation (an optional 'extra' on the 310 and 310-11) as one of several standard engine features. The Turbo-System version first appeared late in 1968, the first production aircraft being delivered in December that year. The Model 310-11 and Turbo-

System T310-11 announced in December 1973 have a higher standard of navaids and radio fitted as standard equipment at the factory including such items of IFR electronics as VOR/LOC and VOR/ILS indicators and an approach coupler for the 400B Nav-O-Matic autopilot. Six individual seats are fitted, the fifth and sixth seats being moved back 4 inches on 1976 models for extra leg room. The standard fuel tankage consists of the two 51 US gallon wing tip tanks, with provision for up to 105 US gallons more optional fuel tankage in the wings. The Riley 65 is basically an updated conversion of the early Cessna 310 models to 310G standard, with a number of new features such as glass-fibre nacelles, but the modifications were so extensive that it was certificated as a new type; it is available with 240hp Continental 0-470-M or fuel injection 10-470-D engines. The Riley Rocket is identical to the Riley 65 except for having 290hp Lycoming -10-540-A1A5 engines and increased fuel capacity, while the Turbo-Rocket is the same as the Rocket except that each engine has two Rajay Turbo 300 exhaust-driven turbosuperchargers.

Convair PBY-5A Catalina

USA

Engines: Two 1,200bhp (max take-off) Pratt & Whitney R-1830-92 Twin Wasp 14-cylinder 2-row radials
Span: 104ft 0in
Length: 63ft 10in
Height: 18ft 10in
Wing area: 1,400sq ft
Weight: 17,564lb (empty)
34,000lb (max gross)
Speed: 196mph (max) at 7,500ft
130mph at 10,000ft (cruising)
Range: 3,100 miles with max fuel

Probably the most famous flying boat ever the Consolidated Model 28 Catalina served in every part of the world with the US Navy, USAAF and half a dozen other Allied air forces, and first flew in prototype form as the XP3Y-1 on 21 March 1935. The major production version, the PBY-5, had two 1,200hp Pratt & Whitney R-1830-82 or -92 Twin Wasps, and RAF Catalinas from Mks 1 to IVB were very similar. The Catalina III was the RAF equivalent of the PBY-5A amphibian which flew in December 1939; the USAAF version was the OA-10A and the Royal Canadian Air Force called it the Canso. Boeing Aircraft of Canada made 240 PBY-5s as the P2B-1. An improved version with some modifications to the hull, a new nose gun position and a new, taller fin and rudder was produced by the Naval Aircraft Factory as the PBN-1 Nomad, and Boeing Canada built the same version as the PB2B-2. Convair produced the PBN-1 as the PBY-6A; this was the last production version, and 3,290 Catalinas altogether were built, plus several hundred more built under licence in Russia since late 1939 as the GST, powered by M62 radials, for the Soviet Navy.

The first civil Catalina, or Model 28-3, was NC777 *Guba* (the Papuan for *squall*) which was used by the Archbold Expedition to New Guinea in the summer of 1939 sponsored by the American Museum of Natural History. This was later employed by BOAC on routes to Lisbon and Lagos from December 1940. BOAC also acquired six other Catalinas, five of which were turned over to Qantas, which used them on what was then the world's longest non-stop air route, totalling 3,513 miles from Perth to Colombo in Ceylon; known as 'The Route of the Double Sunrise' and inaugurated on 10-11 July 1943, this involved a gruelling flight of 27 hours (sometimes over 30) for the few passengers, payload being restricted to 1,200lb with a 3½ton overload of fuel. Qantas also used seven PB2B-2s for some years after the war on regional routes in the Pacific and domestic ones in New Guinea, and TAA also used two Catalinas for services from Port Moresby. Barrier Reef Airways (taken over by Ansett in 1952) flew Catalinas to the Queensland coast holiday resorts, and RAI operated one from Tahiti from 1954. But it was in Alaska and Canada that surplus Catalinas found their most widespread application by airlines, seating up to 22

passengers; some were also used for such jobs as aerial survey, while others were used as water bombers to fight forest fires. During 1960-61 Austin Airways of Toronto helped to develop external underwing water-dropping tanks for its Cansos which enabled 650 gallons of water to be loaded during the take-off run; these tanks could also be adapted for spraying insecticide or fertiliser. A version of the 'Cat' known as the Steward-Davis Super Catalina and powered by two 1,900bhp Wright R-2600-20 Cyclones was used by Alaska Coastal Airlines, which had four. This version had special Sun Domes fitted in place of the blister turrets to give passengers a picture window view of the scenery. The Steward-Davis Skybarge is similar to the Super Catalina, with new cargo doors in the top of the fuselage. A few civil Catalinas served in Latin America, Panair do Brasil using them for services down the Amazon to Manaos from Belem. A number of Catalinas were also used as executive transports in the United States, and the type continued to serve in air forces and navies. A specially-equipped PBY-6A is used in support of Capt Jacques Cousteau's underwater exploration activities.

Convair 240 USA

Photo: Convair 240-1

Engines: Two 2,400bhp (max take-off) Pratt & Whitney R-2800-CA18 Double Wasp 18-cylinder 2-row radials
Span: 91ft 9in
Length: 74ft 8in
Height: 26ft 11in
Wing area: 817sq ft
Weight: 30,345lb (empty equipped)
Capacity payload: 9,600lb
Max take-off weight: 41,790lb
Speed: 347mph (max) at 16,000ft
284mph at 20,000ft (continuous cruising)
Range: 400 miles with max payload
1,025 miles with max fuel

By the end of the war there was an urgent need to replace the many DC-3s in use on major inter-city routes up to about 1,000 miles in the United States with a larger and faster twin-engined type, and early in 1945 American Airlines issued a specification to the US industry for such an aircraft. This resulted in the Convair 240's forerunner, the Model 110, a 30-passenger aircraft generally similar to the 240, with two 2,100bhp Pratt & Whitney R-2800-S1C3-G Double Wasp motors and accommodation for 30 passengers, which first flew on 8 July 1946. This featured a 4in wider diameter fuselage more tapered at the rear than the 240's, with ventral airstairs

folding up under the tail, and large oil cooler intakes under the nacelles. But before the Model 110 flew, American Airlines decided that a slightly larger and more powerful version seating 40 passengers was needed, and placed an initial order for no less than 75 (originally 100) Convair 240s off the drawing board. No prototype was built as such, the first Model 240, which made its first flight on 16 March 1947, being constructed on production jigs and tooling. The 240 was 3ft 8in longer than the Model 110, and was powered by 2,400bhp Double Wasp R-2800-CA18 engines which featured 'aspirated cooling', a form of thrust augmentation in which cooling air and exhaust gases passed through a venturi section before exhausting through twin tailpipes at the rear of the nacelle to give an increase in speed. Hamilton Standard Hydromatic or Curtiss Electric three-blade reversible pitch airscrews were fitted and the cabin was pressurised. Airlines were offered two alternative positions for the integral folding passenger stairway: forward of the wings on the starboard side, or beneath the rear fuselage, or a conventional entrance door aft on the port side could be featured.

American began services with the Model 240 Convairliner on 1 June 1948 and the 240 soon began to attract orders, other US customers being Western Airlines, Continental, Northeast and Pan American, and Trans Australia Airlines, FAMA of Argentina (subsequently operated by Aerolineas

Argentinas), KLM, Swissair, Sabena, Central Air Transport Corp of China, Orient Airways of Pakistan and its successor PIA, Garuda Indonesian Airways and Ethiopian Airlines. Individual customers were identified by a dash number, ie Garuda Indonesian, Model 240-23, Swissair, Model 240-11. Many airlines operated second-hand 240s, including Mohawk Airlines, Trans-Texas Airways, Varig and Cruzeiro of Brazil and LOT of Poland. Ethiopian's two Model 240-25s were fitted with Aerojet 14AS-1000 JATO units under the fuselage for a time to cope with 'hot and high' African airports and Pan Am also tested JATO on its Model 240s at Mexico City's high altitude airport. Many 240s were converted into executive transports, often with weather radar and sometimes with an auxiliary power unit in the extreme tail, while both airline and executive 240s could be fitted with extra tankage in the outer wings to bring the fuel capacity to 1,500 US gallons. Altogether 176 commercial 240s were built, plus 48 unpressurised T-29A navigational trainer versions of the 240 for the USAF, 105 pressurised T-29Bs, 119 T-29Cs with more powerful engines and 93 T-29Ds for the big K-1 bombing system. Built concurrently were 49 C-131A Samaritan aeromedical versions (Model 240-53) and VC-131A staff transports.

Convair 340 USA

Photo: Convair 340-41

Engines: Two 2,500bhp (max take-off) Pratt & Whitney R-2800-CB16 or -CB17 Double Wasp radials
Span: 105ft 4in
Length: 79ft 2in
Height: 28ft 2in
Wing area: 920sq ft
Weight: 32,399lb (empty equipped)
Capacity payload: 13,900lb
Max take-off weight: 47,000lb
Speed: 314mph (max) at 16,000ft
284mph at 20,000ft (continous cruising)
Range: 250 miles with max payload
1,875 miles with max fuel

Success of the Convair 240 led naturally to a stretched version, the Model 340, which had the fuselage lengthened by 4ft 6in to accommodate an extra seat row, bringing the passenger accommodation up to 44, the wing span increased to 105ft 9in, more powerful R-2800-CB16 or -CB17 Double Wasp engines, a new flap arrrangement and an entirely new interior. Longer undercarriage legs and larger tyres were featured, fuel capacity was increased and dihedral on the outer wings was slightly more than on the 240. The standard passenger entrance door with folding airstairs was now on the port side. The Convair 340 made its first flight at San Diego on 5 October 1951, and the first 340 service was flown by United Air Lines, which had ordered 55 of the type, on 28 March 1952. The 340 was also ordered by Braniff, Delta, Hawaiian Airlines and National in the USA, by All Nippon of Japan, Garuda Indonesian Airways, Philippine Air LInes, Saudi Arabian Airlines, by Ansett in Australia, in Europe by Finnair, Alitalia, Lufthansa, JAT of Jugoslavia, KLM and Linjeflyg, and by Avensa of Venezuela, LACSA of Costa Rica, REAL and Cruzeiro of Brazil. Among the operators of second-hand 340s were several US local service airlines such as Frontier, Lake Central, North Central and Ozark. In mid-1962 Caribair, which operated services from Puerto Rico to the US Virgin Islands and the Dominican Republic, had its five second-hand 340s fitted with an Aerojet JATO unit in the extreme end of the tail cone to overcome the temperature and terrain limitations of airports like St Thomas, where hills rise abruptly at the end of the runway. These 340s were later converted to Dart-engined Convair 640s.

Altogether 212 civil 340s were built, and military versions for the USAF included 36 C-131B 48-passenger transports and electronic test beds, some of which had two Solar T41 Mars auxiliary gas turbines in under-wing pods, two YC-131C test beds for the Allison YT56-A-3 turboprop, 33 C-131D and VC-131D 44-passenger transports and 10 TC-131E

electronics countermeasures trainers. For the US Navy, 36 Model 340s were built as R4Y-1 (later C-131F) transports for cargo or 44 passengers or 27 stretcher cases; the R4Y-1Z was a VIP version seating 24 with six berths. One C-131 was modified for zero gravity experiments, and another C-131 was converted by the Cornell Aeronautical Laboratory into a TIFS (Total In-Flight Simulator) to demonstrate the theoretical flight characteristics of large multi-engined aircraft such as the SST and C-5A Galaxy. This featured a second cockpit added ahead of, and slightly below, the normal nose to simulate pilot environment in future large jets, and movable vertical control surfaces on the wings to generate side forces; Allison T56 turboprops replaced the Double Wasps. Six C-131Es were converted to RC-131F photo survey aircraft and one to an RC-131G for navaid calibration for the USAF.

Convair 440 USA

Engines: Two 2,500bhp (max take-off) Pratt & Whitney R-2800-CB16 or -CB17 Double Wasp radials
Span: 105ft 4in
Length: 81ft 6in
Height: 28ft 2in
Wing area: 920sq ft
Basic operating weight: 33,314lb
Max payload: 12,836lb
Max take-off weight: 49,700lb
Speed: 300mph at 13,000ft (max cruising)
289mph at 20,000ft (best economy cruising)
Range: 285 miles with max payload
1,930 miles with max fuel

Further development of the Model 340 resulted in the Convair 440, known as the Metropolitan chiefly by those European airlines which ordered it. The Model 440 had the same overall dimensions as the 340, and the other improvements introduced with it, were a higher all-up weight and optional weather radar of 150 miles range, which increased the length by 2ft 4in. Its chief difference from the 340 was a new thrust-augmenting exhaust system with a rectangular slit-type exit nozzle at the end of the nacelle for the exhaust gases and cooling air, instead of the previous twin tailpipes; soundproofing of the cabin was considerably improved as well. The 440 was offered in a 52-passenger high-density layout as well as the more usual 44-seater, the former having an extra window each side in the forward part of the cabin. The 440 prototype first flew on 6 October 1955 and the first production aircraft on 15 December that year. First services with the 440 were by Continental Air Lines in February 1956, and other US domestic operators of the type were Braniff, Delta, Eastern, Mohawk and National, also Hawaiian Airlines. An unexpected feature of 440 sales, in view of the Viscount's competitive appeal, was the number ordered by European airlines, almost half the 153 built for airline use going to Alitalia, Condor Flugdienst, Finnair, Iberia, JAT of Jugoslavia, Kar-Air of Finland, KLM, Lufthansa, Sabena, SAS and Swissair. Other customers were Avensa of Venezuela, Cruzeiro and REAL in Brazil, All Nippon of Japan, Garuda Indonesian Airways and Ansett ANA. Principal operators of second-hand 440s in the 1960s were the US local service airlines Allegheny, North Central and Ozark, LAN of Chile and SAHSA of Honduras, Aviaco of Spain and Linjeflyg of Sweden, while among present operators of used 440s there are American Inter Island Airways, Aspen Airways of Colorado, Mackey International of Miami, Air-Sea Service of Switzerland, Pyramid Airlines of Cairo and LAGE of Equatorial Guinea. In addition to the 153 built for airlines, 26 more went to other users, executive and military, including the Federal German Luftwaffe, the Italian Air Force, the Royal Australian Air Force, and two, designated C-131G (formerly R4Y-2) for the US Navy Bureau of Aeronautics. Several Convair 340s were modified up to 440 standard.

Convair 540 and 580

Photo: Convair 540
Data: Convair 580

Engines: Two 3,750eshp (max take-off) Allison
501-D13H turboprops
Span: 105ft 4in
Length: 81ft 6in
Height: 29ft 2in
Wing area: 920sq ft
Max payload: 8,870lb
Max take-off weight: 58,140lb
Speed: 342mph at 20,000ft (cruising)
Range: 1,614 miles at 53,200lb weight (5,000lb
payload)
2,866 miles with max fuel

As early as 1950 Convair began considering re-
engining the basic 240 airframe with turboprops to
improve its performance and operating economics,
and no doubt to meet the competitive challenge
already foreseen from the Vickers Viscount. At
Allison's suggestion Convair fitted the first 240 to fly
with two 2,750eshp (max take-off) Allison XT38
turboprops, and it first flew with these on 29
December 1950; it then became known as the
Model 240-21 Turboliner, and T38A-4 (Allison
501-A2) turboprops driving Aeroproducts 4-blade
airscrews soon replaced the original engines. But
flight test results with the T38 engines were not
encouraging, and the Turboliner did not go into
production. It was D. Napier & Son Ltd in the UK
who launched the first successful Convair turboprop
re-engining programme, a Convair 340 being fitted
at Luton with two 3,060ehp Napier NE1 1 Eland
turboprops and first flying in this form on 9 February
1955. This was followed by several more
conversions of 340s and 440s to Eland engines by
PacAero at Los Angeles and Canadair, the type being
known in this form as the Convair 540. The US local
service carrier Allegheny Airlines began operating
one on a trial basis on 1 July 1959, and eventually
operated six as 52-passenger 540s. When 440

production ended, Convair transferred the jigs to
Canadair at Montreal, and they built 10 540s as CC-
109 Cosmopolitans for the Royal Canadian Air Force;
these seated 52 passengers and featured increased
fuel capacity, better braking and faster undercarriage
retraction. Two of the three 540s converted earlier
by Canadair were sold to Quebecair, beginning
services on that airline's routes on 24 August 1960;
these were fitted with an auxiliary power unit in the
tail and had the maker's designation CL-66A, the
CC-109 being known as the CL-66B.

Production and development of the Napier Eland
terminated in 1962, however, and Allegheny's 540s
were converted back to piston power while
Quebecair's were disposed of to the RCAF after a
fairly short time in service as was the third one
converted by Canadair, which had been used as a
demonstrator. The seven remaining CC-109s were
converted to Convair 580 standard in 1966-67, and
are used by No 412 Sqn for VIP transport.
Conversion of Convair 340s and 440s to have two
3,750eshp Allison 501-D13 turboprops driving
Aeroproducts 606 four-blade reversible props
produced the Convair 580, known at first as the
Allison-Convair or Super Convair; re-engining was
done by Pacific Airmotive Corp under sub-contract to
Allison. Other modifications made at the same time
were a slight increase in fin and rudder area and
tailplane span, redesigned engine instrumentation
and —as an optional extra — increased fuel
capacity. The Convair 580 made its first flight on
19 January 1960 and FAA certification was obtained
on 22 April 1960, followed by first delivery, to an
executive owner, on 6 May that year. Airline sales
were slow to materialise because when the 580
came on to the market the Lockheed Electra, which
had the same engines, had suffered two accidents
which resulted in speed restrictions and
modifications. The first airline 580, for the US local
service carrier Frontier Airlines, was modified in
January 1964, and Frontier began 580 services on
1 June that year, eventually having all 32 of its

Convairs converted into 580s. Allegheny, which had operated the 540, introduced the 580 in May 1965, and built up its fleet to 38, these including 10 580s of Lake Central Airlines taken over when it merged with Allegheny in July 1968. North Central introduced the 580 in 1967, eventually operating 33, and Avensa of Venezuela acquired seven 580s, the first in July 1964. Subsequent resales have gone to Aspen Airways of Colorado, Evergreen International, which operates some 580F freighters, the Canadian operator Great Lakes Airlines, Mountain West Aviation and SAHSA of Honduras, amongst others. The FAA has used five 580s for navaid calibration, and altogether 175 Convairs have been converted to 580 standard.

Convair 600 and 640   USA

Photo and Data: Convair 640

Engines: Two 3,025eshp (max take-off) Rolls-Royce RDa10/1 Dart 542-4 turboprops
Span: 105ft 4in
Length: 81ft 6in
Height: 28ft 2in
Wing area: 920sq ft
Basic operating weight: 30,275lb
Max payload: 15,800lb
Max take-off weight: 55,000lb
Speed: 300mph at 15,000ft (max cruising)
Range: 1,230 miles with max payload
1,950 miles with max fuel

In its initial form as installed in the Viscount 700, the Rolls-Royce Dart was not powerful enough for the Convair, but when the higher-rated RDa10/1 developed for the NAMC YS-11 became available it was applied, as the Dart 542-4 developing 3,025eshp. (max take-off) to the Convair family, conversions being done either directly by the Convair Division of General Dynamics, or with the aid of kits supplied by them. The re-engined Model 240 was known as the 240D and later as the Convair 600, and the 340 and 440 were known at first as the Convair 640. The 340 and 440D, and then as the Convair 640. The Darts drove Dowty Rotol four-blade airscrews that were 2ft further forward than on the 240, and up to 52 passengers could be accommodated in the Convair 600, or up to 56 in the 640. Long range tanks could give the 600 a maximum fuel capacity of 2,000 US gallons, or 2,945 US gallons for the 640, and an AiResearch auxiliary power unit could be fitted if desired, as could a forward cargo door. The US local service carrier Central Airlines placed the first order, for 10 600s, and Trans-Texas Airways (now Texas International Airlines) ordered 25. The 600 first flew on 20 May 1965, and received FAA certification on 18 November, going into service with Central on 30 November that year. Caribair ordered seven 640s and Hawaiian Airlines eight, the 640 first going into service with Caribair on 22 December 1965. Subsequent orders were placed by Martinair Holland and Air Algerie, while second-hand 640s were acquired by Seulawah-Mandala of Indonesia, Pacific Western Airlines, Aerolineas Colonia of Uruguay, SMB Stage Lines, which now has 15, and the US supplemental carrier Zantop International, which operates 14, some of which are 640F freighters; several smaller US operators use the type. Altogether 39 Convair 600s and 28 Convair 640s were converted.

Convair 880

USA

Photo and Data: 880M

Engines: Four 11,650lb st General Electric
CJ805-3B turbojets
Span: 120ft 0in
Length: 129ft 4in
Height: 36ft 4in
Wing area: 2,000sq ft
Capacity payload: 23,150lb
Max take-off weight: 191,000lb
Speed: 557mph at 30,000ft (optimum cost
cruising)
Range: 5,056 miles with max fuel

For their entry into the jet airliner field with the
Model 880, Convair sought to build on the success
of the Model 240/340/440 family by offering a high
performance medium jet that filled the gap between
the DH Comet 4 and 4C and the Boeing 707-120,
the 707 and DC-8 still being regarded as too big by
many airlines when the Convair jet was announced
in April 1956. It was designated Model 22, was
initially known as the Convair Skylark and then as
the Golden Arrow, this name being linked with the
idea of anodising the exterior surfaces a golden tint.
When this was abandoned, it became the Convair
600 because of the cruising speed of just over
600mph and finally, when this speed was expressed
in feet per second, it acquired the definitive
designation Convair 880. It had a smaller capacity
than the 707 and DC-8 and could accommodate up
to 88 first-class or 119 tourist passengers in a
fuselage designed for five-abreast seating but not
wide enough for six-abreast — a factor which put it
at a disadvantage to the Boeing 707 and 720. The
preliminary design was schemed around four Pratt &
Whitney J57 jets, but the powerplant finally chosen
was the 11,200lb st General Electric CJ805-3, a
version of the military J79. No prototype was built as

such, the first 880, which was built on production
jigs, making its initial flight on 27 January 1959, and
the initial orders had been placed by TWA, which had
had first refusal of the design, for 30 and by Delta Air
Lines, which ordered 10. FAA certification was
received on 1 May 1960 but it was Delta who
inaugurated 880 services on 15 May that year
because TWA (or rather Howard Hughes) could not
complete the financing of its order and had to
postpone some deliveries, finally starting 880
services on 12 January 1961.

The Convair 880M, also known as the Model 22M
or 31, of which seven were ordered by Capital
Airlines but cancelled on that airline's takeover by
United, was a version tailored for shorter ranges and
reduced turn-around times, with extra fuel tankage in
the centre section, higher weights and 11,650lb st
CJ805-3B turbojets with thrust reversers. The 880M
also had four leading edge slats on each wing, a
power-boosted rudder and larger fin, a strengthened
undercarriage with improved braking and a
retractable tail skid. United had been discussing a
possible order for a developed 880 when Boeing,
working very rapidly, came up in 1957 with a slightly
smaller and lightened version of the 707-120 known
as the 720, which United duly ordered. The
appearance of the 720 was a serious blow to 880
and 990A sales prospects, for 707 operators now
had, in the 720, a type with a high degree of
commonality with their bigger jets. Only 65 880s
were built when production ended in July 1962, of
which 17 were 880Ms, and the 880M was used by
VIASA of Venezuela, Alaska Airlines, Civil Air
Transport of Formosa, Japan Air Lines and Cathay
Pacific of Hong Kong; LANICA of Nicaragua acquired
four 880s, one 880M was used by the FAA, and
880s were also used on lease at various times by
Swissair, Japan Domestic Airways, Air Malta and
Northeast Airlines amongst other operators.

Convair 990A Coronado

USA

Photo: Swissair 990A

Engines: Four 16,050lb st General Electric
CJ805-23B turbofans
Span: 120ft 0in

Length: 139ft 2½in
Height: 39ft 6in
Wing area: 2,250sq ft
Basic operating weight: 120,900lb
Max payload: 26,440lb

Max take-off weight: 253,000lb
Speed: 615mph (max) at 20,000ft
556mph at 35,000ft (long range cruising)
Range: 3,800 miles with max payload
5,446 miles with max fuel

Originally known as the Convair 600, the Model 990 was a growth version of the 880 designed to meet the requirements of American Airlines, which placed an initial order in July 1958 for 25 with 25 more on option; this was later reduced to 20 on order. The 990 had a 10ft longer fuselage seating up to 139 passengers, a maximum weight increased to 244,200lb, four General Electric CJ805-23B turbofans and a modified wing with larger flaps and increased area, giving in effect a thinner section which made possible a cruising speed of up to Mach 0.91 (625mph). To minimise the formation of a transonic shock wave at such speeds, with the resulting drag rise, two anti-shock bodies were featured on the trailing edge of each wing in which 320 and 300 US gallons of fuel could be stored. The first 990, built on production jigs, first flew on 24 January 1961, but during flight testing it was found that excessive oscillation occurred in the outer engine pods at high speeds when the outer anti-shock bodies were filled with fuel and this demanded a shortening of the engine pylon. Further expensive modifications became necessary when flight tests revealed excessive airframe drag which meant that guaranteed speed and range could not be attained. While modifications were devised, contracts with American Airlines and Swissair (which had ordered seven, two of which were later leased to SAS) were renegotiated. The modified version was designated Convair 990A and incorporated five main modifications to the engine nacelles, including extending the engine pod aft, covering the clamshell thrust reversers, installing a leading edge 'glove' over the engine mount and fitting a large terminal fairing extending aft of each inboard nacelle.

American began 990 services with unmodified aircraft on 18 March 1962 and Swissair on 25 February with a service to Rio. Only 37 were built, the other operators, apart from Swissair, being Varig of Brazil and Garuda Indonesian, with three 990As each, and Aerolineas Peruanas SA, while one was acquired for celestial research by NASA. This had windows in the upper fuselage for observation and photography, and was later joined by a second-hand 990A. Another new 990A was acquired by Garrett AiResearch as a flying laboratory. The major operators of used 990As are the Spanish charter airline Spantax, which acquired 14, and the US supplemental carrier Modern Air Transport, which has now ceased operations, with 10; Modern operated its 990As seating 149 passengers — more than any other 990A operator — and also fitted them with auxiliary power units. Alaska Airlines acquired one used 990A and Lebanese International Airways had two, which were destroyed in the Israeli raid on Beirut airport in December 1968, while the Danish charter operator Internord Aviation had three. At various times Air Ceylon, Air France, Ghana Airways, El Al, Balair, Iberia, Thai Airways International, Middle East Airlines and Northeast Airlines have operated 990As on lease. A few 990As are used by US travel clubs. Model 990A production ceased early in 1964 after Convair had lost a great deal of money on its jet airliner programmes.

Curtiss C-46 Commando   USA

Photo: C-46A
Data: Civil C-46A, C-46D or C-46F

Engines: Two 2,000bhp (max take-off) Pratt & Whitney R-2800-51M1 Double Wasp 18-cylinder 2-row radials
Span: 108ft 0in
Length: 76ft 4in
Height: 21ft 9in
Wing area: 1,358sq ft
Weight: 29,100lb (empty)
Capacity payload: 17,600lb

Max take-off weight: 48,000lb
Speed: 269mph (max)
195mph at 9,000ft (best economy cruising)
Range: 1,800 miles with 9,584lb payload

At the time of its debut the largest twin-engined aeroplane in the world, the Curtiss Wright CW-20 resulted from discussions held with several airlines in the United States in 1937 about a pressurised twin-engined airliner larger than the DC-3. The CW-20 prototype was first flown at St Louis on 26 March 1940, and was a 36-seater powered by 1,700hp

Wright R-2600-586-C14-BA2 Cyclones and featuring twin fins and rudders. No airline orders for the CW-20 were placed before Pearl Harbor, but the USAAF saw its possibilities as a military transport, especially for freight, and ordered it as the C-46 Commando. The prototype, now fitted with the single fin and rudder of production aircraft, was transferred to the USAAF under the designation C-55-CS, and was later sold to BOAC as G-AGDI, being delivered in November 1941. The first production version was the C-46, of which 25 were built, which had 2,000hp Pratt & Whitney R-2800-43 Double Wasps and was followed by 1,491 C-46A freighters with a single large loading door and by 1,410 C-46Ds with double loading doors, a modified nose and 2,000hp R-2800-51 engines. The C-46E, of which 17 were built, had a single loading door, whereas the 234 C-46Fs had double doors; both the E and F had 2,000hp R-2800-75 motors. Altogether 3,181 C-46s were built for the USAAF. In addition to up to 16,000lb of cargo, the C-46 could accommodate up to 40 troops on folding seats or 33 stretcher cases; fittings under the fuselage allowed for a complete airscrew to be carried externally. The US Marine Corps used a total of 160 Commandos as the R5C-1.

After the war, many C-46s were disposed of to commercial operators, and its 2,300cu ft capacity main hold made it very useful as a freighter, or for carrying up to 62 passengers. A postwar civil version of the C-46, the CW-20E, was planned seating 36 passengers and featuring a stepped windscreen;

2,100hp Wright R-3350-C18B2 Duplex Cyclones would have been fitted in place of the Double Wasps. But after Eastern Air Lines cancelled an order, the CW-20E was abandoned. Technical difficulties regarding the award of a civil airworthiness certificate led to the US Civil Aeronautics Authority placing the C-46 in the transport category for domestic use only, and because of this its American C of A was never ratified by the British ARB. C-46s were chiefly used in North America, especially by the US 'non-skeds' and freight airlines, and by many Latin American operators, both scheduled and non-scheduled. In the mid-1950s a few C-46s were fitted with a Turboméca Marboré auxiliary jet under each wing, and an improved version, the Smith CW-20T, featured some 30 engine and airframe improvements, including modified and cleaned-up engine cowlings; it was awarded an unrestricted CAA certificate in 1956. In March 1958 approval for another modified version, the Smith Super 46C, was obtained for operating at a maximum weight of 50,100lb, a figure soon increased to 50,650lb. The Riddle C-46R was another version modified along broadly similar lines to the CW-20T by Riddle Airlines Inc (now Airlift International); the C-46R received a transport category C of A in March 1957. The C-46 also served with several air forces postwar, including those of Nationalist China, Japan, South Korea, Dominica, Honduras, Brazil, Uruguay and Peru, as well as with the USAF Tactical Air Command.

Dassault Falcon 20

France

Photo: Fan Jet Falcon
Data: Falcon 20F

Engines: Two 4,315lb st General Electric CF700-2D-2 turbofans
Span: 53ft 6in
Length: 56ft 3in
Height: 17ft 5in
Wing area: 440sq ft
Weight: (empty) 15,350lb (Falcon 20DC)
Max payload: 3,320lb
Max take-off weight: 28,660lb

Speed: 536mph at 25,000ft (max cruising)
466mph at 40,000ft (best economy cruising)
Range: 1,400 miles with max payload (Falcon 20DC)
2,000 miles with max fuel (Falcon 20DC)

Widely used as an executive jet with standard accommodation for 8-10 passengers and two crew, or up to 14 in an alternative layout, the Dassault Falcon 20, or Fan Jet Falcon, was originally known as the Mystère 20, this name still being used in France. Pan American's Business Jets Division

placed an initial order for 54, plus 106 on option, in August 1963 and marketed the Mystère 20 in the USA as the Fan Jet Falcon. By October 1977 total orders for the type stood at 427, including 239 for US civil operators and 41 for the US Coast Guard, and 366 had been delivered. A few have been used by airlines, in particular Air Nauru in the Pacific, Touraine Air Transport on certain French domestic routes, and Federal Express Corporation for air mail services in the States, while Air France has used up to five Falcon 20s for airline crew training and Japan Air Lines has three for the same purpose. Development of the Mystère 20 was undertaken jointly with Sud-Aviation, and the prototype first flew on 4 May 1963 powered by two 3,300lb st Pratt & Whitney JT12A-8 turbojets with SNECMA thrust reversers; it was later re-engined with General Electric CF700-2B turbofans which were standard on production aircraft, first flying with these engines on 10 July 1964. Other changes made in production aircraft included a 3ft 3in increase in span to reduce the approach speed, an 18in increase in cabin length, and the use of twin wheels instead of single ones on all three undercarriage units. The first production Mystère 20 flew on 1 January 1965, and French certification and US Transport Category Type Approval was granted on 9 June that year.

Current production version is the Falcon 20F which has 4,315lb st CF700-2D-2 turbofans in place of the earlier 4,200lb st CF700-2C engines, increased wing fuel capacity and high-lift devices to improve take-off and landing. These take the form of non-slotted slats inboard of the wing fences and slotted slats outboard of them. Deliveries of the Falcon 20F began in July 1970. The type has also been used for navaid calibration, for aerial surveys and photography and as a systems trainer; two, designated Falcon ST, have been fitted with Mirage III-E combat radar and navigation systems for the French Air Force, and two of this version have also been supplied to the Libyan Republic Air Force. Seven Falcon 20s are used by the Royal Canadian Air Force's No 412 Sqn as VIP transports. A Falcon 20 was converted to cargo configuration under contract from Pan American by Little Rock Airmotive Inc, the prototype first flying on 28 May 1972. This version was soon ordered by a US third-level airline, Federal Express Corporation, which acquired 33 of the Falcon 20DC, or Falcon D Cargo Jets. These were modified by Little Rock Airmotive to have an upward-opening cargo door 6ft 2in × 4ft 9in in the port side, and a strengthened freight floor, with floor-mounted rollers optional. Federal's Falcons fly parcel, mail and freight services by night from its home base at Memphis, Tennessee, to no fewer than 130 towns and cities all over the USA. The Falcon 20G Guardian is a maritime surveillance version of which 41 have been ordered for the US Coast Guard, and will be powered by 5,050lb st Garrett AiResearch ATF3-6 turbofans. These engines can be retrofitted to existing Falcons, and the next production version of The Falcon 20 will have these powerplants. Three Falcon 20s are used by the RAAF's No 36 Sqn as VIP transports.

De Havilland DH89A Dragon Rapide   UK

Data: Mk 6

Engines: Two 205hp (max take-off) de Havilland Gipsy Queen III 6-cylinder air-cooled in-line motors
Span: 48ft 0in
Length: 34ft 6in
Height: 10ft 3in
Wing area: 340sq ft
Weight: 3,230lb (empty)
5,550lb (max gross) (Mks 1 to 4)
6,000lb (max gross) (Mk 6)
Speed: 150mph (max) (Mk 4)

140mph (cruising) (Mk 4)
Range: 520 miles (Mk 4)

The Dragon Rapide was a development of the DH84 Dragon intended, like the latter, to provide air transport that would pay its way on a very limited flow of passenger traffic without subsidy; it had more powerful DH Gipsy Six engines instead of the Dragon's Gipsy Majors, and featured tapered wings based on those of the DH86 Express. Known at first as the Dragon Six, the prototype DH89 made its first flight on 17 April 1934 and the type was soon selling

steadily, especially to the smaller operators in Britain and the British Empire territories; just over 200 had been built by the outbreak of war. The DH89A introduced in 1937 featured small split flaps and a prototype DH89M military version was built to Spec 18/35 for GR duties with Coastal Command — a requirement for which the Anson was eventually ordered. The DH89B, later named the Dominie, was used by the RAF in two main versions, the Mk I radio trainer to Spec 29/38 (a similar version was also used for navigational training) and the Mk II communications version to Spec 21/38. Altogether 475 Dominies were built, production being transferred in 1943 from Hatfield to the Brush Coachworks Ltd at Loughborough, and many prewar civil Rapides were impressed into RAF service. DH89 production did not end until 1945, when the 737th

and last left the assembly line, and many surplus DH89s were acquired by commercial operators after the war. Three Rapides and a Percival Proctor delivered to Portugal in November 1945 were the first British commercial aircraft to be exported after the war. The Rapide's combination of carrying capacity (6-8 passengers), low first cost, simple fabric-covered wooden construction and reliable Gipsy Queen III engines giving up to 1,000 hours between overhauls made it for a long time almost impossible to replace; over 80 were still in airline service 20 years after the war ended. Many of these, known as Rapide 4s, were fitted with Gipsy Queen II engines driving constant-speed airscrews, while the Mk 6 featured Fairey Reed X5 two-blade fixed pitch airscrews giving a take-off weight increased to 6,000lb and improved payload.

De Havilland DH104 Dove and Devon   UK

Photo: Dove
Data: Dove Mk 8

Engines: Two 400bhp (max take-off) de Havilland Gipsy Queen 70 Mk 3 6-cylinder air-cooled in-line engines
Span: 57ft 0in
Length: 39ft 3in
Height: 13ft 4in
Wing area: 335sq ft
Weight: 6,325lb (empty equipped)
Max take-off weight: 8,950lb
Speed: 230mph (max)
210mph at 8,000ft (max cruising)
Range: 880 miles with max fuel

Designed to meet the Brabazon Committee's Type VB specifications the DH104 Dove, which made its first flight on 25 September 1945, was conceived as

an 'airliner in miniature' embodying the latest and most modern concepts in its design. It embodied a number of 'big aircraft' features hitherto usually absent in light transports of the feeder-line category, such as geared and supercharged engines, braking airscrews, a nosewheel undercarriage, power-operated flaps and advanced all-metal structural techniques such as Redux bonding. The commercial success of this formula was soon apparent, and the Dove's position as the best-selling British transport aircraft (altogether 542 were built) has only recently been taken over by the Islander; the Dove was also the first British airliner to break into the US markets, which it did as an executive type. The prototype did not at first have the dorsal fin standard on production versions; the 8-11 passenger Mk 1 and the executive Mk 2 seating, typically, five people had 330bhp Gipsy Queen 70 Mk 3s while the Mks 1B and 2B featured 340bhp Gipsy Queen 70 Mk 4 powerplants.

The Mk 3 was an air survey version with provision for one Williamson vertical camera, a camera operator's position and oxygen for a service ceiling of 24,000ft, while the Mk 4 air ambulance could take four stretcher cases, a doctor and two medical attendants; in actual practice, these mark numbers were not used. More powerful 380bhp Gipsy Queen 70 Mk 2 engines powered the Dove 5 airliner and the executive Mk 6, otherwise the same as the Mks 1 and 2; the Mks 5A and 6A were versions for the United States market, the Mk 6BA being the Dove 2 fitted with the more powerful engines. The Dove 7 airliner (Mk 7A for the US market) introduced 400bhp Gipsy Queen 70 Mk 3s in new low-drag cowlings with exhaust augmentors and a deeper, Heron-type cockpit canopy; the maximum weight went up from the Mk 1's 8,500lb to 8,950lb. The Mk 8 was the executive version, known as the Mk 8A, and also as the Dove Super Custom 800, for US customers.

Meanwhile a military transport version of the Dove 1 to Spec C13/46 for RAF use and known as

the Devon C Mk 1 was produced, the first of 30 (actually the 48th production Dove) being delivered in 1948; Devons were used by Communications Flights of the various Command HQs and by Air Attaches abroad. Passenger seating was reduced to seven, and the Devon featured several other minor internal changes from the Dove; the Royal Navy's Sea Devon C Mk 20 is very similar. Devons were supplied to the Royal New Zealand Air Force, and Doves have also been delivered to more than a dozen air arms; those of the Royal Swedish Air Force were designated Tp 46. The Riley 400 is a modified version of the Dove by Riley Aeronautics Corp of Fort Lauderdale, Florida, which has two 400hp Lycoming 10-720 engines and a swept fin as well as a number of other airframe changes; Doves could be converted completely to Riley 400 standard or in six individual stages, any one of which could be incorporated on its own in a standard Dove. In 1964 McAlpine Aviation acquired sole rights to carry out Riley 400 conversions in all countries outside North and South America.

De Havilland DH114 Heron

UK

Photo: Mk 1B
Data: Mk 2

Engines: Four 250bhp (max take-off) de Havilland Gipsy Queen 30 Mk 2 6-cylinder air-cooled in-line engines.
Span: 71ft 6in
Length: 48ft 6in
Height: 15ft 7in
Wing area: 499sq ft
Weight: 8,666lb (empty equipped)
Capacity payload: 3,750lb
Max take-off weight: 13,500lb
Speed: 183mph at 8,000ft (cruising)

Range: 500 miles with max payload
1,785 miles with max fuel

The Dove's success as a feederliner led naturally to thoughts of a larger development, and the DH114 Heron was a scaled-up four-engined version of the Dove with an 8ft 6in longer cabin seating 14-17 passengers and, in the Mk 1, a fixed nosewheel undercarriage for simplicity and ease of maintenance; the Gipsy Queen 30 Mk 2 engines drove DH 2-blade non-feathering airscrews. The prototype Mk 1 first flew on 10 May 1950 and Mk 1s were used by BEA, Jersey Airlines, Braathens SAFE of Norway, Gulf Aviation, NZNAC of New

49

Zealand and a number of other operators. But before long the Mk 1 was succeeded in production by the Heron 2 with a retractable undercarriage giving a 20mph increase in cruising speed but at a small increase in empty weight; feathering propellers were now fitted. The Mk 2 made its first flight on 14 December 1952 and proved popular not only as an airliner but as an executive type seating 6-8 people; some were supplied to foreign air forces and also to the Queen's Flight, which used four specially-equipped Herons with VIP interiors, one of these being a Heron C4. The Sea Heron C20 was a version of the Mk 2 used by the Royal Navy for communications duties.

Altogether 148 Herons were built, and about 80 of these were still in airline service by the beginning of 1970; during the 1960s the type became increasingly popular among the US third-level or commuter airlines. But already several operators had felt the need for more modern powerplants to extend the Heron's useful life and improve its performance, and the Japanese carrier Toa Domestic Airlines had five of its Heron 1Bs converted by Shin Meiwa during 1965 to have 260hp Continental IO-470-D 'flat six' engines, in which form they were known as the Tawron. Connair Pty Ltd, the Alice Springs-based Australian airline serving mostly the Northern Territory, had several of its Herons converted by Riley Aeronautics to have Lycoming IO-540-G1A5 'flat six' engines, and Riley produced a conversion of the Heron with Lycoming IGO-540-B1A5 powerplants known as the Riley Turbo-Skyliner, the first of which was delivered to the US third-level operator Colorado River Airlines. In Canada Saunders Aircraft began converting Heron 2s into ST-27s with two Pratt & Whitney PT6A-34 turboprops.

De Havilland DHA-3 Drover

Australia

Photo and Data: Mk 3

Engines: Three 180hp Lycoming 0-360-A1A 4-cylinder horizontally-opposed air-cooled engines
Span: 57ft 0in
Length: 36ft 6in
Height: 10ft 9in
Wing area: 325sq ft
Weight: 4,600lb (empty equipped)
6,500lb (max loaded)
Speed: 158mph (max)
140mph (cruising)
Range: 900 miles

The DHA-3 Drover was designed by DH's Australian subsidiary, de Havilland Aircraft Pty Ltd, as a simple light transport to replace the DH84 Dragon in Australian conditions, the emphasis being on ruggedness and a good climb-out performance with one engine inoperative. After a number of layouts were investigated, the design emerged as a three-engined, fixed undercarriage development of the DH104 Dove seating up to eight passengers and incorporating the Dove's well established structural features, lower-powered (145hp) Gipsy Major 10 Mk 2 engines replacing the latter's Gipsy Queen 70s. The prototype Drover first flew on 23 January 1948

and production deliveries began in 1949. Only 20 aircraft had been built when production ended in 1953, the Drover 1 being succeeded by the Mk 2 with double slotted flaps. The type was used by Trans-Australia Airlines for its multi-stop routes in Queensland, Fiji Airways, Air Melanesiae and its predecessor New Hebrides Airways, in the New Hebrides islands, Qantas, and by the New South Wales and Queensland sections of the Royal Flying Doctor Service. The latter's seven aircraft were later re-engined with 180hp Lycoming O-360-A1A 'flat four' engines, driving Hartzell feathering airscrews, thus becoming Drover 3s; the first Mk 3 conversion being delivered on 4 June 1960. The air ambulance Drover could carry two stretcher cases and two medical attendants.

De Havilland DHC-2 Beaver

Canada

Photo: Beaver Seaplane
Data: Mk I

Engine: One 450bhp Pratt & Whitney Wasp Junior R-985-SB3 9-cylinder radial
Span: 48ft 0in
Length: 30ft 4in
Height: 9ft 0in
Wing area: 250sq ft
Basic operating weight: 3,000lb
Max take-off weight: 5,100lb
Speed: 163mph (max) at 5,000ft
135mph at sea level (max cruising)
Range: 483 miles with max payload
778 miles with max fuel

Air transport in Canada's far north, which often had the task of serving communities for whom the aeroplane was virtually the only link with the outside world, had traditionally demanded rugged and reliable single-engined STOL transports, capable of operating on wheels, floats or skis. To replace older types like these, such as the Fairchild 82 or Noorduyn Norseman which were now obsolescent the DHC-2 Beaver was designed especially for

Canadian bush operations as a seven-passenger utility transport with a 450hp Pratt & Whitney Wasp Junior R-985 engine. The prototype first flew on 16 August 1947 and a Canadian Department of Transport type certificate was granted on 12 March 1948. The Beaver soon gained acceptance among civil operators and large orders were placed by the US Army for the type under the designation L-20A-DH (now U-6A); altogether 968 U-6A Beavers have been supplied, mostly to the Army but a few to the USAF (originally designated C-127) for use as utility transports by Strategic Air Command. Another 46 were supplied to the British Army as the Beaver AL Mk 1, and some 16 other air arms have also acquired Beavers. Twenty years after its first flight, the Beaver was in civil and military service in 65 different countries, and nearly 150 were in airline service, mostly in Canada and Alaska but also in South America, Africa, the Far East and Australasia. STOL performance is ensured by slotted ailerons interconnected with the slotted flaps so that they droop up to 15° when the flaps are fully lowered. The cabin seats up to seven passengers in lightweight collapsible bush seats and the cabin doors, one on each side, are wide enough to roll a

45-gallon petrol drum into the cabin on its side. Hatches in the rear wall of the cabin are provided to enable long pieces of freight, such as 10ft long drilling rods, to be loaded and stowed, and the floor is stressed for freight carrying.

Twin Edo floats can be fitted in place of the wheels, or fixed skis or a combination wheel-ski gear of DH design. The Beaver amphibian has rectractable nose and main wheels in each float, the former retracting upwards and over on to the top of the float. A rack for a supply container can be fitted under each wing and under the fuselage, and the Beaver can be equipped for crop spraying or dusting, aerial survey, cable- or wire-laying, paratroop dropping, the carriage of stretcher cases or for 'sky shouting' using a loud hailer. A single Beaver II was produced in 1953 by fitting a Beaver with a 550bhp

Alvis Leonides 502/4 radial driving a de Havilland 3-blade airscrew, and a taller fin and rudder was featured. Design work on the DHC-2 Mk III Turbo-Beaver began in June 1963 and this flew for the first time on 30 December that year, powered by a 578eshp Pratt & Whitney PT6A-6 turboprop driving a three-blade Hartzell reversible-pitch prop. First deliveries of the Turbo-Beaver took place in December 1964, and this version could be produced both as a new aircraft and by converting existing Beavers. The forward fuselage is extended to bring the cockpit ahead of the wing, and a new swept fin and rudder of greater area is featured. Up to nine passengers can be carried in the cabin (plus one beside the pilot) or up to 1,800lb of freight. Altogether 1,657 Beavers were built.

De Havilland DHC-3 Otter
Canada

Photo: Otter Amphibian

Engine: One 600hp Pratt & Whitney R-1340-S1H1-G or S3H1-G Wasp 9-cylinder radial
Span: 58ft 0in
Length: 41ft 10in
Height: 12ft 7in (landplane)
Wing area: 375sq ft
Basic operating weight: 4,431lb
Max take-off weight: 8,000lb
Speed: 160mph (max) at 5,000ft 132mph at sea level (max cruising)
Range: 875 miles with 2,100lb payload 945 miles (max)

The success of the Beaver led naturally to consideration of a larger development designed, like the Beaver, for Canadian conditions but suitable for bush and outback operators anywhere in the world. According to a joke in the old *de Havilland Gazette*, the Otter was designed for the sort of pilot who

comes into town once a year for a C of A and a shave, and this certainly sums up its ability to give trouble-free operation in arduous climatic conditions for long periods away from base. Compared with the Beaver the Otter (originally known as the King Beaver) is more powerful, with a 600hp Pratt & Whitney R-1340 Wasp, and can seat up to 10 passengers. (or 11, with one beside the pilot) against the Beaver's seven. The Otter prototype first flew on 12 December 1951, and the type received its Canadian Certificate of Airworthiness as both a landplane and seaplane in November 1952. The Otter soon attracted the interest of military customers as well as civil, a total of 223 being supplied to the US Army as the U-1A, and some to the US Navy as the U-1B (previously UC-1). Otters were used by the US Navy's Operation Deep-freeze expedition to the Antarctic in 1956-58, and nine other countries, including Britain, have used Otters and Beavers in Antarctica. The Canadian Armed Forces' 69 Otters have been used for Arctic search and rescue operations, paratroop dropping and for

aerial photography; some have been used on behalf of the United Nations. Other military operators of the Otter include the Royal Australian Air Force and the air forces of Burma, Chile, Colombia, Ghana, India, Indonesia and Norway.

Civil Otters have been used by many Canadian airlines and bush operators, but few have gone into airline service outside Canada; Otter seaplanes were used by Wideroe's Flyveselskap A/S for domestic services in northern Norway, and as a landplane the type has been employed by Philippine Air Lines on domestic routes, by Qantas and TAA for routes in New Guinea and Papua, by Aigle Azur in Indo-China and by Aero Contractors in Nigeria. About 50 Otters

were in airline service in 1970. The cabin normally accommodates nine passengers on folding seats, with provision for a tenth seat; six stretchers and four passengers or sitting casualties can be carried, or three stretchers and seven passengers. The cabin floor is reinforced for freight carrying and there is a cargo drop hatch, camera hole or paratroop exit in the floor. Instead of wheels, twin Edo floats can be fitted or fixed skis of DH design. The amphibious version features standard Edo floats modified to take retractable nose and main wheels; the floats are lengthened and the nosewheels retract up and over into their top decking, retraction of all four wheels being by hydraulic power.

De Havilland DHC-4 Caribou Canada

Engines: Two 1,450bhp (max take-off) Pratt & Whitney R-2000-7M2 Twin Wasp radials
Span: 95ft 7½in
Length: 72ft 7in
Height: 31ft 9in
Wing area: 912sq ft
Weight: 16,920lb (empty)
28,500lb (max gross)
Speed: 216mph at 6,500ft (max cruising)
181mph at 7,500ft (best economy cruising)
Range: 372 miles with 8,620lb payload OR 1,280 miles with 5,152lb payload

The Caribou had its genesis in design studies by de Havilland Aircraft of Canada for a twin-engined version of the Otter weighing 13,000lb, with two Otter-type powerplants and a fixed undercarriage. But early US and Canadian Army interest led to the incorporation of rear loading, and the result was a much larger design aimed at combining DC-3 load-carrying capabilities with Beaver and Otter-type STOL performance. The decision to proceed was made in 1955 and the prototype DHC-4 Caribou, the

first of three, first flew on 30 July 1958. Exceptional STOL performance and single engined handling were achieved with the aid of full-span double slotted flaps and the big single fin and rudder. The DHC-4 received US Type Approval at a gross weight of 26,000lb and the DHC-4A at a gross weight of 28,500lb. Five Caribous were evaluated by the US Army as the YAC-1A tactical transport, the first of these being delivered on 8 October 1959, and this led to an order for 159 CV-2s (previously AC-1s); the CV-2A was equivalent to the DHC-4 while the CV-2B corresponded to the slightly heavier DHC-4A. Later 134 of the US Army's CV-2s were transferred to the USAF and redesignated C-7As. Nine Caribous were ordered by the Royal Canadian Air Force under the designation CC-108. The Caribou can accommodate 32 troops or 26 fully-equipped paratroops or 22 stretcher cases, four sitting casualties and four medical attendants; up to three tons of cargo or two fully-loaded jeeps can be carried in the freighter role, while for airline use seats for up to 30 passengers can be fitted. Production aircraft have a 3ft 9in longer fuselage than the prototypes and the Caribou was ordered by a number of foreign air forces in addition to the US Army. Biggest customer was the Royal Australian Air Force, which bought 25, followed by the Indian Air Force with 16 and eight for the Ghana Air Force. Smaller numbers were ordered by the air forces of Kuwait, Zambia, Zaire, Kenya, Tanzania (which now has 12 Caribous), the Uganda Police Air Wing and the Royal Malaysian Air Force, which now has 12. The Swedish Air Board acquired one which was later sold to Ansett-MAL for use in Papua New Guinea, but there have been only a few other Caribou civil sales: three for Civil Air Transport in Formosa and two (plus six more leased),

for Air America. One CV-2 was converted into a flying command post by the Collins Radio Co for use by the 1st (Air) Cavalry Division in Vietnam, and the prototype was later fitted with two 2,850hp General Electric T64-GE-4 turboprops to test these engines for the DHC-5 Buffalo, first flying with T64s on 22 September 1961. Other sales of the military version have been to the air forces of Spain (2), Muscat and Oman and the Abu Dhabi Defence Force. Single examples of the civil version are flown by Air Cargo America, Air Gabon, Intermountain Aviation (now sold), while Guyana Airways has two.

De Havilland DHC-6 Twin Otter Canada

Photo and Data: Series 300

Engines: Two 652eshp Pratt & Whitney PT6A-27 turboprops
Span: 65ft 0in
Length: 51ft 9in
Height: 18ft 7in
Wing area: 420sq ft
Basic operating weight: 7,320lb
Max payload: 4,430lb
Max take-off weight: 12,500lb
Speed: 210mph (max cruising)
Range: 115 miles with max payload
1,103 miles with max fuel

The success of the DHC-3 Otter had led naturally to studies of the possibilities of a twin-engined development, and de Havilland Aircraft of Canada's first thoughts in this direction had led eventually to the DHC-4 Caribou. The Twin Otter, design work on which began in January 1964, was much smaller and was intended to use many of the DHC-3 Otter's wing and fuselage components. It was aimed especially at the commuter and third-level airline markets, and to operators flying routes of low traffic density in undeveloped areas and using small and restricted airfields. Using the same fuselage cross-

section as its single counterpart, the Twin Otter has a cabin lengthened to seat up to 20 passengers on each side of a central aisle, with a redesigned tail unit and a new nose; the wing is very similar to the Otter but increased in span to 65ft and with double-slotted full span trailing edge flaps, with ailerons that droop when these are lowered. Design work was quickly completed, construction of an initial batch of five Twin Otters beginning in November 1964, and the prototype first flew on 20 May 1965. The first three aircraft had 579shp Pratt & Whitney PT6A-6 turboprops but production aircraft, later known as Series 100s, were fitted with the improved PT6A-20 of the same power. Type approval was granted in May 1966 and the first deliveries were made in July, the Twin Otter soon attracting worldwide sales interest from third-level and other small airlines; first of a number of military customers was the Chilean Air Force, with an order for eight. The US Army acquired two, designated UV-18A, and the Canadian Armed Forces have eight, designated CC-138. Like the single-engined Otter, a wheel ski undercarriage could be fitted or twin floats; all floatplanes have the short Srs 100 nose, Series 200s or 300s as well as Series 100s. Ten of the 12 supplied to the Peruvian Air Force have floats for operations along the Amazon.

Production of the latter totalled 115 and the

Series 200, deliveries of which began in April 1968, was the same except for a lengthened nose fairing with increased baggage capacity. Altogether 115 of this version were built and the Series 300 differed in having 652eshp PT6A-27 turboprops and a maximum take-off weight increased by 1,500lb to 12,500lb. A ventral pannier carrying up to 600lb of baggage or freight can be fitted, as can low pressure tyres for operating off rough strips. Twin Otters have been used for such jobs as freighting, aerial surveys, oilfield support operations and by corporate and executive owners, and over 500 have now been built. Six of a special STOL version, the Twin Otter 300S, were ordered for Air Canada subsidiary AirTransit Canada's experimental STOL services between Montreal and Ottawa. Starting on 23 July 1974 and running until April 1976, this service used STOL ports close to the centres of both cities, each with a single 2,000ft paved strip. The 300S had upper wing spoilers ahead of the flaps, higher capacity brakes and an anti-skid braking system, advanced avionics for IFR operation, improved engine fire protection and other systems changes, and passenger seating was reduced to 11 in airline-style seats. These Twin Otters operated up to 30 flights daily on a half-hour schedule.

Dornier Do28D Skyservant West Germany

Engines: Two 380hp Lycoming IGSO-540-AIE 6-cylinder horizontally-opposed air-cooled engines
Span: 51ft 0in
Length: 37ft 5in
Height: 12ft 9in
Wing area: 302sq ft
Weight: 5,066lb (empty equipped)
8,470lb (max gross)
Speed: 201mph (max) at 13,100ft
186mph at 13,100ft (cruising)
Range: 1,255 miles with max fuel

The Dornier Do28 was evolved as a straightforward twin-engined development of the Do27 using virtually the same basic structure, the engines being mounted on stub wings set well forward with fixed undercarriage units at the extremities. The prototype Do28, with two 180hp Lycoming O-360-AIAs, first flew on 29 April 1959, and was followed by a second prototype with 250hp Lycoming O-540-A1D engines and an increase in wing span. The Do28A-1, the first production version, started coming off the line in 1960 and seating up to six passengers in the rear cabin, plus one beside the pilot, was similar to the second prototype. A combination of full span fixed slots and double-slotted flaps with inner portions of the ailerons drooping as flaps ensured an exceptional STOL performance, and a wheel/ski gear could be fitted if desired. The Do28A-1-S was a floatplane conversion of the A-1 by the Jobmaster Co of Seattle under contract to Hamilton Aviation Ltd of Edmonton, Alberta; the prototype flew in 1964. The Do28B-1 with two 290hp Lycoming IO-540-A engines first flew in April 1963, and had an increased gross weight and payload, an enlarged tailplane, a redesigned nose, auxiliary fuel tanks in the wing tips, improved electrically-acutuated flaps, a redesigned instrument panel and minor detail improvements. The Do28B-2 is the B-1 with turbo-supercharged engines and the Do28B-1-S was a projected seaplane conversion by the Jobmaster Co. The Do28C was a proposed pressurised version of the B-1 with two 530hp Turbomeca Astazou II turboprops, larger vertical tail surfaces and a span reduced to 37ft 5in.

The Do28D Skyservant is a completely new design with only the Do28's basic configuration; it has a very similar wing and a completely new square section fuselage seating up to 11 passengers in the 12ft 6in long cabin (plus one beside the pilot), and there is a large double-opening side door measuring 4ft 2in × 4ft 4in. More powerful Lycoming IGSO-540 engines are fitted driving Hartzell three-blade airscrews, and the tailplane is a one-piece all-moving surface. The first of three Do28D prototypes first flew on 23 February 1966, and both German and

American airworthiness certification was granted in 1967, production deliveries beginning that year. A wheel/ski gear or floats can be fitted. Up to 13 people can be carried in inward-facing folding seats, or five stretcher cases and five sitting casualties and attendants in folding seats; the cabin can be stripped and used for cargo. Both the Do28 and Do28D have been supplied to third-level and air taxi operators as well as to various government, corporate and executive customers, and have served with airlines from Canada and the Netherlands Antilles to Laos and Indonesia. Military users include the West German Luftwaffe, which acquired 121 Do28Ds, and the Kriegsmarine, which has 27 Do28D Skyservants. The Do28D-5 TurboSky, which first flew in April 1978, has two 620ehp Lycoming LTP101-600 AIA turboprops.

Douglas DC-3 USA

Engines: Two 1,200hp Pratt & Whitney Twin Wasp R-1830-90, -9OC, -90D or -92 14-cylinder 2-row radials
Span: 95ft 0in
Length: 64ft 6in
Height: 16ft 11$\frac{1}{2}$in
Wing area: 987sq ft
Operating weight: 17,720lb (empty)
Max payload: 6,600lb
Max take-off weight: 25,200lb
(US Passenger Operations)
28,000lb (British C of A, freighting)
Speed 215mph (max)
165mph at 6,000ft (best economy cruising)
Range: 350 miles with max payload
1,510 miles with max fuel

Famous as the world's most widely used airliner in civil or military service, the Douglas DC-3 had its origins in an American Airlines requirement of 1934 for a developed DC-2 with a wider fuselage to accommodate 14 passengers in sleeping berths and to replace the Curtiss Condor biplanes used on American's Boston-Dallas-Los Angeles sleeper services. At first Douglas was reluctant to go ahead with the new project, as the DC-2 had only made its first flight on 11 May 1934 and sales had hardly started (200 DC-2s were sold in all). The new DST (Douglas Sleeper Transport), as the DC-3 was initially designated, had a longer fuselage than the DC-2 with 26 inches more internal width, increased wing span, an enlarged tail unit (the characteristic dorsal fin was added three months after the first flight), more engine power and a stronger undercarriage. After an initial American order for 10 DSTs in July 1935, the prototype DST made its first flight from Santa Monica on 17 December that year; the DST was certificated (ATC607) on 29 April 1936 at a gross weight of 24,000lb initially, later raised to 25,000lb and then 25,200lb when more engine power became available. American's first DST was delivered on the day of certification, and its first DC-3, the so-called 'day plane' version of the DST with accommodation for 21 passengers, and with the DST's four 'bunk' windows deleted, on 18 August. American inaugurated DST services between New York and Chicago on 25 June 1936, and on the transcontinental route to Los Angeles on 18 September.

At first 920hp Wright GR-1820-G5 Cyclones were fitted to the DST, but several other models of the GR-1820 giving 1,000, 1,100 or 1,200hp could also be fitted to both the DST and DC-3, and also the DC-3B. Pratt & Whitney R-1830 Twin Wasps of 1,000hp became available for the DC-3A and DST-A, and again several different models of the R-1830 giving 1,050 or 1,200hp could be fitted; the Twin Wasp was to become by far the commonest powerplant, being fitted to most of the military versions. The DC-3 had proved to be an immediate success and orders flowed in, a total of 507 having been built by the end of 1941, of which 434 went to airlines; these included 50 DST and DST-A versions for American, Eastern, United, TWA and Western Air Express. About 100 DC-3s were exported, of which 63 were sold through and assembled by Fokker for European airlines such as KLM, Swissair and ABA of Sweden. The first two military versions for the USAAC, a C-41 and C-41A similar to the DC-3A, had been delivered in 1938-39 and the first big military order, for 545 C-47 Skytrains, was placed on 16 September 1940 (30 went to the US Navy as

R4D-1s); to handle military production new facilities were built at Long Beach and Oklahoma City. Pending the first C-47 deliveries, some 149 airline DC-3s on order were taken over by the USAAC under the designations C-48, C-49, C-50, C-51, C-52, C-68 and C-84. The 965 C-47-DLs built at Long Beach were 27-seaters with double cargo doors and strengthened freight floor and a 12-volt electrical system; they were followed by 2,954 C-47A-DLs and 2,300 Oklahoma-built C-47A-DKs which were the same but for a 24-volt electrical system, and by 300 C-47B-DLs and 3,064 C-47B-DKs. The B had supercharged R-1830-90 or -90B engines for flying over the 'Hump' from northern Assam into China, as well as cabin fuel tanks and a different cabin heating system. The C-53 Skytrooper, of which 395 were built, was a 28-seat carrier without the C-47's double cargo doors or floor; it entered service in October 1941. More than 1,200 C-47s and C-53s were supplied under Lend-Lease to the RAF, who named the type Dakota, the Dakota I corresponding to the C-47, the Mk II to the C-53, the Mk III to the C-47A and the Mk IV to the C-47B. Many Dakotas and C-47s were used as glider tugs, as well as paratroop transports, freighters and air ambulances. A final batch of 28 civil DC-3Ds were built at Santa Monica in 1946, these being assembled from C-117A components, and the last of these was delivered to Swissair in May that year. Total DC-3 production from 1935-46 amounted to 10,655, while in Japan the type was built in modified form for the Japanese Navy, about 571 of the L2D family being completed by Showa and Nakajima. The Russian-built DC-3, powered by Shvetsov M-621R or M-63R radials, was known as the Lisunov Li-2 (NATO codename Cab); it differed in details from the DC-3 and had the entry door to starboard. Over 2,700 Li-2s are believed to have been built, and 707 US-built C-47s went to Russia under Lend-Lease, Aeroflot also acquiring a few DC-3s in 1937 under the designation PS-84.

After the war thousands of DC-3s became available at cheap war surplus prices, equipping many small charter operators as well as larger airlines; the vast majority were conversions of C-47s, C-47As, C-47Bs or Dakotas. Many operate at gross weights of 28,000lb, and some at 32,000lb. The DC-3 reached its numerical peak in 1948, when there were 1,740 in commercial service, this number falling to about 1,300 by 1960 and to just over 500 today. Several major airlines produced their own improved versions of the DC-3, such as BEA's 'Pionair'-class variant and Pan Am's Hi-Per DC-3, and features like airstairs and picture windows were sometimes added by US operators, especially to the many DC-3s converted into executive transports. Others were used for air survey, often carrying special equipment such as an MAD boom, and even for aerial agriculture, while a recent illegitimate use has been for drug smuggling across the Mexican border into the States. Hardly an air force in the world has not had DC-3s in its inventory at some time, and in the mid-1960s there were some two dozen different versions of the basic C-47 serving the USAF and US Navy, mostly postwar variants such as the EC-47D for airways checks, HC-47 for search and rescue and Navy LC-47H and J for cold-weather operations and SC-47H and J search and rescue variants. Best known was the AC-47 'Puff the Magic Dragon' gunship, usually armed with three 7.62mm miniguns and used against ground targets in Vietnam. The Nigerian Air Force used DC-3s as makeshift bombers during the Biafran war, dropping 220lb bombs out of a crude shute from the cargo doors. Late in 1974 the US third-level operator Pilgrim Airlines became the first to operate the Turbo-Three, or Turbo DC-3, a version with two Rolls-Royce Dart turboprops. A still later version has three Pratt & Whitney PT6 turboprops.

Douglas DC-4   USA

Engines: Four 1,450bhp (max take-off) Pratt & Whitney R-2000-2SD13-G Twin Wasp 14-cylinder 2-row radials
Span: 117ft 6in
Length: 93ft 5in
Height: 27ft 7in
Wing area: 1,463sq ft

Weight: 46,000lb (empty equipped)
Max payload: 14,200lb
Max take-off weight: 73,000lb
Speed: 265mph (max)
207mph at 10,000ft (cruising)
Range: 1,150 miles with max payload
2,180 miles with max fuel

So successful were the new generation of twin-engined all-metal monoplane airliners exemplified by the Boeing 247 and Douglas DC-2 and DC-3 that thoughts soon started to turn to a four-engined version of this formula for trunk routes, particularly those across the USA. In mid-1935, before the DC-3 had even flown, discussions started between Douglas and five US airlines, United, American, TWA, Eastern and Pan American about a new four-engined airliner, and the airlines each put up $100,000 towards the cost of a prototype. The latter, known as the DC-4E, made it first flight on 7 June 1938 and was virtually a different aeroplane to the eventual production DC-4. It was larger, with a wing 20ft 9in greater in span, very similar in plan form to that of the later XB-19 bomber, and had inward retracting mainwheels, a backward retracting nosewheel, triple fins and rudders (a single fin and rudder was later fitted) and 1,400bhp Pratt & Whitney Twin Hornet R-2180-S1A1-G engines; up to 52 passengers could be accommodated. After evaluation the five sponsor airlines decided that the DC-4E was really too big for their needs. The production DC-4, designated DC-4A, was scaled down, with a tapered wing of 1,463sq ft area that was to remain almost unchanged right through to the DC-7B, four 1,350bhp Pratt & Whitney R-2000 Twin Wasps, a single fin and rudder, main wheels retracting into the nacelles, and accommodation for 42 passengers in an unpressurised cabin.

Orders for 61 were placed off the drawing board by American, United and Eastern but Pearl Harbour intervened and the type was taken over by the USAAF, the 24 DC-4As on the line being completed as C-54 Skymaster military transports, the first of these flying on 14 February 1942. These were followed by 207 C-54As (US Navy R5D-1) with a large cargo door and strengthened freight floor, 220 C-54Bs (R5D-2) with increased fuel capacity, the VC-54C VIP version for President Roosevelt, 350 C-54Ds (R5D-3), as the B but with an engine change, 75 C-54Es (R5D-4) with various interior changes and provision for carrying certain external loads, such as airscrews, under the fuselage, and 76 C-54Gs (R5D-5) with different engines to the E and a revised interior. C-54s were widely used as long haul transports and many surplus ones were adapted for civilian use after the war, providing the first four-engined equipment for a great many airlines starting to expand their routes, as well as for charter operators and the US 'non-skeds'. Up to 86 passengers could be accommodated in coach-class seating, although more usually 40-60 people were carried in first/tourist interiors. The first commercial operator of the DC-4 was American Export Airlines, which flew the first postwar landplane service across the Atlantic, from New York via Gander and Shannon to Hurn on 23-24 October 1945. The DC-4 pioneered long haul freighting, for which its double cargo doors were very suitable, and it was the first type to fly racehorses across the Atlantic. Some DC-4s were used as VIP or executive transports, sometimes with exotic interiors; that used by King Ibn Saud featured a throne room, while another was reputed to contain a gold-plated bathroom. Military versions continued to appear postwar, including the C-54M modified from the E for the Berlin airlift, the HC-54D air-sea rescue variant and TC-54D trainer,

Below: *DC-4*

the EC-54D special electronics version for MATS, and the EC-54U and RC-54V for reconnaissance serving with the US Coast Guard. DC-4s have also served with nearly 20 other air forces since the war. DC-4 production ended in August 1947 after 79 of a postwar civilian version designated DC-4-1009 had been completed; altogether 1,163 DC-4s were built and over 60 are still in airline service. A swing tail conversion of a DC-4 was produced by Sabena for Air Congo in 1966-67, and the DC-4-ME2 Super Skymaster was a variant re-engined in 1966 with 1,500bhp (max take-off) Wright R-2600-35MI Cyclones by Charlotte Aircraft Corp, giving improved performance and overcoming the shortage of R-2000 Twin Wasp spares; this version could be produced by kits.

Douglas DC-6   USA

Photo and Data: DC-6B

Engines: Four 2,500bhp (max take-off with water injection) Pratt & Whitney R-2800-CB17 Double Wasp 18-cylinder 2-row radials
Span: 117ft 6in
Length: 105ft 7in
Height: 29ft 3in
Wing area: 1,463sq ft
Basic operating weight: 58,635lb
Max payload: 24,565lb
Max take-off weight: 107,000lb
Speed: 360mph (max) at 18,100ft
307mph at 22,400ft (best economy cruising)
Range: 3,000 miles with max payload (no reserves)
4,720 miles with max fuel (no reserves)

During the closing months of the war it was clear to Douglas that while the unpressurised DC-4 would suit the postwar requirements of a great many airlines, there was a need for a larger and faster pressurised development for trunk routes, especially for the US transcontinental routes, to meet the challenge of the Lockheed Constellation. Design work on the DC-6 began in 1944, and this was a straightforward development of the C-54B Skymaster with a 6ft 9in longer fuselage, pressurisation and 2,400bhp (max take-off with water injection) Pratt & Whitney R-2800-CA15 Double Wasps; the same wings and a similar undercarriage to the C-54B were used, and the tail surfaces were slightly enlarged. Various systems and structural improvements were also featured, and reversible-pitch Hamilton Standard airscrews became available for retrofitting about a year after

DC-6 commercial deliveries started. The USAAF ordered a prototype of the DC-6 as the XC-112A-DO, and this made its first flight on 15 Feburary 1946 powered by 2,100bhp R-2800-34 engines. A month later there were over 100 DC-6s on order from the airlines, American Airlines placing the initial order for 50. First DC-6 deliveries, one each to American and United, were made on 27 November 1946. American flew the first DC-6 service, from Chicago to New York, on 27 April 1947. Fuel capacities were 3,322 US gallons for the domestic DC-6 and 4,722 US gallons for the overwater version; up to 68 passengers four-abreast could be carried, or 26-39 in sleeper berths, or up to 90 in a coach-class interior. Following two accidents caused by fuel venting into the cabin heater intakes and causing fires, all 97 DC-6s were grounded on 12 November 1947 for four months while modifications were made.

Altogether 175 DC-6s had been delivered when production ended in May 1952; one of these, designated C-118-DO and named 'The Independence', was a VIP version for President Truman. DC-6s were ordered by overseas airlines such as SAS, KLM, Sabena, FAMA of Argentina and Philippine Air Lines, as well as by US carriers such as United, National and Delta. Many surplus DC-6s were sold to charter operators and a few have had freight doors fitted. During 1948 work began on a stretched version of the DC-6 with uprated engines and increased fuel tankage and gross weight; the fuselage was lengthened by 5ft and 2,500bhp R-2800-CB17 Double Wasps were fitted; this new version was developed in parallel freighter and passenger forms as the DC-6A Liftmaster and DC-

Above: *DC-6*

6B. The prototype DC-6A first flew on 29 September 1949 and this version had a strengthened floor and a 7ft 7in wide × 5ft 7in high loading door ahead of the wings and a second cargo opening, 10ft 4in wide × 6ft 6in high aft, with a forward door opening sideways and a much larger one opening upwards. Slick Airways began DC-6A services on 16 April 1951, but DC-6As were often used as passenger aircraft seating up to 105 people. The DC-6C was a convertible passenger-freighter version of which a few were built, the first being delivered to Sabena in November 1953. Altogether 74 commercial DC-6As and DC-6Cs were built, plus 101 DC-6As for the USAF as the C-118A-DO and 65 for the US Navy as the R6D-1 (later C-118B), also used as VC-118A and VC-118B staff transports and the aeromedical MC-118A, which can carry 60 stretcher cases. Military DC-6As and DC-6Bs, in some cases ex-civil aircraft, have served the air forces of Belgium, France, West Germany, Italy, Portugal, Jugoslavia and Mexico.

The DC-6B was the same as the DC-6A but without the cargo doors and other special freight features; it was powered by R-2800-CB16 or -CB17 engines which allowed take-off weights of respecitvely 100,000lb and 106,000lb. The DC-6B first flew on 2 February 1951 and American operated the first services with it on 29 April that year. It was ordered by many airlines, and production, which totalled 287, did not end until 1958; it was widely regarded as being the most economical to operate of postwar airliners, and was very reliable. Largest operator was Pan American, which ordered 45 primarily for its tourist-class traffic, and had these modified up to 'Super Six' standard with increased payload and performance and larger fuel capacity. From 1954 weather radar could be fitted to DC-6Bs, and in 1957 airscrew spinners became available as an 'extra'. Many surplus DC-6Bs were acquired by both scheduled and charter airlines and freight operators, a few being fitted with DC-6A type cargo doors. Two DC-6Bs were converted by Sabena to swing-tail freighters under the designation DC-6BST.

Douglas DC-7 — USA

Photo and Data: DC-7C

Engines: Four 3,400bhp (max take-off) Wright R-3350-988TC18EA-1 or EA-4 Turbo Compound 18-cylinder 2-row radials
Span: 127ft 6in
Length: 112ft 3in
Height: 31ft 8in
Wing area: 1,637sq ft
Basic operating weight: 80,000lb
Max payload: 21,500lb
Max take-off weight: 143,000lb
Speed: 405mph (max) at 22,700ft
345mph (cruising)
Range: 3,610 miles with max payload
5,642 miles with max fuel

Such was the competitive rivalry between the three major airlines on US transcontinental routes, American, United and TWA, that design work on a direct development of the DC-6B to an American Airlines specification started in 1951, the year that

American had been the first to put the DC-6B into service. The Super Constellation had flown in October 1950 and the DC-7, as the DC-6B development was designated, had the same Wright R-3350 Turbo Compound engines, of the 3,250bhp (max take-off) R-3350-972TC18DA-2 model, a 3ft 4in increase in fuselage length over the DC-6B, the new cabin seating up to 98 passengers in a coach-class layout, and increased fuel capacity to give non-stop transcontinental range. The wing and tail unit were the same as the DC-6B. The first DC-7, which was built on production jigs, made its initial flight on 18 May 1953, by which time 58 had already been ordered by American, United, Delta and National. FAA certification was completed by November that year and American operated the first DC-7 service on the 29th of that month between Los Angeles and New York, making the journey non-stop in both directions for the first time. From 1955 airscrew spinners and weather radar could be fitted to DC-7s, of which 105 were built altogether, and DC-7Bs. Next version was the DC-7B (there was no DC-7A), a

long range version of the DC-7 with fuel capacity increased to 6,400 US gallons by four external saddle tanks forming part of the rear of the engine nacelles, and extra tankage in the wings. More powerful 'DA-4 Turbo Compounds were fitted, the flap linkage system was redesigned and structural modifications incorporated allowed higher gross weights.

Altogether 110 DC-7Bs were delivered to Pan American, Panagra, Eastern Air Lines, National, Delta, Continental, American and South African Airways; some of these did not have all the DC-7B's new features, such as the saddle tanks'. Pan Am's seven DC-7B's inaugurated the first non-stop New York-London service on 13 June 1955, with one stop in the westbound direction, and so it was logical that the next version should be designed for the long-sought goal of non-stop transatlantic capability in both directions all the year round against the strong westerly headwinds. The DC-7C Seven Seas had an increase in wing span of 10ft in the form of a wing root centre section housing more fuel, the tankage now totalling 7,860 US gallons; 3,400bhp EA-1 Turbo Compounds were fitted, the inboard engines now being 5ft further away from the fuselage to reduce cabin noise levels. The fuselage was lengthened by 3ft 6in enabling up to 105 passengers to be carried, and tailplane span and fin and rudder height were increased. The first DC-7C

made its initial flight on 20 December 1955 and Pan Am was the first customer, beginning DC-7C transatlantic services on 1 June 1956; a dozen more airlines ordered DC-7Cs, including European carriers such as SAS, Swissair, Sabena, KLM, Alitalia, TAI of France and BOAC, the latter acquiring 10 as stop-gap aircraft pending the introduction of Britannias on the North Atlantic. BOAC considered having its 10 fitted with Rolls-Royce Tyne Turboprops, in which form they would have been known as the DC-7D, but this idea was abandoned. From 1959 DC-7s and DC-7Bs rendered surplus by turboprops and jets were converted to freighters by Douglas with DC-6A type cargo doors, a strengthened floor and — a later innovation — mechanised pallet loading. A number of DC-7Cs were similarly converted, usually by Douglas but sometimes by airlines themselves, and all freighter versions (these differed according to individual airline requirements) were officially known as the DC-7F, although the designations DC-7BF and DC-7CF are more frequently used. DC-7Cs sold off by the major airlines were used by a great many charter, supplemental and all-freight operators as well as occasionally for scheduled services in Latin America and elsewhere, and by several US travel clubs. Altogether 121 DC-7Cs were built.

Below: *DC-7*

Embraer EMB-110 Bandeirante   Brazil

Photo: EMB-110P2
Data: EMB-110C

Engines: Two 680shp Pratt & Whitney PT6A-27
turboprops
Span: 50ft 3in
Length: 46ft 8¼in
Height: 13ft 6½in
Wing area: 312sq ft
Weight: 7,451lb (empty equipped)
Max take-off weight: 12,345lb
Speed: 270mph (max) at 15,000ft
262mph at 15,000ft (max cruising)
Range: 153 miles with max payload
1,379 miles with max fuel

In the same class as the Beech 99, which it closely
resembles in size, type of engines and performance,
the Embraer EMB-110 Bandeirante is the first
transport aircraft of indigenous South American
design to be sold to operators in Europe. Named
after the pioneer Brazilians who explored and
colonised the western part of the interior in the 17th
century, the Bandeirante was designed to a Brazilian
Ministry of Aeronautics specification for a multi-
purpose aircraft suitable for a variety of roles in
addition to carrying passengers, such as aeromedical
work and navigation training. The design team was
initially under the leadership of the French engineer
Max Holste, who had been responsible for the Nord
262, and Embraer (Empresa Brasileira de
Aeronautical) was formed at Sao Paulo in 1969 to
handle production. The prototype, with the Brazilian
Air Force designation YC-95, first flew on 26
October 1968, followed by the second prototype on
19 October 1969 and the third on 26 June 1970.
These three had Pratt & Whitney PT6A-20
turboprops, circular cabin windows, and mainwheels
that were partially exposed when retracted. A
Brazilian-type certificate was granted, the first
production EMB-110 flying on 9 August 1972, and
the first three off the Embraer line being delivered to
the Brazilian Air Force, who had ordered 60 of the

basic 12-seater EMB-110 under the designation C-
95, on 9 February 1973; the Chilean Navy also
ordered three of these. Production aircraft had a
slightly longer fuselage with square cabin windows,
more powerful PT6A-27 engines and redesigned
nacelles in which the wheels were completely
enclosed when retracted.
  Of conventional construction, with glass fibre
used for certain parts such as wing tips and the
dorsal fin, the Bandeirante seats up to 15 passengers
in the EMB-110C airline variant, which first entered
service with Transbrasil on 16 April 1973; the
downward-hinged door on the port side has built-in
airstairs, and RCA AVQ-47 weather radar is optional.
The similar EMB-110P third-level variant developed
from the C seats 18 passengers in six rows of three;
five of these were delivered to the Belem-based
Transportes Aereos da Bacia Amazonica by early
1976. Four stretcher cases can be carried in the
aeromedical version, the EMB-110E is an executive
version seating up to seven passengers and the
EMB-110F an all-cargo version. Specialist variants
are the EMB-110A for navaid calibration, of which
the Brazilian Air Force has two designated EC-95;
the EMB-110B for aerial photogrammetric survey, of
which the Air Force uses six designated RC-95, and
VASP Aerofotogrametrica SA has one; and the EMB-
110S geophysical survey variant. The EMB-110K, of
which 20 are being delivered to the Air Force, is the
same as the C but with an enlarged fuselage door,
and the EMB-110K1 is a proposed version of the K
with a 2ft 9in longer fuselage. By March 1976 74
Bandeirantes had been delivered out of 135 on order
by the Air Force, executive owners and Brazilian
government agencies, the Uruguayan Air Force,
which had five, and airlines such as Transbrasil,
third-level operators such as Transportes Aereos
Regionais (an affiliate of VASP), Rio-Sul (part-owned
by Varig) and air taxi firms such as Taxi Aero Sagres.
The first European customer was the French third-
level airline Air Littoral, which ordered two EMB-
110P2s in 1977. The EMB-110P2 has the K1's
longer fuselage and 750shp PT6A-34 turboprops,
and seats 21 third level passengers.

Faucett-Stinson F19   Peru

Engine: One 600hp Pratt & Whitney
R-1340-S1H1-G Wasp 9-cylinder radial
Span: 58ft 0$\frac{3}{4}$in
Length: 38ft 8in
Height: 14ft 4in
Wing area: 435.8sq ft
Weight: 5,088lb (empty)
7,583lb (loaded landplane)
8,750lb (loaded seaplane)
Speed: 161mph (max) at 6,400ft
155mph (cruising)
Initial rate of climb: 787ft/min
Service ceiling: 15,000ft

In the pioneering years of air transport just after
World War I several aircraft manufacturers formed
their own airlines to operate the transport aircraft
they had produced; thus, there was Junkers
Luftverkehr and its numerous associates, Handley
Page Transport and Lignes Aeriennes Farman. But
the process in reverse, whereby an airline developed
an aircraft to its own requirements and built it in its
own workshops, was less usual; this process led to
the creation of the Peruvian Faucett-Stinson F19 for
that country's leading domestic airline. Elmer J.
Faucett was a US citizen who had come to Lima in
1920 as a Curtiss representative and in the next few
years made a number of pioneering civil flights in
Peru; on 15 September 1928 he formed Compania
de Aviacion Faucett SA to operate domestic services.
A long multi-stop route down the Peruvian coast was
started using two Stinson Detroiters initially, and
both of these were modified in the airline's
workshops in the light of its operational experience.
The Stinsons performed well enough in the
mountainous conditions of Peru but after several
years a replacement was needed and Faucett could
find no type that really suited his airline's

requirements; US manufacturers were at this time
going over to twin-engined designs such as the
Lockheed 10A Electra and Boeing 247, while the
single-engined types available mostly seemed
underpowered and lacking in payload. So Faucett
made an agreement with Stinson and, with the help
of some Stinson engineers, started the design of a
type to meet his requirements. The result was the
Faucett-Stinson F19, which made its first flight on
20 September 1934 and was an eight-passenger
high wing monoplane with a 600hp Pratt & Whitney
R-1340-S1H1-G Wasp radial; the F19 was very
similar to the much later DHC-3 Otter in terms of
size, power and carrying capacity — it even had the
same engine. It was of mixed construction with
wooden wings and a welded steel tube fuselage and
tail surfaces, the whole being fabric-covered.

Thirty F19s were built in the Faucett workshops at
Santa Cruz on the outskirts of Lima, where the
company had its own airport, and production
continued until 1947, six being built for the Peruvian
Government. Virtually every new F19 incorporated
improvements over its predecessors and a few were
fitted with floats for operation from the Amazon and
its many tributaries, while a later landplane version
was fitted with the 875hp Pratt & Whitney Hornet R-
1690-S1E3-G radial. The F19s enabled new routes
into the interior of Peru to be opened, and four F19s
were still in use in the early 1960s, not being finally
retired from scheduled service until mid-1964,
largely because they could operate into airfields too
small for DC-3s. An F19 made the first non-stop
flight between Lima and Buenos Aires in 1937, and
the type was used briefly as a military transport
during the war of 1941 between Peru and Ecuador.
The F19 was a very successful example of the 'do it
yourself' approach, and had it gone into large-scale
production might well have sold steadily in other
Latin America countries, Canada and Alaska.

Fokker-VFW F27 Friendship and Fairchild Hiller F-27/FH-227

Netherlands/USA

Photo: F27A-200
Data: F27 Series 200

Engines: Two 2,020ehp (max take-off) Rolls-Royce RDa7 Dart 528 or 2,105ehp RDa7 Dart 528-7E or 2,230ehp RDa7 Dart 532-7 turboprops
Span: 95ft 2in
Length: 77ft 3½in
Height: 27ft 11in
Wing area: 753.5 sq ft
Operating weight: 24,600lb (empty)
Max payload: 10,340lb
Max take-off weight: 45,000lb
Speed: 302mph (cruising)
Range: 1,285 miles with max payload
1,374 miles with max fuel

Continuing in the prewar tradition of such widely-used Fokker airliners as the FVII and FVIIb/3m, the F27 Friendship has become the most widely sold turboprop airliner, nearly 700 having been ordered by the end of 1977, of which some 490 were from Fokker and 208 from Fairchild (later the Fairchild Hiller Corp) in the USA. Just after the war Fokker had resumed its aeronautical activities, and one of its tasks was the refurbishing of war-surplus DC-3s for airline use; in 1950 Fokker asked some of the airlines, who had been its customers for this work, to outline their ideas for a DC-3 replacement. A number of design studies resulted from this market survey, one of which was the P275 of August 1950, which was a 32-seater shoulder wing project powered by two Rolls-Royce Dart turboprops, and this led eventually to the F27 in 1952. The latter had a high wing, a circular-section pressurised fuselage with accommodation for up to 40 passengers, double-slotted flaps for a good short-field performance and a range with full payload of 300 miles.

Dutch government backing was secured for the construction of two prototypes and two static test airframes; the first of these prototypes flew on 24 November 1955 with two 1,540ehp RDa6 Dart

507s and was at first unpressurised. The second prototype, which first flew on 31 January 1957, had 1,720ehp RDa6 Dart 511s, which were later fitted to the first prototype, and a 3ft longer fuselage which enabled seating capacity to be increased from 32 to 36; this fuselage stretch was made standard on production aircraft, which also had single-slotted instead of double-slotted flaps. The initial gross weight was 35,700lb, later raised to 37,500lb for the production F27 Friendship 100, and eventually to 40,500lb. Fokker flew the first production aircraft on 23 March 1958, and in April 1956 an agreement had been concluded with the Fairchild Engine and Airplane Corp (later Fairchild Hiller) for manufacture of the F27 under licence, especially for the US local service airlines, then almost wholly equipped with DC-3s. The initial Fairchild-built version, the F-27, had a number of changes, such as seating for up to 40 passengers, increased fuel capacity, and a nose lengthened for weather radar, which was also fitted to Fokker aircraft. The first Fairchild F-27 flew on 12 April 1958 and the F-27 received FAA Type Approval on 16 July, entering commercial service with West Coast Airlines, one of a number of local service carriers to order the type, on 27 September 1958.

Initially Fairchild F-27s had Dart 511s and a gross weight of 35,700lb, but the Dart 511-7E with higher power for hot day conditions could later be fitted, and with the 'wet-boosted' Dart 514-7s gross weight went up to 39,400lb. Fokker F27 Srs 100s also had the Dart 511-7E engines and a gross weight of 39,000lb, which went up to 40,500lb when Dart 514-7s were installed. Aer Lingus was the first to put this version into service, beginning Friendship flights on 15 December 1958. The F27 Srs 200 featured the uprated 2,020ehp RDa7 Dart 528 engines, test flown in the first prototype, and these gave better performance under 'hot and high' conditions, and enabled the gross weight to go up to 42,000lb; later, RDa7 Dart 532-7 engines were fitted to Srs 200s. With Dart 528s the Fairchild F-27

Above: *F27-600*

became the F-27A, and could later be fitted with the Dart 528-7E of 2,105ehp. By now both Fairchild and Fokker had sold executive as well as airline versions of the Friendship, and the F27 Srs 300, also known as the Combiplane, had a 7ft 7½in × 5ft 10in cargo door in the port side and a strengthened freight floor for mixed passenger/cargo operations. Its Fairchild equivalent was the F-27B Freightship, which entered service with Northern Consolidated Airlines in Alaska in November 1958; the F-27B, like the F-27, could also be fitted with Dart 514-7s, the Srs 300 and F-27B having the same engines as the Srs 100 and F-27. A quick-change version of the Srs 300 with palletised seating was later produced. The F27 Srs 400 was a Combiplane version of the Srs 200, with the same cargo door; it had no Fairchild equivalent. The F27M Troopship was a military version based on the Srs 400 and able to carry 45 paratroops or 24 stretcher cases and up to seven attendants, or 13,800lb of freight.

The F27 Srs 600 has the same cargo door as the 300 and 400, but without the watertight and strengthened floor; the same engines as the Srs 400 are fitted, and Srs 600s have also been supplied to a number of air forces. The Srs 700, not built, was the same as the 600 but with the lower-powered Darts of the Srs 100. Meanwhile Fairchild had produced in 1961 the F-27F for executive customers, with 2,190ehp RDa7 Dart 529-7E engines; fuel capacity was increased and extra tankage could be installed for extended range. The F-27G was a projected freighter version of the F-27F, and in 1965 there followed the F-27J with 2,250ehp RDa7 Dart 532-7 engines and a gross weight of 42,000lb; the later F-27M (not to be confused with the Troopship) had RDa7 Dart 532-7N engines. The M was the last short-fuselage version produced by Fairchild, which

built 128 of this kind. A stretched version of the Friendship had been proposed in 1961, but it was not until 1966 that the first order for the F27 Srs 500, as it was known, was placed for the Air France Postale de Nuit night air mail service, these 500s being equipped for in-flight mail sorting. The Srs 500 had a 4ft 11in longer fuselage allowing up to 56 passengers to be accommodated instead of the maximum of 48 on earlier versions; the forward cargo door of the Srs 300 is featured and RDa7 Dart 532-7 turboprops, while gross weight went up to 45,000lb. The first Srs 500 flew on 15 November 1967 and deliveries of this version began in June 1968.

Fairchild produced its own stretched version as the FH-227, with a 6ft longer fuselage, Dart 532-7s and a gross weight of 43,500lb. The first FH-227 prototype flew on 27 January 1966, and the FH-227A was a projected version with another 3ft fuselage stretch and more powerful RDa10 Dart 542-7 engines. The FH-227B was similar to the FH-227, but had a higher gross weight, new wheels and brakes and some structural modifications; this version became the FH-227D when fitted with uprated Dart 532-7L engines and other improved features. Some FH-227s were later converted to the FH-227C with some of the FH-227B's features but retaining the original weights, or to FH-227E standard with Dart 532-7L engines. Fairchild built 78 of the FH-227 versions altogether. Fokker now offers a long-stroke, rough-field undercarriage for all F-27 versions, as well as a revised flight deck, while the F27MPA Maritime is a special version of the Srs 600 for coastal patrol duties.

Fokker-VFW F28 Fellowship   Netherlands

Photo: F28-1000
Data: F28 Series 4000

Engines: Two 9,850lb st Rolls-Royce Spey 555-15H turbofans
Span: 82ft 3in
Length: 97ft 1¾in
Height: 27ft 9½in

Wing area: 850sq ft
Operating weight: 37,736lb (empty)
Max take-off weight: 73,000lb
Speed: 530mph at 21,000ft (max cruising)
Range: 1,162 miles with max payload
2,560 miles with max fuel

Within a year or two of entering airline service the

F27 Friendship had attracted sufficient sales interest from airlines for Fokker to embark on a new short-haul jet airliner that would complement it. This was the F28, later named Fellowship, announced in April 1962 when it was revealed as a jet slightly smaller than the BAC One-Eleven 200, with accommodation for 65 passengers and emphasis on a good short-field performance. It was originally conceived as a 50-passenger aircraft with two rear-mounted Bristol-Siddeley BS75 turbofans operating over ranges of up to 1,000 miles, but the choice of powerplant soon shifted to the Rolls-Royce RB183 Spey Junior, a simpler and less powerful version of the Spey powering the Trident and One-Eleven. An unusual feature were the hydraulically-operated petal type air brakes which formed the aft end of the fuselage. Production began to get under way in July 1964 with financial backing from the Dutch government and risk-sharing participation in production by Short Bros of Belfast, the German firms HFB (now MBB) and VFW (later to merge with Fokker) and major equipment manufacturers such as AiResearch, Dowty Rotol, Goodyear and Jarry Hydraulics. Three prototypes were built, these flying on 9 May, 3 August and 20 October 1967 respectively and the first production aircraft, for the German charter and IT operator Lufttransport-Unternehman — LTU, which had ordered two, was delivered on 24 February 1969, the day on which Dutch certification was granted.

Initial production aircraft were known as the Mk 1000, and seat up to 65 passengers five-abreast, the gross weight, originally 62,000lb, having been increased in 1969 to 65,000lb. Sales followed the Friendship pattern of a slow but steady trickle of orders in ones and twos and threes rather than a few much bigger purchases. Plans for Fairchild Hiller to build the F28 under licence in the USA to follow its production of F-27s were cancelled in 1968; these

would have been powered by the new Rolls-Royce Trent three-spool turbofan, development of which did not proceed. A stretched version, the Mk 2000, was developed by Fokker with a 7ft 3in increase in fuselage length and accommodation for up to 79 passengers. The first prototype F28 was modified to a Mk 2000 and as such first flew on 28 April 1971, the first production 2000 being delivered to Nigeria Airways that October. The next versions were the Mks 5000 and 6000, equivalent respectively to the Mks 1000 and 2000, but with the wing span increased by 6ft 11½in, with wing leading edge slats to allow operation from shorter runways, and improved Spey 555-15H turbofans fitted with 'hush kits'. The Mk 2000 prototype was fitted with the extended wings and made its first flight as a Mk 6000 on 27 September 1973. But it was found that the short-field performance of the slatted versions was needed in only a few potential applications which limited their market, and so two further versions were offered, the Mks 3000 and 4000 corresponding respectively to the 1000 and 2000 (both of which are now out of production) having the extended span wings without slats and the same Spey 555-15H engines. The Mks 4000 and 6000 can accommodate up to 85 passengers in high-density seating at 29in pitch. The 6000 prototype has been operated on lease by the Swedish airline Linjeflyg with the slats wired shut, and the 6000J is a version currently being offered to the Japanese domestic airlines as a YS-11 replacement. The Mk 1000-C is a mixed passenger/freighter version of the 1000 with a forward cargo door measuring 8ft 2in × 6ft 1½in; this door can be retrofitted to existing 1000s. Altogether 130 F28s have been ordered, of which about 100 are in airline service and a dozen or so are operated by various governments as VIP aircraft. A proposed 115-seat derivative known as the F29 (formerly the Super F28) is being studied.

Ford Tri-motor

USA

Photo: Model 5-AT
Data: Model 5-AT-B

Engines: Three 425hp Pratt & Whitney Wasp C 9-cylinder uncowled radials
Span: 77ft 10in
Length: 49ft 10in
Height: 13ft 8in

Wing area: 835sq ft
Weight: 7,800lb (empty)
13,250lb (loaded)
Speed: 135mph (max)
115mph (cruising)
Range: 500 miles

First flown in 1926, and popularly known as the 'Tin

Goose', the Ford Tri-motor was one of the most important airliners in US domestic air transport in the late 1920s and early 1930s, and was also used by a number of airlines abroad. It was designed by Bill Stout for the Ford Motor Co, which at that time operated air mail services connecting Chicago and Cleveland with Detroit, and the Tri-motor first went into service on 14 December 1926 with Stout Air Services. The eleven-passenger Model 4-AT Tri-motor was the first production version, and was available with three 235hp Wright Whirlwind R-975 uncowled nine-cylinder radials as the Model 4-AT-B, or with three 300hp Wright Whirlwind R-975-J6 engines as the Model 4-AT-E. The Tri-motor was of all-metal construction, with unstressed duralumin corrugated skin covering the load-bearing internal metal structure, and was very strong, no Tri-motor reputedly having had a structural failure in flight. The Model 5-AT Tri-motor introduced in August 1928 was a more powerful version of the 4-AT with a larger wing of 3ft 10in increased span and greater area (835sq ft instead of 785sq ft), and accommodation for 13 passengers. The Model 5-AT-B had three 425hp Pratt & Whitney Wasp C nine-cylinder radials or 450hp Wright Whirlwinds. The Model 6-AT was similar to the 4-AT-E but had the larger wing of the 5-AT and accommodation for 13 passengers. Altogether 199 Tri-motors were built, (116 of them the 5-AT Model), production in 1929 reaching the very high rate of four a week.

The Tri-motor was robust, uncomplicated and easy to maintain, with a roomy cabin albeit a noisy one, and these qualities led to its widespread use by the pioneer US domestic airlines, by Pan American and its associates NYRBA (predecessor of Panair do Brasil) and Panagra, by the TACA group of airlines in Central America and by several other Latin American operators such as Avensa of Venezuela, Mexicana and a few airlines in Canada and Alaska; Avensa's three Tri-motors were used to carry freight to the oilfields, and were fitted out to seat six passengers. A few airlines used the Tri-motor outside the Americas; the Spanish airline CLASSA (a predecessor of Iberia) acquired one in 1930 that was the first US airliner to enter service in Europe, and Guinea Airways used four in New Guinea. After the war the Tri-motor continued in airline service; a small Mexican carrier, Transportes Aereos Terrestres, operated a daily Model 5-AT-B service from Tayoltita to Mazatlan until about 1963 and Island Airlines Inc (previously known as Sky Tours Inc), a US air taxi operator, flies two Model 4-AT-Bs over a ten-mile route from Port Clinton, Ohio, to the Bass Islands in Lake Erie; the surviving Ford was recently damaged in an accident but is to be repaired. Early in 1976 Scenic Airlines Inc of Las Vegas acquired the 11th production 5-AT-B from a museum in South Carolina and refurbished it for scenic flights over the Grand Canyon in Arizona under the name Grand Canyon Airlines. It had been fitted with three 450hp cowled Wasp Juniors from Vultee BT-13 trainers several years ago, but these were replaced by Scenic with the original uncowled engines for authenticity. This Ford was used by President Roosevelt in his 1932 election campaign, and has since been joined in Scenic's fleet by a Model 5-AT-C that was originally a floatplane.

Grumman G-21 Goose

USA

Photo and Data: G-21A

Engines: Two 450bhp (max take-off) Pratt & Whitney R-985-AN6 Wasp Junior 9-cylinder radials
Span: 49ft 0in
Length: 38ft 4in
Height: 15ft 0in
Wing area: 375sq ft

Weight: 5,425lb (empty)
8,000lb (loaded)
Disposable load: 2,575lb
Speed: 201mph (max) at 5,000ft
191mph at 5,000ft (cruising)
Range: 800 miles

Intended for airline and executive use, the 6/7-seater

Grumman G-21 Goose amphibian first flew in June 1937 with two 450hp Pratt & Whitney R-985-SB Wasp Juniors, R-985-SB2 engines being made standard after a few aircraft had been delivered, and loaded weight increased by 500lb to produce the G-21A. The G-21B was a pure flying boat version with the undercarriage removed. The Goose soon attracted military interest, 26 being ordered in 1938 by the US Army Air Corps as the OA-9 (plus five more civil G-21As impressed as OA-9s), and these were followed by five more OA-13As and OA-13Bs during the war, the B being the same as the Navy JRF-5. A single G-21A evaluated by the US Navy as the XJ3F-1 in 1938 was followed by an order for 10 as JRF-1 8-seat utility transports, and 10 more for the US Coast Guard for air-sea rescue as JRF-2s and -3s, the -3 having anti-icing equipment and an autopilot for use in northern waters. The JRF-1A was fitted for target-towing and photography and another 10, designated JRF-4, were equipped for the ASW role; both these were Navy versions, as was the JRF-5. The -5 was by far the most numerous, 190 being built, and this utility version was fitted with cameras; the JRF-5G was a Coast Guard air-sea rescue variant. The JRF-6 had later electrics and radio, and the -6B was a navigational trainer variant; 56 JRF-5Gs and JRF-6Bs were supplied to the RAF in 1943 as the Goose 1 and 1A. The Royal Canadian Air Force also acquired 29 of the type. The Goose could also be used for ambulance work, and in the ASW role carried two 250lb bombs under the wings. Altogether 345 of the type were built, and after the war many were acquired by airlines, chiefly in Canada, Alaska and the Caribbean; there were still about 50 in airline service in 1970.

Some were also used by US executive owners, and for this market McKinnon Enterprises has since 1958 produced several modified versions of the Goose, including a retractable float conversion and a four-engined version, the G-21C, produced to special order with 340hp Lycoming GSO-480-B2D6 powerplants and, on later production conversions, designated G-21D, a 3ft longer bow enabling 14 instead of 12 passengers to be carried; retractable floats are featured. The G-21E Turbo Goose has the Wasp Juniors replaced by two 579eshp Pratt & Whitney PT6A-20 turboprops in new engine locations, and driving Hartzell reversible propellers; McKinnon claims the Turbo Goose can taxi and take off on one engine. The original conversion was undertaken jointly with Alaska Coastal Airlines, which operated a fleet of piston-engined G-21As. The G-21E seated up to 12 people whereas the G-21F had a 4ft 3in longer fuselage forward of the flight deck and can seat 17 people. Its span (and that of the G-21E) is now 50ft 9in, the F's take-off weight, at 12,200lb, is more than half as much again as the piston-engined G-21A and cruising speed is 190mph. The G-21G Turbo Goose has two 715eshp Pratt & Whitney PT6A-27s.

Grumman G-44 Widgeon   USA

Data: G-44A

Engines: Two 200hp Ranger 6-440C-5 6-cylinder inverted in-line air-cooled engines
Span: 40ft 0in
Length: 31ft 1in
Height: 11ft 5in
Wing area: 245sq ft
Weight: 3,240lb (empty)
4,525lb (loaded)
Speed: 160mph (max)
130mph at 65% power (cruising)

Designed as a four-seat amphibian for executive and private owner use, the G-44 Widgeon first flew in July 1940. The first production version was the J4F-1 three-seat utility transport and anti-submarine patrol model for the US Coast Guard, of which 25 were delivered in 1941. In the ASW role the J4F-1 could carry a single depth bomb under the starboard wing root, the crew being reduced to two members. The USAAF version of the J4F-1 was the OA-14, of which 16 were built, and the major military version was the J4F-2 five-seat utility transport, of which 135 were built; it could also be used as an

instrument trainer. Fifteen J4F-2s were transferred to the Royal Navy and known at first by the British name Gosling I, later changed to Widgeon I; these were mainly used for communications in the West Indies. Widgeons were also used in small numbers by the Royal Canadian Air Force, the Brazilian Air Force and the Portuguese Naval Air Service. The G-44A postwar civil version had a modified hull for improved water handling characteristics; about 50 of these were built. A number of ex-military Widgeons were modified for airline use, chiefly in Alaska and Canada, and also for executive use, mainly in the United States. The New Zealand airline NZ Tourist Air Travel operated Widgeons, of which it had six altogether, on local services and sightseeing flights from Auckland and other parts of New Zealand from 1954 until its absorbtion into Mount Cook Airlines in 1969. The latter used them until retiring them in April 1975, and three of them had been converted to Super Widgeon standard from 1962 by the fitting of

260hp Continental 10-470-D engines in place of the Ranger 6-440C-5 in-line powerplants.

In France, SCAN (Société de Constructions Aéro Navales) built 40 G-44A Widgeons under licence with two 220hp Mathis 8GB22 eight-cylinder inverted vee engines in place of the Rangers. These were intended for the French Navy and for civil operators, but the French-built aircraft were eventually sold to the USA and re-engined with 300hp Lycoming R-680-E3 nine-cylinder radials as the Gannet Super Widgeon. McKinnon Enterprises have produced another version, also known as the Super Widgeon, with two 270bhp Lycoming GO-480-B1D 'flat six' engines giving a 60mph increase in cruising speed and a gross weight increased to 5,500lb. Retractable wing tip floats and a number of optional 'extras' can be featured, and over 70 of these conversions were produced. Altogether 286 Widgeons were built.

Handley Page HP81 Hermes 4   UK

Engines: Four 2,100bhp (max take-off) Bristol Hercules 763 radials
Span: 113ft 0in
Length: 96ft 10in
Height: 30ft 0in
Wing area: 1,408sq ft
Weight: 51,665lb (empty)
Capacity payload: 17,000lb
Max take-off weight: 86,000lb
Speed: 266mph at 20,000ft (max weak mixture cruising)
Range: 2,000 miles with 14,400lb payload 3,700 miles (max)

The Hermes 4 was the first British four-engined airliner of postwar design to enter service with BOAC and the basic Hermes design was a pressurised development of the Hastings military transport. The HP68 Hermes 1 prototype was completed in 1945 but crashed on its first flight on 2 December that year. The HP68 Hermes 1A was a proposed civil version of the Hastings with four 1,675hp Bristol Hercules 101 radials and intended primarily as a freighter; the Hermes 1B was a passenger version

with 2,000hp Hercules 733s. Both these were very similar to the Hastings C1 which first flew in prototype form on 7 May 1946. Only one HP74 Hermes 2 was built, to Spec 33/46, this having a 15ft longer fuselage with the additional length distributed evenly fore and aft of the wings, and retaining the tailwheel undercarriage; 1,715hp Hercules 121 engines were fitted. The Hermes 2 was used to test various features of the Mk 4 such as pressurisation, air conditioning and soundproofing and the Hercules 763 engines. The projected HP79 Hermes 3 was to have had the Mk 2's longer fuselage and Bristol Theseus turboprops, this being a free turbine engine designed for a low fuel consumption. The Mk 3 was superseded by the HP82 Hermes 5, two of which were built to Spec 32/46, which were similar to the Hermes 4 but with 2,490ehp Theseus 502 turboprops, being used as test beds for these engines. The HP81 Hermes 4 to Spec 37/46 was a development of the Mk 2 with a nosewheel undercarriage, larger tail surfaces and 2,100bhp Hercules 763 engines. BOAC ordered 25 Hermes 4s for its African routes on which services began, after some delays, on 6 August 1950; they

were operated as 40-passenger aircraft although up to 74 passengers could be accommodated.

But by the time the Hermes entered BOAC service it was already surpassed by the DC-6 and Constellation, with the result that BOAC was the only airline to order the type, and it was withdrawn from service in October 1953, to be put back on to the East African routes between July and December 1954 after the Comet 1 was grounded. BOAC sold off its Hermes fleet to British independents; those using the type were Airwork Ltd, Air Safaris, Air Links, Britavia, Falcon Airways, Silver City Airways and Skyways, these operators using them extensively for trooping, when up to 68 servicemen could be carried, and also for other charter work.

Skyways leased two of its Hermes to Middle East Airlines for a time in 1955-56, and two others of its fleet were used by Bahamas Airways Ltd in 1959-60 when Skyways had a controlling interest in that airline. Some Skyways Hermes were converted to freighters to operate London-Singapore cargo services under contract to BOAC. A number of Hermes 4s were converted to Hermes 4A standard, with slightly more powerful Hercules 773s developing 2,125bhp. A projected development of the Mk 4 was the HP91 Hermes 6, with 2,100hp Hercules 783s, increased all-up weight and payload, and redesigned flaps and ailerons plus a larger fin and rudder.

Handley Page Herald   UK

Photo: Herald 209
Data: Series 200

Engines: Two 2,105ehp (max take-off) Rolls-Royce RDa7/2 Dart 527 turboprops
Span: 94ft 9in
Length: 75ft 6in
Height: 24ft 1in
Wing area: 886sq ft
Weight: 24,400lb (empty equipped)
Max payload: 11,242lb
Max take-off weight: 43,000lb
Speed: 307mph (max)
275mph at 15,000ft (max cruising)
Range: 700 miles with max payload
1,760 miles with max fuel

Designed as a private venture DC-3 replacement seating 40-44 passengers in a pressurised cabin, the HPR3 Herald's design was made the responsibility of Handley Page (Reading) Ltd which was the former Miles Aircraft company. In its initial form the Herald was powered by piston engines, the first of two prototypes, which made its first flight at Woodley on 25 August 1955, being powered by four 825bhp

(max take-off) Alvis AleM 1-1 Leonides Major 701 radials; a second prototype made its initial flight in August 1956. Orders had already been received for a total of 29 Heralds from Queensland Airlines, Australian National Airways and Lloyd Aereo Colombiano before the first prototype flew, but as the flight test programme progressed the success of the Viscount and the growing number of orders for the Fokker Friendship rendered future sales prospects for the piston-engined Herald increasingly marginal. So in May 1957 Handley Page announced plans for an alternative version of the Herald with two Dart turboprops, and the piston-engined version was later abandoned. Both prototypes were re-engined with two 2,105ehp Rolls-Royce RDa7/2 Dart 527s, flying with these engines on 11 March and 17 December 1958 respectively; the type was originally known as the Dart Herald. The first production aircraft, known as a Series 100, made its first flight on 30 October 1959 and was used as a company demonstrator, being followed by three Herald 101s seating up to 47 passengers ordered by the Government for use by BEA on its Highlands and Islands routes in Scotland. The major production version was the Herald 200 with a 3ft 6in longer

forward fuselage which could seat up to 56 passengers in compact seats, although usually 44 passengers were carried.

The second prototype Dart Herald was converted to Srs 200 standard, first flying in this form on 8 April 1961. Jersey Airlines (now British Island Airways) placed the first order for six Srs 200s in September 1960, but only 36 Srs 200s had been built when Handley Page went out of business in mid-1968. These were used by Eastern Provincial, Maritime Central and Nordair in Canada, the Italian domestic airline Itavia, Alia of Jordan, Arkia of Israel, the Swiss charter operator Globe Air, British Midland Airways, Bavaria Fluggesellschaft, Sadia of Brazil, Air Manila and Far Eastern Air Transport of Formosa; BUA used one as an executive transport. Subsequent Srs 200, 101 and 400 resales have gone to British Air Ferries, Brymon Airways, Air Ecosse, Express Air Freight and Intra Airways in the UK, Nile Valley Aviation of Egypt, Europe Aero Service of France and Lineas Aereas La Urraca of Colombia. The Srs 400

was a military transport version of the 200, of which eight were supplied to the Royal Malaysian Air Force. This had a strengthened floor, a fuselage door openable in flight for dropping supplies or paratroops, and accommodation for 50 troops in rear-facing seats or 24 stretcher cases and attendants or freight. The Srs 500 was a projected military version similar to the 400, but with more powerful RDa12 Darts and lift-dumping devices for improved STOL performance. The projected Srs 600 had more powerful Dart 532/9 engines, a 5ft longer fuselage accommodating 64-68 passengers and increased fuel capacity, while the Srs 700, another project, was similar to the 600 but without the fuselage stretch and seated 52-60 passengers. The Brazilian airline VASP originally ordered 10 Srs 700s, but later chose YS-11s instead. The Srs 800, also not built, was a military transport version of the 700. Total Herald production numbered 50 aircraft.

Below: *Herald 214*

Hawker Siddeley Comet 1 and 2

UK

Photo: Comet 1
Data: Comet C2

Engines: Four 7,300lb st Rolls-Royce Avon
117/118 turbojets
Span: 115ft 0in
Length: 96ft 0in
Height: 29ft 6in
Wing area: 2,027sq ft
Weight: 120,000lb (max gross)
Max payload: 13,500lb
Speed: 508mph (max) at 40,000ft
488mph at 36-40,000ft (max cruising)
Range: 2,535 miles (max stage length with full
payload)

Forever famous as the type that operated the world's
first jet airliner services, the de Havilland DH106
Comet had its genesis in the first Brabazon
Committee, which in February 1943 had
recommended the development of a jet powered
mailplane for postwar use on North Atlantic routes
to be made by DH. But during 1944 the de
Havilland team under Mr R. E. Bishop became
convinced that a true airliner, seating around 40
passengers, could be a practical proposition
designed around four de Havilland Ghost turbojets.
With BOAC showing an interest, de Havilland was
authorised in February 1945 to proceed with the
design of a jet airliner. Several different projects
were studied under the designation DH106, and the
relative merits of conventional twin boom and
tailless layouts were investigated before the Comet's
final configuration was agreed in August 1946. On
21 January 1947 the first Comet orders were
placed, for two prototypes, eight for BOAC and six for
British South American Airways, the BOAC total
becoming nine after its takeover of BSAA in July
1949.

The prototype Comet 1 first flew on 27 July 1949
followed by the second, which flew one year later to
the day, and which had four-wheel bogie main
undercarriage units instead of the single mainwheels
of the first. Engines were four 5,050lb st Ghost 50
turbojets, and the first prototype had a small faired-
over nacelle between each pair of jet pipes which

was intended to house a 5,000lb st de Havilland
Sprite 'cold' liquid fuel rocket motor to improve take
off performance from 'hot and high' airports. But the
idea of using Sprites was abandoned, being
overtaken by water methanol injection and later,
more powerful engines. On 22 January 1952 the
Comet 1 received its normal category C of A from
the ARB, and on 2 May BOAC inaugurated the
world's first jet airliner service from London to
Johannesburg via Rome, Beirut, Khartoum, Entebbe
and Livingstone. The Comet was an instant success:
its average load factors were some 80% over all
BOAC routes and a profit was made during the first
year of operation. The nine Comet 1s for BOAC were
followed by 10 Mk 1As, featuring an extra 1,000
Imperial gallons of fuel, and seating 44 instead of 36
passengers. The latter variant was ordered by Air
France, UAT, Canadian Pacific and the RCAF. UAT
began Comet services over the Paris-Casablanca-
Dakar route on 19 February 1953, and later started
Paris-Jo'burg flights; Air France began Comet
services to Beirut on 26 August 1953, Canadian
Pacific in the end did not put the type into service
and South African Airways leased BOAC Comets for
its own Jo'burg-London flights.

After the two BOAC Comet 1 accidents on
10 January and 8 April 1954 due to pressure cabin
fatigue all Mk 1 and 1A operations ceased, except for
the RCAF's two Mk 1As. The Comet 2, a prototype of
which had flown on 16 February 1952, was already
in production; this had a 3ft fuselage stretch to
increase the seating to 44 passengers, and 6,500lb
st Rolls-Royce RA7 Avon 502s (later 7,100lb st
RA25 Avon 503s). BOAC ordered 12 Mk 2s and
other customers for this version, whose orders later
lapsed, were Air France, Canadian Pacific, British
Commonwealth, Pacific Airlines, Japan Air Lines,
LAV of Venezuela and Panair do Brasil. The first of
10 Mk 2s laid down for BOAC were completed and
delivered to RAF Transport Command's No 216 Sqn
in mid-1956; the first two were Comet T2s for crew
training and did not have the strengthened freight
floor of the eight others, designated C Mk 2s, which
carried 36-44 passengers or 11,200lb of freight. All
10 were structurally strengthened as a result of the
1954 accidents, and had elliptical cabin windows to

reduce stress levels at corner cut-outs. No 216's Comets were not finally retired until April 1967. Three more structurally unmodified 2s were used by RAF Signals Command on radar and electronics development as Comet 2Rs. Two Comet 2Es were used as engine test beds with 10,500lb st RA29 Avon 524s in the outboard positions, these being the

Above: Comet C Mk 2

engines of the Comet 4; later, both were used for radio and navaid development, testing amongst other things Dectra and the Decca Navigator, and a few ex-airline Mk 1s were also employed on similar development work.

Hawker Siddeley Comet 4, 4B and 4C   UK

Photo: Comet 4
Data: Comet 4C

Engines: Four 10,500lb st (max take-off) Rolls-Royce RA29/1 Avon 524 turbojets
Span: 115ft 0in
Length: 118ft 0in
Height: 29ft 6in
Wing area: 2,121sq ft
Basic operating weight: 78,500lb
Max payload: 28,950lb
Max take-off weight: 162,000lb
Speed: 535mph (max cruising)
526mph at 33,000ft (best economy cruising)
Range: 4,310 miles with max fuel

First major stretch of the basic Comet airframe had been the Comet 3 intended for transatlantic routes; this had an 18ft 6in longer fuselage seating 58 first-class or up to 78 tourist passengers, an extra 1,000 Imperial gallons of fuel in pinion tanks on the wing leading edges, and increased wing and flap area. Uprated Avons were fitted, initially 9,000lb st RA16s

and later 10,000lb st RA26 Avon 524s. The Mk 3 prototype first flew on 19 July 1954 and this also served as the prototype for the Mks 4 and 4B, being designated Mk 3B when fitted with the short-span (108ft) 4B wings, first flying in this form on 21 August 1958. Pan American had ordered three Mk 3s, with seven more on option, in October 1952 followed by Air India and BOAC, and Pan Am would have been the first operator of this version. The Comet 4 incorporated all the structural knowledge gained from the 1954 accidents, and differed little from the Mk 3 except for having 10,500lb st RA29 Avon 524s, a gross weight of 158,000lb, later raised to 162,000lb, and accommodation for up to 81 economy passengers or 63 in a mixed-class interior. BOAC had ordered 19 Mk 4s only a month after the 1954 accident enquiry's verdict was made known, and the first of these flew on 27 April 1958. The Comet re-entered airlines service on 4 October that year when BOAC inaugurated London-New York flights via Gander three weeks ahead of Pan Am with 707-121s; the Comet 4s were later deployed on routes to India and the Far East, to Australia and to

South America, and BOAC's last Comet service was flown on 24 November 1965. Aerolineas Argentinas ordered six Mk 4s, and one Mk 4C later, and inaugurated jet services over the South Atlantic on 19 May 1959, followed by Buenos Aires-New York flights on 7 June. East African Airways, which ordered three, was the only other Mk 4 customer, beginning jet services to London on 17 September 1960.

Perhaps even more significant than Pan Am's earlier order for Mk 3s was the Capital Airlines order, announced on 24 July 1956, for 10 of a new short-haul variant, the Mk 4A, and four Mk 4s; this was the first ever order for a short-haul jet by any airline. The Mk 4A featured a 7ft shorter wing span to increase speed at lower altitudes, and a 3ft 4in fuselage stretch enabling up to 92 passengers to be seated five-abreast. But Capital's financial troubles which led to its takeover by United in 1961 led it to cancel its Comet order and the Mk 4A was not built. It was developed into the Mk 4B for BEA which had a 6ft 6in longer fuselage than the Mk 4 and could accommodate up to 102 passengers with the wing pinion tanks removed. The Mk 4B first flew on 27 June 1959, and BEA began Mk 4B services between London and Moscow on 1 April 1960,

Above: *Comet 4C*

having ordered 14 altogether; the only other Mk 4B customer was Olympic Airways, which ordered four and had operated some of BEA's on lease. Final production version was the Comet 4C, which first flew on 31 October 1959, and which combined the Mk 4B's longer fuselage with the Mk 4's larger wing and fuel tankage; altogether 28 were built. The Mk 4C was ordered by Mexicana, United Arab Airlines (now Egyptair), Middle East Airlines, Kuwait Airways and Sudan Airways; in addition, five were supplied to the RAF as Comet C4s for use by No 216 Sqn, one was used by the Ministry of Aviation for long range navaid research and one VIP Mk 4C went to King Ibn Saud of Saudi Arabia. Malaysia-Singapore Airlines AREA of Ecuador and Dan Air Services started Comet operations with ex-BOAC Mk 4s, and BEA Airtours and Channel Airways did likewise with ex-BEA Mk 4Bs. Dan-Air is now the only Comet operator, having acquired virtually all the surviving 4s, 4Bs and 4Cs as well as the RAF's C4s; it now operates 10 chiefly on charter and IT work. Altogether 74 Comet 4s, 4Bs and 4Cs were built, plus two unsold Mk 4C airframes rebuilt into the Nimrod prototypes.

Hawker Siddeley HS748

UK

Photo and Data: Series 2A

Engines: Two 2,280eshp Rolls-Royce RDa7 Dart 532-2L or 532-2S turboprops
Span: 98ft 6in
Length: 67ft 0in
Height: 24ft 10in
Wing area: 810.75sq ft
Basic operating weight: 26,700lb
Max payload: 11,800lb
Max take-off weight: 46,500lb
Speed: 278mph at 10,000ft (max cruising)
Range: 683 miles with max payload
1,080 miles with max fuel

First revealed on 9 January 1959, the Avro Type 748 (A. V. Roe & Co Ltd later became part of Hawker Siddeley Aviation) is a private venture short/medium haul transport in the DC-3 replacement category, and had its origins in the 1957 Defence White Paper's prediction that there would be no more new manned military aircraft for the RAF. Avro decided to re-enter the civil market and made a number of design studies, especially of Heron/Viking/DC-3

replacements, and by mid-1958 the first project under the Avro type number 748 had been schemed. This was for an 18,000lb, 20-seat airliner with two 1,000shp turboprops on a 75ft span wing, proposed in low wing and high wing forms. From airline reactions to this, it became clear that to be saleable, the new type would have to be powered by Rolls-Royce or Pratt & Whitney engines; as a result Dart turboprops were chosen and the project became considerably larger, seating 36 passengers four-abreast and with a gross weight of 33,000lb, tailplane position and nacelle shape later being revised. The Type 748 was now a competitor with the Fokker F27 Friendship then about to enter airline service, and to ensure that the 748 sold, Avro sought to offer a cheaper price and better performance than the Dutch aircraft. The possibility of licenced production in India, whose Air Force had a potential requirement for 100 or more to replace its many DC-3s, was a major factor in going ahead with the Type 748, which the Indian Government duly selected for construction in a new factory at Kanpur to be managed by Hindustan Aeronautics Ltd. The first Indian-assembled 748 Series 1 flew on 1 November

1961, and the first Series 2 (with Dart 531s built by HAL) on 28 January 1964.

The first prototype made its initial flight on 24 June 1960, followed by the second on 10 April 1961; the latter was later used as a demonstrator and leased to a number of airlines pending delivery of the first 748s they had on order. The 748 was unusual at the time in having a fully fail-safe structure, instead of the safe-life kind, and field performance was enhanced by a feature of the Fowler flaps in which the rear 35% of flap chord was made up of a four-piece tab on each side which came down automatically with full flap to increase drag without destroying lift. Both prototypes were powered by 1,740ehp RDa6 Dart 514 engines, as was the first production version, known as the Series 1, the first of which flew on 30 August 1961. Skyways Ltd, which ordered three, was the first customer and used its 748s on low-fare coach-air services between London and Paris. Aerolineas

Argentinas, which ordered nine (plus three more later) was the first export customer, beginning 748 domestic services on 2 April 1962. The major production version, introduced after only 18 Series 1s had been built, was the 748 Series 2 with uprated 2,105ehp RDa7 Dart 531 engines; the wing was slightly stiffer and the gross weight, initially 36,000lb, went up to 38,800lb and then, in 1965, to 44,495lb, while up to 62 passengers could be carried. The second prototype Series 1 was re-engined and first flew as the prototype Series 2 on 6 November 1961; the first production Series 2 flew in August 1962. In mid-1967 the 2,280ehp RDa7 Dart 532-2L and 532-2S became available and the fitting of these engines resulted in the Series 2A, giving increased performance and improved economics. Fuel capacity had also been increased, an extra 260 Imperial gallons having been offered

Below: *HS748*

to 748 operators from late 1963, and fuel capacity went up to 1,440 Imperial gallons with the increase in gross weight to 44,495lb.

First of several military customers was the Brazilian Air Force, which designated its Series 2s C-91s, and several air force 748s were VIP versions for heads of state; the Royal Australian Air Force used eight of its 10 Series 2s as navigation and air electronics trainers. The 748 supplied to King Bihendra of Nepal featured a rear freight door for paratrooping and supply dropping and a VIP interior; this 8ft 9in wide × 5ft 8in high door, which first flew in a Series 2A on 31 December 1971, was developed to meet military requirements, together with a strengthened floor and optional cargo hoist. Over 20 rear door-equipped Series 2As have been ordered, and the civil version so equipped is sometimes known as the Series 2C. An earlier and more drastic redesign of the basic 748 for freighting

produced the Type 748MF Andover, with an upswept rear fuselage 11ft longer incorporating rear loading doors and an integral loading ramp, more powerful 3,245eshp RDa12 Dart 201s and a 'kneeling' undercarriage; 31 Andovers were supplied to the RAF and a proposed civil version was the Type 748CF (later HS780). The Andover CC Mk 2 is a special VIP version of the Series 2 for the Queen's Flight, and several Series 2s and 2As have been supplied as corporate and executive transports, while both Britain and Germany use the 748 for radio and navaid calibration. The Coastguarder is a maritime patrol version of the HS748 first flown on 18 February 1977. By the beginning of 1979 a total of 339 748s and Andovers had been sold to operators in some 40 different countries. The Series 2B, available from 1979, has 2ft extensions to both wing tips and Dart 536-2 engines for improved performance in 'hot and high' conditions.

Hawker Siddeley Argosy

UK

Photo: Argosy C1
Data: Argosy 220

Engines: Four 2,230eshp Rolls-Royce Dart 532/1 turboprops
Span: 115ft 0in
Length: 86ft 9in
Height: 29ft 3in
Wing area: 1,458sq ft
Weight: 48,920lb (empty equipped)
Max payload: 32,000lb
Max take-off weight: 93,000lb
Speed: 282mph (max cruising)
Range: 485 miles with max payload
1,760 miles with max fuel

The AW650 Argosy was designed as a private venture by the former Sir W. G. Armstrong Whitworth Aircraft Ltd, one of the Hawker Siddeley Group companies, as a large-capacity freighter for both civil and military use. The AW650, originally named Freightliner, was pressurised, had four Rolls-Royce RDa7/2 Dart 526 turboprops, and was

intended to be the first of six versions of the basic design. The others were the AW651 with two Rolls-Royce RTy1 Tyne turboprops; the AW660 Argosy C1 military transport version with 'beaver tail' rear doors with integral ramp; the AW661, similar to the AW660 but with two RTy1 Tynes; the AW670 Air Ferry, a car ferry version with four Dart 526s and a longer fuselage 14ft 6in wide at floor level, intended to take up to six large cars two-abreast and 30 passengers, and the AW671 Airbus, an air coach version with the AW670's extra-wide fuselage. Of these versions, only the AW660 was built, and was preceded by the production batch of 10 AW650 Argosy 100s, of which the first three served as prototypes, the first of these making its initial flight on 8 January 1959. In 1961 these were bought by BEA and used, as Argosy 102s, with the 'Rolamat' cargo handling system, on domestic and European routes until they were traded in, in part exchange for the Argosy 222s.

The first customer to order the Argosy 100 had been the Miami-based Riddle Airlines Inc (now Airlift International), which took delivery of the first of

seven Argosy 101s in December 1960 for its Logair military contract flights in the States for the USAF's Military Air Transport Service. In July 1962 these were sold back to the manufacturer because of Riddle's financial difficulties, and five were taken over by Capitol International Airways for its Logair flights linking USAF bases in the States, the other two going to Zantop Air Transport of Detroit, which also flew Logair services and later acquired the five Capitol aircraft. The first of 56 Argosy C1s made its initial flight on 4 March 1961. This version could accommodate up to 72 fully-armed troops or 54 paratroops or 48 stretcher cases, or such loads as a 105mm howitzer. The nose door featured on the AW650 was deleted, weather radar being mounted in the nose, and the wing structure was strengthened, while more powerful (2,680ehp) RDa8 Dart 101 turboprops were fitted. An in-flight refuelling probe could be fitted, and 14 Argosy C1s were later converted into Argosy T1 navigator trainers. Next civil version was the Argosy 200,

which featured a box-spar wing making the entire airframe fail-safe, and integral fuel tanks instead of the Srs 100's bag-type tanks. The first Srs 200 first flew on 11 March 1964 and was soon converted into a Srs 220, this differing in having Dart 532/1 turboprops, wider front and rear door apertures and increased weights and performance. BEA ordered six Argosy 222s which entered service in February 1965, these being sold off in 1970 when four went to Midwest Aviation of Winnipeg, one later going to the Irish operator Aer Turas, and two others to TransAir of Canada, these both later being sold to SOACO in the Gabon. SAFE Air in New Zealand uses two Srs 222s, and the Australian operator IPEC Air has three. The British independent ABC Carriers operates three of the Srs 101/102s, while an ex-RAF Argosy C1 has been acquired by Philippine Air Lines. Two more ex-RAF aircraft are operated by Otras Range Air Services in support of the German-controlled rocket range in Zaire.

Hawker Siddeley Trident UK

Photo: Trident 3B
Data: Trident 2E

Engines: Three 11,960lb st Rolls-Royce RB 163-25 Spey 512-5W turbofans
Span: 98ft 0in
Length: 114ft 9in
Height: 27ft 0in
Wing area: 1,461sq ft
Basic operating weight: 73,250lb
Max payload: 29,600lb
Max take-off weight: 143,500lb
Speed: 596mph (max cruising)
505mph (long range cruising)
Range: 3,155 miles with max payload
3,558 miles with max fuel

The de Havilland DH121 Trident had its origins in a BEA outline specification of July 1956 for a short/medium haul 600mph jet airliner, broadly able to carry up to 100 economy passengers or 70-80 in

a two-class interior over stage lengths of from 300 to about 1,200 miles. To meet this need de Havilland first projected the DH119 with four Rolls-Royce RA29 Avons, and this was followed by the DH120 which was intended to meet both BEA's requirement and BOAC's need for a long haul jet that was eventually satisfied by the VC10. These differing needs could not be combined satisfactorily in the DH120, and the DH121 was evolved to meet the BEA specification. In two respects the latter pioneered new trends; it featured three rear-mounted engines and it was the first airliner in which full all-weather operations, using automatic blind-landing equipment, were made a design objective. Three engines were chosen, partly because four engines giving the required cruising thrust would have made the aircraft overpowered on take-off, while only two would have had to be more powerful than otherwise needed in cruising flight to cater for engine failure on take-off. BEA announced its choice of the DH121 in February 1958 and was allowed to

place a provisional order for 24 that month only after a political controversy. This led to the formation of the Airco consortium by de Havilland, Fairey Aviation and Hunting Aircraft to produce and market the DH121; Airco was set up to meet the then Government's desire for larger groupings in the aircraft industry but, paradoxically, it was dissolved later in 1959 because the constituent companies were now in different groups of the rationalised industry.

When ordered by BEA, the DH121 was a 111-passenger aircraft with three 13,790lb st Rolls-Royce RB141/3 Medway by-pass engines and a range of 2,070 miles; the Medway would soon be developing 14,000lb or more, and the DH121's size and range could be stretched to meet this growth. BEA considered whether to do this but, tragically, concluded that the RB141 engine was rather too large and that the DH121 should be scaled down; this resulted in the British jet being heavily outsold by the Boeing 727-100 which, in its original form, it had so closely matched in terms of size and power. The now smaller DH121 was powered by three 9,850lb st RB163/1 Spey 505/5 engines, seated 97-103 passengers, had a wing span reduced to 89ft 10in from the original 107ft, and a take-off weight of 115,000lb instead of the original 122,500lb. The type was named Trident in September 1960 and the first one (there was no prototype) made its initial flight on 9 January 1962. British certification was received on 18 February 1964, and BEA made its first revenue Trident flight on 11 March, with full scheduled operations starting on 1 April that year. The Trident 1C, with 1,000 Imperial gallons extra fuel tankage, became the standard version instead of the Mk 1, all BEA's 24 being delivered as Mk 1Cs. With the Smiths Autoland system, BEA's Tridents were approved in September 1968 for automatic landings in ICAO Category II weather conditions.

The Trident 1E was the export version, with 11,400lb st RB163-25 Spey 511-5 engines, a wing of 5ft 2in greater span with full span leading edge slats instead of the leading edge droop of the Mk 1, increased wing tankage and a gross weight raised to 128,000lb. The 1E seated 115 passengers, or up to 140 in a high density interior for Channel Airways, whose five 1E-140s were later disposed of to Air Ceylon, and BKS/Northeast. Altogether 15 Mk 1Es were built for Kuwait Airways (3), Iraqi Airways (3) and Pakistan International (4), the latter's being sold to CAAC of China in 1970. The Trident 2E, of which BEA ordered 15 in 1965, was similar to the 1E, with no fuselage stretch but with uprated 11,960lb st RB163-25 Spey 512-5W engines, low drag wing tips increasing the span to 98ft, increased fuel tankage for non-stop London-Middle East operations, and a gross weight of 143,500lb. Up to 149 passengers could be carried, and BEA began scheduled services with the 2E on 18 April 1968. Cyprus Airways bought two 2Es but the major export customer was CAAC of China, which ordered a total of 33, the first of which was handed over on 13 November 1972. First stretched version was the Trident 3B, of which BEA ordered 26; this has a 16ft 5in longer fuselage to seat up to 180 passengers, and to improve take-off performance at higher operating weights a 5,250lb st Rolls-Royce RB162-86 booster jet was installed at the base of the rudder, while some changes were made in the wing control surfaces. The 3B first flew on 11 December 1969 and the first BEA 3B entered service on 1 April 1971, approval for 'zero zero' autoland operations in full Category IIIA conditions being granted that December. Two Super Trident 3Bs were ordered by CAAC in 1972, these having extra fuel tankage and gross weight increased by 8,000lb to 158,000lb. Mk 2Es and 3Bs of British Airways have had Trident 1-type wing tips retrofitted as part of the wing fatigue crack modifications.

Hunting-Percival Prince

Photo: Prince 6E
Data: Prince 5 (President)

Engines: Two 540/560bhp Alvis Leonides 504/5A 9-cylinders radials.
Span: 64ft 6in
Length: 46ft 0in
Height: 16ft 1in
Wing area: 400sq ft
Weight: 8,545lb (empty)
Capacity payload: 2,244lb
Max take-off weight: 13,500lb
Speed: 222mph (max) at 6,000ft
187mph at 4,000ft (continuous cruising)
Range: 714 miles with max payload
817 miles with max fuel

The Prince light and executive transport was a development of the Percival P48 Merganser, a 5-8 seat high wing monoplane with two 296hp DH Gipsy Queen 51 in-line engines, a span of 47ft 9in and a gross weight of 7,000lb. The Merganser prototype first flew on 9 May 1947 but non-availability of the DH Gipsy Queens, then earmarked for the DH Dove,

led to production plans being abandoned in favour of a larger version known as the Prince and seating 8-10 passengers, with two Alvis Leonides radial engines, a span of 56ft 0in and a higher gross weight. The Prince prototype first flew on 13 May 1948, and the Prince I and 2 production versions had 520hp Leonides 501/4 engines, the Mk 2 having main spar modifications to increase all-up weight from 10,659lb to 11,000lb, as well as a sloping windscreen. The Prince 3 had more powerful Leonides 502/4 engines and increased all-up weight; a long or short nose could be featured, and an air survey version, the P54 had a transparent lengthened nose with a camera operator's position. Retrospective modifications, involving different series engines and improved braking to give higher all-up weight, resulted in the Mk 4, with Leonides 503/4s or 5s and an all-up weight of 11,500lb, and the Mk 6 with Leonides 504/5As and an all-up weight of 11,800lb. The Prince 5, a civil version of the Pembroke, was renamed President. Most Princes were sold to corporate and executive owners, or

Below: *President*

were used for jobs such as aerial survey or — by the Ministry of Civil Aviation Flying Unit — for navaid calibration. The Brazilian airline Aeronorte (Empresa de Transportes Aereos Norte do Brasil) operated seven Prince 2s for a time around 1952 on domestic routes in the north-eastern 'shoulder' of Brazil radiating from Sao Luiz. Polynesian Airlines began operating services in 1959 between Apia, the capital of Western Samoa, and Pago Pago, the capital of American Samoa, using an ex-Royal Australian Air Force Prince 3, and two more Princes, a Mk 6E and a Mk 4E, were delivered to the airline in April 1961.

The Sea Prince C1 was a Navy staff transport version of the Prince 2, the Sea Prince C2 being an improved version based on the Prince 3 with increased disposable load. The Sea Prince T1 was a navigational and radar operator trainer, 41 of which were built, with radar in the nose and accommodation for an instructor and four pupils. The P66 Pembroke C1, which first flew on 20 November 1952, is a development of the Prince 3 with an 8ft 6in increase in wing span, a 2,000lb higher loaded weight, a strengthened fuselage floor and long-stroke twin wheel main undercarriage legs. The RAF ordered 46 Pembrokes as staff transports, two of these being diverted to the Royal Rhodesian Air Force; six were also supplied to the RAF as a dual-purpose communications/photographic variant, the C(PR) Mk 1, with provision for cameras in the fuselage. Export versions of the Pembrokes were supplied to the air forces of Belgium (12 C51s), Sweden (20 C52s, also designated Tp 83 by the Swedish Air Force), Finland (C53), the German Federal Republic (33 C54s) and the Sudan (C55). The Pembroke could carry 8-12 passengers in rear-facing seats, or up to six stretcher cases or 2,500lb of freight. Those for Belgium had a transparent nose similar to the P54 air survey version, and camera hatches in the fuselage.

Ilyushin Il-12 and Il-14

USSR

Photo: Il -14
Data: Il -14M

Engines: Two 1,900hp Shvetsov ASh-82T 14-cylinder 2-row radials
Span: 104ft 0in
Length: 73ft 2in
Height: 25ft 11in
Wing area: 1,075sq ft
Weight: 27,776lb (operational equipped)
Max take-off weight: 39,683lb
Speed: 259mph (max)
239mph (high speed cruise)
Range: 810 miles with max payload
1,988 miles with max fuel

Intended to succeed the many Lisunov Li2s (licence-built DC-3s) in military and airline service in the Soviet Union, the Ilyushin Il-12, design work on which began in 1943, is closely comparable to the Saab 90A-2 Scandia in terms of size, payload and horsepower, and has less power and a smaller payload than the Convair 240. First flown in prototype form in 1945, the Il-12 (NATO codename Coach) was powered in production form by two 1,775hp Shvetsov ASh-82FNV radials and in airline service seated 27-32 passengers and a crew of four, or only 18 in a de luxe version; it was not pressurised. The military version had large double cargo doors in the port side and featured observation blisters aft of the flight deck for use by a paratroop drop controller. It could carry up to 26 fully-equipped troops, 20 paratroops, or 16 stretcher cases and six sitting casualties or medical attendants, or up to 8,800lb of freight; it could also be used as a glider tug. A photo survey version fitted with cameras was also produced. The Il-12 was Aeroflot's first-line equipment until the early 1950s, and it was also used in small numbers by LOT of Poland, the Czech airline CSA, TAROM of Rumania and TABSO of Bulgaria. Some Aeroflot Il-12s were later used as freighters, and also for such jobs as forest fire patrols and air ambulance work. Over 3,000 Il-12s are believed to have been built when production ended in 1956.

The II-12 was gradually replaced by the II-14 (NATO codename Crate), which first flew in prototype form in 1952 and differed from it in having uprated 1,900hp ASh-82T engines, a redesigned fin and rudder with a squared-off top, a refined structure, fewer cabin windows, some aerodynamic improvements and a form of thrust augmentation similar to that of the Convair 240. There were two main versions, the standard II-14P as used by Aeroflot and seating only 18-32 passengers, and the stretched II-14M, which appeared in 1956, with a 3ft 4in extension of the forward fuselage, a higher all-up weight, and various detailed improvements; the wing leading edge extension between the fuselage and engine nacelles of the II-14P and II-12 was replaced by a large wing root fillet on each side. The M also featured revised fuel tankage and a reduced structure weight, and could accommodate 24-32 passengers. Many II-14Ps and Ms were later converted into freighters with double cargo doors in the port side under the designation II-14T, and over 3,500 II-14s are believed to have been built in the Soviet Union, many being military versions of both

Above: *II-12*

the II-14P and M. Eighty II-14Ps were built under licence by the VEB Flugzeugwerke in East Germany during 1956-59, seating 18 or 26 passengers and also being used by Interflug for all-cargo services. The II-14P was also built under licence in Czechoslovakia as, the Avia 14, about 50 being built from 1955 before production of the II-14M as the Avia-32 began, with accommodation for 32 passengers; Czech production ended in 1962. The Avia 14-32A, which appeared in 1958, featured local strengthening to allow operation at an increased all-up weight, the Avia 14T was a freighter version and the later Avia 14 Salon featured circular cabin windows and a revised fuel system featuring wing tip tanks; accommodation for 36, 40 or 42 passengers could be provided. II-14s were supplied to many Communist airlines and air forces, and to those of a number of Third World countries; VIP versions were also donated to the heads of several Third World states.

Ilyushin Il-18   USSR

Photo: Yemeni II-18
Data: II-18D

Engines: Four 4,250ehp Ivchenko AI-20M turboprops
Span: 122ft 8½in
Length: 117ft 9in
Height: 33ft 4in
Wing area: 1,507sq ft
Weight: 77,160lb (empty equipped)
Max payload: 29,750lb
Max take-off weight: 141,000lb
Speed: 419mph (max cruising)
388mph (best economy cruising)
Range: 2,300 miles with max payload
4,040 miles with max fuel

In the same category as the Vickers Vanguard and Lockheed Electra, the Ilyushin II-18 (NATO codename Coot) was the first postwar Russian airliner to compare favourably with its western contemporaries in terms of technical sophistication or seating capacity and decor, and the first to be ordered by non-Communist airlines. The prototype II-18, known as the *Moskva*, made its first flight in July 1957, powered by 4,000ehp Kuznetsov NK-4 turboprops and was followed by two pre-production aircraft; production was under way while flight testing progressed. The first 20 production aircraft, with accommodation for 75 passengers, were powered alternately by the NK-4 turboprop and the Ivchenko AI-20 of similar power, the latter engine becoming standard on the 21st and subsequent

aircraft. The Il-18 flew its first scheduled passenger service with Aeroflot over the Moscow-Alma Ata route on 20 April 1959; this followed a series of proving flights in the Ukraine carrying freight and mail. The initial version was soon succeeded by the Il-18B which had accommodation for 84 passengers and the maximum take-off weight increased from 130,514lb to 134,923lb.

In 1961 the Il-18B was followed by the Il-18V, with accommodation for 90-110 passengers, and 4,000ehp AI-20K engines; fuel capacity was 5,213 Imp gallons. The 110-seat mixed tourist/economy interior has 24 passengers six-abreast in the forward cabin, 71 six-abreast in the main cabin and 15 five-abreast in the rear cabin. In 1965 the Il-18D (previously the Il-18I) entered Aeroflot service, this having 4,250eshp. AI-20 M turboprops, additional centre section tankage increasing the fuel capacity to 6,600 Imp gallons, and increased all-up weight. Up to 122 passengers can be accommodated in the three main cabins by lengthening the pressurised section of the fuselage by removing the 250cu ft unpressurised cargo hold in the tail. It was also possible to accommodate 122 passengers in the summer peak periods by removing the two large

wardrobes in line with the airscrews, and replacing them by two six-abreast seat rows. A 65-seat layout at reduced seat pitch was also available made up mostly of five-abreast rows. Entering service about the same time as the D was the Il-18E (also known in Russia as the Il-18Ye), which has the same engines as the D but the lower fuel capacity of the Il-18V. Il-18s are flown by a flight crew of five. Total Il-18 production is believed to number 565, of which over 450 are in Aeroflot service, being extensively used on domestic routes, and having been replaced on international routes by jets. Over 100 have been exported outside as well as inside the Soviet bloc countries, to Air Guinee, Air Mali, Air Mauritanie, Ghana Airways (which had eight, but returned them all to Russia), Egyptair and Yemen Airways. Il-18s were also supplied to Cubana, CAAC of China, Balkan Bulgarian (formerly TABSO), CSA of Czechoslovakia, Interflug, LOT of Poland, Malev and Tarom. VIP versions have been supplied to Kruschev, President Tito, the Indian President, the Algerian Government and small numbers serve the air forces of Afghanistan, Bulgaria, China, Czechoslovakia and Poland. Other users include CAAK of North Korea and Hang Khong of Vietnam.

Ilyushin Il-62 USSR

Engines: Four 23,150lb st Kuznetsov NK-8-4 turbofans
Span: 141ft 9in
Length: 174ft 3½in
Height: 40ft 6¼in
Wing area: 3,010sq ft
Operating weight: 153,000lb (empty)
Max payload: 50,700lb
Max take-off weight: 357,000lb
Speed: 528-560mph at 33-39,400ft (cruising)
Range: 4,160 miles with max payload
5,715 miles with max fuel

Russia's equivalent of the Vickers VC10, the Ilyushin Il-62 was the first long haul four-engined jet to go into production in the Soviet Union, and it entered airline service with Aeroflot more than three years later than the British jet had done with BOAC,

although the VC10 had first flown only some seven months earlier than the Il-62's maiden flight in January 1963. Intended to replace the Tu-114 on such routes as Moscow-Montreal and Moscow-Tokyo, the Il-62 (NATO codename Classic) was first revealed on 24 September 1962, when the prototype was inspected at Moscow by Mr Kruschev and other Soviet leaders. Because the new 23,150 st Kuznetsov NK-8-4 turbofan developed for the Il-62 was not ready in time, the prototype first flew powered by 16,535lb st Lyulka AL-7 turbojets, being followed by a second prototype and three pre-production aircraft. Some of these were fitted with the NK-8-4 engines which had now become available, thrust reversers being fitted on the outer engines only, and the first NK-8 powered Il-62 flew late in 1964. The development programme was made protracted by the fact that the Il-62, like other

rear-engined T-tailed aircraft, had inadequte control margins at low speed and to rectify this and achieve desirable stalling characteristics the wing was modified by the fitting of a fixed, drooped extension on each leading edge outer portion. The Il-62 was the largest high performance aircraft to have fully manual flying controls on all three surfaces, and these must also have involved a good deal of development flying. There are two spoiler sections forward of the flaps, which are double-slotted, and an automatic flight control system for use under conditions similar to ICAO Category II standards is featured.

There is accommodation in two main cabins for 186 passengers six-abreast, 72 in the forward cabin and 114 in the rear one, or 168 passengers at an increased seat pitch; 122 people can be carried in a mixed-class interior, with 20 four-abreast in the forward cabin and 102 six-abreast in the rear. After proving flights carrying freight, the Il-62 began regular scheduled services with Aeroflot between Moscow and Montreal on 15 September 1967, to Delhi on 17 October that year and to New York on 15 July 1968, and later to Tokyo and over other domestic and international routes, including those to Havana and Lima (Peru). The Czech airline CSA leased an Il-62 from Aeroflot for its Prague-London services in May 1968, and later ordered seven, followed by Interflug, which began services early in

1970 with the first of six, LOT, which has acquired seven in all, beginning services in May 1972; and Tarom, which began Il-62 flights with two in 1973, and has since acquired two more. Both CSA and LOT operate their Il-62s to New York, while Cubana flies its four Il-62s to Prague and Montreal and CAAC of China, which had five, flew Il-62 services to Tirana (Albania) and Bucharest. Egyptair also used seven Il-62s for a time, but returned them to Russia and replaced them by 707-320Cs. All those exported were the original Il-62 version; in 1970 an improved model, the Il-62M (also known as the Il-62M-200) was evolved, with four 23,350lb st Soloviev D-30KU turbofans, seating for up to 186 passengers, a tank in the fin to provide additional fuel capacity, and an improved range of up to 6,400 miles; maximum gross weight has gone up to 363,760lb. The new turbofans have an improved fuel consumption and there are now clamshell-type instead of cascade-type thrust reversers on the outer engines, allowing the engine pod to be of lower cross-sectional area. Changes have been made to the flight deck, and spoilers are now used for lateral control at low speeds. Aeroflot began operating the Il-62M early in 1974, and now has about 100 of both versions; the M version has not yet been exported. Newest version is the Il-62MK with a strengthened wing structure, modified undercarriage and seating capacity increased to 195.

Israel Aircraft Industries Arava

Israel

Photo: IAI-201

Engines: Two 750shp Pratt & Whitney PT6A-34 turboprops
Span: 68ft 9in
Length: 42ft 9in
Height: 17ft 1in
Wing area: 470.2sq ft
Basic operating weight: 8,816lb
Max payload: 5,184lb
Max take-off weight: 15,000lb
Speed: 203mph (max) at 10,000ft
193mph at 10,000ft (best economy cruising)
Range: 174 miles with max payload
812 miles with max fuel

In very much the same class as the Short Skyvan, the IAI Arava was designed as a light transport with STOL performance and rough-field landing capabilities, and a twin-boom layout was chosen for easy rear loading. Design work started in 1966 and construction of a prototype, which was used for structural testing, began towards the end of that year. The first flying prototype made its maiden flight on 27 November 1969, followed by a second prototype on 8 May 1971. Two main versions are offered, the IAI-101 civil transport, seating up to 20 passengers and type certificated in April 1972, and the IAI-201 military version, the prototype of which first flew on 7 March 1972. In the 12ft 8¼in long

cabin the IAI-201 can accommodate 24 fully-equipped troops or 17 paratroops and two dispatchers in inward-facing seats, or 12 stretcher cases and two sitting patients or medical attendants or just freight. The aft end of the fuselage swings open for loading and unloading, and there is an outward-opening door at the rear of the cabin plus an emergency exit and cargo door on the starboard side. An optional 'extra' is a 0.50in Browning machine gun pack, mounted on each side of the fuselage above a pylon containing a pod for seven 68mm rockets; there is also provision for an aft-firing machine gun. Lift spoilers above the wings and double-slotted flaps, together with Hartzell

reversible-pitch airscrews driven by the Pratt & Whitney PT6A-34 turboprops, combine to achieve STOL performance. Three Aravas were operated on lease by the Israeli Air Force during the 'Yom Kippur' war of October 1973, and IAI's sales efforts have concentrated so far on military customers in the Latin American countries, 50 Aravas being sold by the beginning of 1976. The type has been ordered by the air forces of Israel, Bolivia, Guatemala, Honduras, Mexico, Nicaragua and El Salvador, and by the Ecuadorean Army. The Arava has obvious possibilities as a civil freighter, and for such jobs as the carriage of livestock.

Junkers Ju52/3m   Germany

Photo: French-built Ju52/3m

Engines: Three 830hp BMW132T 9-cylinder air-cooled radials
Span: 95ft 10in
Length: 62ft 0in
Height: 14ft 10in
Wing area: 1,190sq ft
Weight: 12,346lb (empty)
24,317lb (loaded)
Speed: 190mph (max)
154mph at 8,200ft (cruising)
Range: 808 miles

Standard equipment of Deutsche Luft Hansa in the 1930s, making up 75% of its fleet, and used in all the major German airborne assaults of World War II, the Junkers Ju52/3m started life as the single-engined Ju52. A prototype of this made its first flight on 13 October 1930, powered by a BMW VI engine; later a Rolls-Royce Buzzard was fitted and the one and only Ju52 was sold to Canada as CF-ARM, where it was used as a freighter by Canadian Airways Ltd, a predecessor of the present CP Air. The

Ju52/3m first flew in May 1932 and was fitted with three 600hp BMW Hornets or 725hp BMW132As or 830hp BMW132Ts, the BMW132 being the most widely used powerplant; these were nine-cylinder radials and alternative engines in this category were the 925hp Bristol or PZL-built Pegasus, 750hp ENMASA Beta E-9C (for Spanish-built Ju52s) and the 710hp Wright Cyclone, while the Junker Jumo 5 diesel, the Jumo 206 or BMW VI in-line engines were other alternatives. As a 15-17 passenger airliner, the Ju52/3m was the mainstay of Deutsche Luft Hansa, who had 67 of the type in their fleet in mid-1938; Ju52s were also used by other European airlines such as OLAG of Austria, Sabena, Aero O/Y of Finland, Hungary's MALERT, Poland's LOT, ABA of Sweden, DDL and DNL who came together to form the present SAS, and the prewar British Airways, who had three. Outside Germany, South African Airways, with 11 Ju52s in 1939, was the largest prewar operator, while in South America Lloyd Aereo Boliviano of Bolivia, Syndicato Condor (now Cruzeiro do Sul) and VASP in Brazil and Uruguay's CAUSA used the type, the latter flying two Ju52/3mW seaplanes on services across the River Plate.

In 1935 the first Luftwaffe bomber squadrons were equipped with the Ju52/3mg3e, which carried 3,307lb of bombs and had a dorsal gun position and ventral 'dustbin' turret; this version also served in the Spanish Civil War with the Kondor Legion and Nationalist forces, while Ju52s were also used in this conflict as troop transports, freighters and for casualty evacuation. The 'Tante Ju' ('Auntie Ju') or 'Iron Annie' as it was known to German servicemen, continued in these roles throughout the war. It was also used as a glider tug, and for mine countermeasures work, and armament, when fitted, was usually one 13mm MG 131 firing from the open dorsal position, and two 7.92mm MG 15s manually aimed from the cabin windows. The former Amiot company built 400 Ju52/3ms as AAC1

Toucans, the 'AAC' standing for Ateliers Aeronautiques de Colombes. In Spain, Construcciones Aeronauticas SA built 170 as CASA 352-Ls for the Spanish Air Force, which used them until 1975 as transports under the designation T2B, the last one being completed in 1952. German production totalled 4,845 Ju52s and AAC1s served in small numbers in the early postwar years, being used mostly by French charter operators, but also by Air France, British European Airways, which used 11 Ju52s as the 'Jupiter' class on various Scottish and Irish Sea services, by JAT of Jugoslavia and Air Liban. DNL of Norway used its Ju52/3mW seaplanes for domestic services down the Norwegian coast, while in New Guinea Gibbes Sepik Airways Ltd did not retire its last two Ju52s until 1960.

Let L-410 Turbolet

Czechoslovakia

Data: L-410A

Engines: Two 715ehp Pratt & Whitney PT6A-27 turboprops driving Hamilton Standard or Hartzell 3-blade reversible airscrews
Span: 57ft 4$\frac{1}{4}$in
Length: 44ft 7$\frac{3}{4}$in
Height: 18ft 6$\frac{1}{2}$in
Wing area: 353.70sq ft
Basic weight: 7,495lb (empty)
Max payload: 4,078lb (cargo version)
Max take-off weight: 12,566lb
Speed: 230mph at 9,845ft (max cruising)
Range: 186 miles with max payload
807 miles with max fuel

In the same category as the Twin Otter and Short Skyliner, the 15-19 passenger L-410 Turbolet feederliner is the first indigenous design from the Kunovice factory of the Czech National Aircraft Industry, or Let (short for Letecké Zavody, Narodni Podnik, or Aviation Works, National Corporation). Design of the L-410, which can also be used in the

executive, aerial survey, air ambulance, radio/navigational trainer and other roles and is intended for operation from grass airfields, was started in 1966 and the prototype, powered by Pratt & Whitney PT6A-27 turboprops, first flew on 16 April 1969. Development of a suitable Czech turboprop for the L-410, the Motorlet M601A, started while the aircraft was on the drawing board, but the next three prototypes and the initial production version, designated L-410A, were powered with PT6A-27s. This version featured a small increase in wing span and overall length, and seated 15-19 passengers, or 12 in a de luxe layout; in the ambulance role six stretcher cases, five sitting patients and a medical attendant can be carried, while the cabin can quickly be converted to carry freight. There are double upward-opening doors aft on the port side, and both can be removed for paratroop training.

The first L-410A deliveries were to Slov-Air, an associate of the Czech airline CSA, the former putting L-410As into service at Bratislava in 1971 on third-level routes; at the beginning of 1976 CSA

took over Slov-Air and the 12 L-410As it had, continuing to use them on domestic routes. During 1973 five L-410As underwent hot and cold weather trials, and route evaluation in the Soviet Union, in anticipation of a possible Aeroflot order, but deliveries to Russia, where some are now in service with Aeroflot, were delayed until the Czech engines became available. The L-410M has two 549ehp M601A turboprops driving Avia V508 3-blade reversible airscrews, and this version was scheduled to enter service in 1975, two aircraft

being used for certification. Forty L-410As, including the prototypes, had been built by the summer of 1975. A photo survey version known as the L-410AF has a larger, wider and extensively glazed nose section with a vertically-mounted camera and an inward-facing seat for the navigator/camera operator. The nosewheel cannot be retracted in flight; the L-410's main wheels retract inwards into stub fairings, and a ski landing gear can also be fitted. One L-410AF was sold to Hungary in 1974.

Lockheed 10 Electra and 12

USA

Photo and Data: L-10A Electra

Engines: Two 450bhp (max take-off) Pratt & Whitney Wasp Junior R-985-SB2 9-cylinder radials
Span: 55ft 0in
Length: 38ft 7in
Height: 10ft 1in
Wing area: 458sq ft
Weight: 6,450lb (empty)
Capacity payload: 2,400lb
Max take-off weight: 10,500lb
Speed: 202mph (max) at 5,000ft
180mph at 9,600ft (cruising)
Range: 713 miles at 75% power

Having made their name with a series of fast single-engined transports such as the Vega and Orion, Lockheed turned their attention to a larger twin-engined development for 8-10 passengers. This, the Model 10 Electra, made its first flight on 23 February 1934 powered by Pratt & Whitney R-985 Wasp Juniors, and it was noteworthy for featuring twin fins and rudders instead of the single vertical tail surfaces it had in the initial design stages. The Electra's speed made it immediately popular with US and foreign airlines, and it was ordered not only by leading US operators such as Braniff, Delta, Northwest and National, but by several European airlines, including the prewar British Airways, who had seven, LOT of

Above: *L-12A*

Poland, Aeroput of Jugoslavia and LARES of Roumania. Others served with airlines in Canada, Latin America, Australia and New Zealand and with corporate and executive users; altogether 148 Electras were built. Most common version was the Model 10A, with 450hp Wasp Junior R-985-SB2 radials; the Model 10B had 440hp Wright Whirlwind R-975-E3 engines, the 10C had 450hp Wasp Junior R-985-SC1s and the 10E had 600hp Wasp R-1340-S3H-1 motors. A ski-equipped Model 10E was bought by the Soviet Amtorg Trading Corp in 1937 to search for the Russian aviator Levaneffsky and his crew missing on a trans-Polar flight. Miss Amelia Earhart was lost in the Pacific on 2 July 1937 in her Model 10E on a round-the-world record flight. Military versions included the pressurised XC-35 with a fatter fuselage, deeper nose, very small windows and 550hp Wasp XR-1340-43 turbo-supercharged engines; the C-36 series and UC-37 light transports and the US Navy's R20-1, R20-2 and R30-1. In recent years most Model 10s have been used as executive transports although a few have served with third-level and other small airlines.

The Lockheed Model 12 was a smaller and lighter version of the Electra which first flew in 1936, seating up to six passengers; it was faster and had a longer range. Its speed made it more popular as an executive type, although it was used by a number of airlines and several air forces. About 112 were built in all. The principal version was the Model 12A with 400hp Wasp Junior R-985-SB engines, or 450hp Wasp Junior R-985-SB2s in later production aircraft; the Model 12B had 450bhp Wright Whirlwind R-975-E3 engines. The Model 212A was an armed version for the Netherlands East Indies Army Air Corps, with one 0.303in machine gun in a dorsal turret and a second fixed to fire forward from the nose; up to eight small bombs could be carried under the centre-section. The C-40 and UC-40 series were military transports, the single C-40B having a nosewheel undercarriage, and the JO-1 and JO-2 were similar versions for the US Navy. Mr Sidney Cotton in his specially equipped Model 12A made several unauthorised reconnaissance flights over Germany just before war broke out, securing pictures of the German fleet which the Air Staff had not been able to obtain; as a result, the Heston Flight was formed which eventually became the Photographic Reconnaissance Unit. Using another specially modified 12A after the war Mr Cotton explored the development of blind landing equipment.

Lockheed 14 Super Electra

USA

Photo: Lockheed 414 Hudson III
Data: Model 14-G3B

Engines: Two 900bhp (max take-off) Wright Cyclone GR-1820-G3B 9-cylinder radials
Span: 65ft 6in
Length: 44ft 2½in
Height: 11ft 10½in
Wing area: 551sq ft
Weight: 11,025lb (empty)
17,500lb (loaded)
Disposable load: 6,475lb
Speed: 257mph (max) at 9,300ft
237mph at 13,800ft (cruising)
Range: 1,705 miles

Named the Super Electra, although more usually known just by its designation, the Lockheed Model 14 was a larger, faster and more powerful development of the Models 10 and 12, seating up to 11 passengers and a crew of three. A mid-wing position was chosen, chiefly to give ground clearance to the big Lockheed-Fowler area-increasing flaps when lowered, and the Model 14 was the first airliner to have two-speed superchargers, feathering airscrews and under-floor freight holds. The prototype first flew on 29 July 1937 and three alternative production models were offered: the 14-H2 with 875bhp Pratt & Whitney Hornet R-1690-S1E2-G engines, the 14-F62 with 900bhp Wright Cyclone GR-1820-F62s and the 14-G3B with 900bhp Cyclone GR-1820-G3B engines.

Model 14s were used by a number of airlines, including British Airways, who used one to fly Neville Chamberlain to his historic Munich meeting with Hitler in 1938, and by LOT of Poland and LARES of Roumania; three of the latter's were still in use by its successor TARS (the present-day Taron) in the early postwar years. Trans-Canada Air Lines found its Hornet-powered 14-H2s underpowered, and had all 14 of them re-engined with 1,200bhp Pratt & Whitney R-1830-SIC3-G Twin Wasps, in which form they were redesignated Model 14-08s, being very similar to the Model 18-08 Lodestar. The prewar Japan Airways had used the Model 14 on domestic routes and services to China, 29 being supplied, and 56 more were built under licence during 1940-1 by Kawasaki as Model 14-WG3 military transports for the Japanese Army. Production was then handed over to Tachikawa, who built 688 more in the next three years; these were given the Allied code name 'Thelma'. A redesigned version by Kawasaki with a lengthened fuselage to accommodate additional cargo, and modified Fowler flaps went into production in 1941 as the Ki 56, later codenamed 'Thalia'; 119 of these were built.

By far the best known military version was the Model 414 Hudson, hastily produced for the British Purchasing Commission, and used for maritime reconnaissance by RAF Coastal Command and a number of Allied air forces. The Hudson first flew on 10 December 1938 and the initial RAF order for 200 was increased just over tenfold in later years; No 224 was the first Hudson squadron. A Hudson shot down the first German aircraft to be claimed by the RAF during the war — a Dornier Do18 — over Jutland on 8 October 1939 and in August 1941 another Hudson forced a U-boat to surrender to it after attacking the submarine. From 1942 Hudsons also made night landings in occupied France to deliver and collect agents and supplies for the Resistance. Later marks of Hudson had ASV radar, rocket projectiles or airborne lifeboats and the A-28 and A-29 were USAAF versions, the US Navy's PBO-1 corresponding to the A-29; the AT-18 and AT-18A were respectively gunnery and navigational trainers. Production ceased on 30 June 1943 after 2,584 Hudsons had been built. After the war, a few Hudsons were converted for airline use and aerial survey work; the Australian operator East-West Airlines used three on routes in New South Wales, the last two being sold in 1963.

Lockheed 18 Lodestar

USA

Photo: Learstar
Data: L-18-56

Engines: Two 1,200bhp (max take-off) Wright Cyclone GR-1820-G205A 9-cylinder radials
Span: 65ft 6in
Length: 49ft 9¾in
Height: 11ft 10½in
Wing area: 551sq ft
Weight: 11,790lb (empty) 18,500lb (max loaded)
Useful load: 5,654lb
Speed: 272mph (max) at 15,300ft 248mph at 19,000ft (cruising)
Range: 1,890 miles

The Lodestar was a development of the Model 14 with a longer fuselage capable of accommodating 14 passengers, and double taper on the wing trailing edges. Production aircraft had the tailplane raised

slightly to avoid buffeting when the Fowler flaps were lowered. The prototype, which first flew on 21 September 1939, was actually rebuilt from a Model 14-H2 of Northwest Airlines Inc, and after flight testing was completed, was sold to British West Indian Airways in 1940. As with the Model 14, a choice of different powerplants was offered to prospective customers: the Model 18-07 had two 875bhp Pratt & Whitney R-1690-S1E3-G Hornets, the Model 18-08 1,200bhp Twin Wasp R-1830-S1C3-G radials, the 18-10 had 1,050bhp Twin Wasp R-1830-SC3-Gs, the 18-14 had 1,200bhp Twin Wasp R-1830-S4C4-Gs, the Model 18-40 had 1,100bhp Wright Cyclone GR-1820-G102A radials, the 18-50 had 1,200bhp Cyclone GR-1820-G202As and the Model 18-56, the most numerous Lodestar variant, had 1,200bhp Cyclone GR-1820-G205A engines. The first airline customer for the Lodestar was South African Airways, which ordered 28 in April 1940. BOAC operated a sizeable Lodestar fleet, mostly on wartime routes in the Middle East and

Africa, and the RAF used four squadrons of the type in the Middle East as Lodestar CIs, IAs and IIs for air ambulance and general transport work, these corresponding to the USAAF's C-56, C-59 and C-60 respectively.

There was a multiplicity of USAAF versions, differing chiefly in type of engine fitted and cabin interiors: C-56 variants to C-56E were Cylone- and Hornet-powered, the C-57 series had Twin Wasps, the C-59 was Hornet-powered and the C-60, C-60A and XC-60B had Cyclones, while the single C-66 had Twin Wasps. Many of these variants were civil models impressed into military service, and could seat up to 18 troops; by far the most numerous was the C-60A, of which 325 were built as standard US Army/Navy troop transports, the Navy designation being R50-6; as a glider tug this version could tow as many as three gliders. Orders for 691 C-60Cs, a C-60A with large loading doors, were cancelled. The US Navy R50-1, -2, -5 and -6 corresponded to the C-56, C-59, C-60 and C-60A, the R50-3 and -4 being 4-7 seat VIP/executive versions of the Models 18-10 and 18-56; about 100 of all six series were built for the Navy. After the war Lodestars continued in airline use, but many were used as executive transports, sometimes with weather radar, a few for aerial survey and one, in New Zealand, for aerial topdressing. The Learstar Mk 1, which appeared in the summer of 1954, was a modification of the Model 18-56 by Lear Inc with many drag-reducing features and new systems that gave a substantially improved performance; the prototype first flew on 19 May 1954 and production deliveries began that October. The Learstar Mk II was very similar, with extra fuel capacity in the outer wings. Pacific Airmotive took over Learstar conversions in 1956. Other high speed executive modifications of the basic Lodestar airframe were produced by Howard Aero (now the Business Air Craft Corporation) as the H-250, H-350, H-500 and the pressurised H-400 (redesignated BA-400), the last three being remanufactured versions of the Ventura bomber. A new tri-gear version of the H-250 appeared in 1965 with a 4ft longer nose and a reconditioned Douglas A-26 nosewheel, as well as new nacelles for the Wright Cyclone R-1820-56A or -72A engines.

Lockheed Constellation

USA

Photo: L-749
Data: L-749A

Engines: Four 2,500bhp (max take-off) Wright Duplex Cyclone GR-3350-749C18BD-1 18-cylinder 2-row radials
Span: 123ft 0in
Length: 95ft 1$\frac{1}{4}$in
Height: 23ft 0in
Wing area: 1,650sq ft
Weight: 60,141lb (empty)
107,000lb (max gross)
Max payload: 20,276lb
Speed: 304mph at 20,000ft (continuous cruising)
Range: 3,800 miles with max payload
4,840 miles with max fuel

The Constellation had its origins in an earlier four-engined project, the Model L-44 Excalibur, and design work on the former began in April 1939 to a specification issued by TWA for an airliner to fly the US transcontinental routes. Four of the new 2,200bhp Wright R-3350 Duplex Cyclones were chosen, and novel features included the so-called 'lifting fuselage' with a cambered centre-line to give an aerofoil-like profile in side view, hydraulic power-boosted controls and reversible-pitch airscrews. The prototype Constellation first flew on 9 January 1943 and flight tests soon showed it to have an outstanding performance. Both TWA and Pan American had placed orders for the type in 1940, but waived their rights to the Constellation in favour of the USAAF, and 20 production aircraft laid down for TWA were completed as C-69-1-LO and C-69-5-LO 63-seat troop transports and one as a C-69C-1-LO 43-passenger version, 49 more of the C variant being cancelled. Fifteen of the C-69s were refurbished for civil use and sold off to TWA, BOAC, El Al Israel Airlines and Capital Airlines. The first true commercial version was the Model L-049, which received its CAB type approval on 11 December 1945 at a maximum gross weight of 90,000lb, and successive gross weight increases up to 96,000lb in the 049D and 98,000lb in the 049E were affected by minor undercarriage and structural strengthening.

TWA began North Atlantic services with its 049s

89

on 5 February 1946 and US transcontinental flights 10 days later; Pan Am had begun Atlantic flights on 20 January that year and 049s were soon in service with major operators such as Air France, BOAC, KLM and Panair do Brasil. Altogether 66 049s were built in addition to those converted from C-69s. The Model L-149 was created by fitting the 049 with the Model 749's outer wings to increase the fuel capacity to 5,820 US gallons; a few 049s were so converted. Next commercial version was the L-649 with more powerful Wright GR-3350-749C18BD-1 engines, improved passenger accommodation, new propellers and wing tankage increased to 4,690 US gallons. Eastern Air Lines, which ordered 14 L-649s, was the only customer as both this and the 649A (not built) which had a higher gross weight were soon superseded by the Model L-749. This was a long-range version of the 649 with the same BD-1 engines, wing tankage increased to 5,820 US gallons and a maximum gross weight of 102,000lb

(later increased to 105,000lb); the first 749 was delivered to Air France on 18 April 1947. Both the 649 and 749 could carry the Speedpak under-fuselage freight container (also carried by a few 049s) which could take up to 8,200lb of freight. A further gross weight increase to 107,000lb resulted in the Model L-749A; many 749s were converted to 749A standard by airlines using kits. Several 749As were later fitted with a forward or rear freight door and strengthened freight floors. The PO-1W (later WV-1), two of which were built, was a US Navy early warning version of the 749A with dorsal and ventral radomes similar to the later WV-2/EC-121 variants. Ten C-121s, a military version of the 749, were also built, eight being C-121A-1-LO personnel and staff transports, one a VC-121A-1-LO and one VC-121B-1-LO VIP transports for commanders-in-chief. Including the military variants, 131 Model 749s and 749As were built.

Lockheed Super Constellation USA

Photo: L-1049H
Data: L-1049G

Engines: Four 3,250bhp (max take-off) Wright Turbo Compound R-3350-972TC18DA-3 18-cylinder 2-row radials.
Span: 123ft 0in
Length (with weather radar): 116ft 2in
Height: 24ft 9in
Wing area: 1,650sq ft
Weight: 79,237lb (equipped)
137,500lb (max gross)
Max payload: 24,293lb

Speed: 370mph (max) at 20,000ft
310mph at 20,000ft (cruising)
Range: 4,160 miles with max payload
4,810 miles with max fuel

Successive increases in maximum gross weight (and corresponding increases in payload) had taken the Constellation from 90,000lb to 107,00lb without any fuselage stretch, and so a stretched version would have obvious possibilities. This materialised as the Model L-1049A Super Constellation with an 18ft 4$\frac{3}{4}$in increase in fuselage length made by adding two constant-diameter fuselage sections fore and aft of

Above: *L-1049E*

the wing spars. The structure was strengthened and rectangular cabin windows replaced the circular ones of earlier models. The Constellation prototype was converted into a Super Constellation, and made its first flight in this form on 13 October 1950. Eastern ordered 14 L-1049As and was the first to operate Super Constellation services when this variant began New York-Miami flights on 17 December 1951. TWA ordered 10 1049As, being the only other customer. The 1049A did not have Turbo Compounds but 'conventional' Wright R-3350-956C18CB-1 engines of 2,700bhp and with these it was underpowered; maximum gross weight was 120,000lb and fuel capacity was 6,550 US gallons.

The first Turbo Compound-engined variant was the US Navy's R7V-1 transport (later C-121J), which had 3,250bhp R-3350-34W engines and the wing structure redesigned for a maximum gross weight of 130,000lb (later increased to 133,000lb). Of 50 R7V-1s ordered, 33 later were turned over to the USAF as C-121Gs, while the Model L-1049F or C-121C was the USAF version of the R7V-1, 33 being built; this F model had structural reinforcement for the higher gross weight of 137,500lb. The L-1049B was a commercial freighter version of the R7V-1 with a gross weight of 130,000lb and two upward-opening cargo doors; Seaboard & Western Airlines's order of four for its New York-Europe routes was changed to the L-1049D which superseded the B and had a gross weight of 133,000lb. The first civil Turbo Compound version was the L-1049C, with 3,500bhp R-3350-972TC18DA-1 engines, a

maximum gross weight of 133,000lb and fuel capacity of 6,550 US gallons. The prototype 1049C, for KLM, made its first flight on 17 February 1953 and this model was soon followed by the L-1049E, which was the same as the C with the same gross weight, but incorporating all structural modifications (except to the undercarriage) for an eventual gross weight of 150,000lb. There were 74 1049Cs and 1049Es built, and some Es were later modified to 1049G standard with or without wing tip tanks; a few Cs were also modified to E standard and a number of 1049As, Cs and Es were later converted into freighters.

Other military transport versions included a single VIP VC-121E for President Eisenhower's use, plus two R7V-2 and two YC-121F test beds for the Pratt & Whitney T-34 turboprop, while a prolific family of AEW and electronic warfare variants for both the Navy and USAF started with the WV-2 (later EC-121K). The Model L-1049G or Super G was a development of the 1049E with more powerful R-3350-972TC18DA-3 Turbo Compounds, a gross weight of 137,500lb and two 600 US gallon wing tip tanks as an optional 'extra', weather radar could also be fitted and 104 Super Gs were built, some later being converted to freighters. The L-1049H was a freighter version of the Super G with the same freight doors and heavy-duty floor of the earlier 1049D and more powerful EA-3 or EA-6 Turbo Compounds; it could also be used to carry up to 118 passengers and 53 were built in all.

Lockheed L-1649A Starliner   USA

Engines: Four 3,400bhp (max take-off) Wright Turbo Compound R-3350-988TC18EA-2 18-cylinder 2-row radials.
Span: 150ft 0in
Length: 116ft 2in
Height: 23ft 9in
Wing area: 1,850sq ft
Weight: 85,553lb (empty)
Capacity payload: 23,000lb
Max take-off weight: 160,000lb
Speed: 377mph (max) at 18,600ft
323mph at 20,000ft (continuous cruising)

Range: 5,400 miles with max payload
6,280 miles with max fuel

The ultimate stretch of the basic Constellation airframe was the Model L-1649A Starliner, previously known as the Super Star Constellation, which featured a completely new and redesigned wing of 150ft span, higher aspect ratio (12.15 instead of 9.7) and thinner section and with integral tankage for 9,600 US gallons of fuel to make possible non-stop operation of the North Atlantic route in both directions all the year round, with the

ability to make the east-to-west crossing against winter headwinds without loss of payload. There were two intermediate stages from the Super Constellation to the L-1649A: the Model L-1449 project, which would have had a 4ft 7in fuselage stretch over the 1049G Super Constellation, a strengthened undercarriage and 6,000ehp Pratt & Whitney PT2F-1 turboprops (a civil version of the military T-34), and the Model L-1549 project, which would have had a 10ft 9in fuselage stretch, the same PT2F-1s and a maximum gross weight of 187,500lb. Several alternative powerplants were considered for the 1449, including the Pratt & Whitney T-52, Allison T-56, Rolls-Royce RB109 Tyne and Bristol BE25 Orion, but in the end the lack of a suitable turboprop led to the abandoning of both the 1449 and 1549. The Model L-1649A reverted to Wright R-3350-988TC18EA-2 Turbo Compounds mounted 5ft further outboard on the wings, and this time there was no fuselage stretch over the Super Constellation. The prototype first flew on 11 October 1956 and first deliveries to TWA, which had ordered 25, followed in April 1957; Air France ordered 10 and Lufthansa and LAI of Italy (in which TWA had a 40% holding) ordered four each, the LAI aircraft being taken over by TWA following the merger of LAI into Alitalia.

Only 43 L-1649As were built (plus the prototype)

as the redesign of the wing and non-availability of the turboprop chosen for the L-1449 meant that the Starliner was a whole year later than the DC-7C in entering North Atlantic service, and sales suffered accordingly. Typical cabin layouts accommodated up to 64 first-class or 99 coach passengers, or 26 first-class and 45 tourist. Two of Lufthansa's 1649As were later converted to freighters with upward-opening cargo doors fore and aft, as were six of TWA's (plus a further six later), a strengthened freight floor being fitted. The 1649As were in service only a few years before being displaced on international routes by 707s and DC-8s, and second-hand examples were sold off to Trans Atlantica Argentina, Lineas Aeres Patagonica Argentinas, Trek Airways of South Africa (operating three jointly with Luxair), Alaska Airlines, Red Dodge Aviation, World Airways Inc, Air Korea and several non-airline operators and travel clubs. Air Afrique, Candor Flugdienst, Trans Mediterranean Airways and the Argentine carrier Aerovias Halcon also used the 1649A on lease at various times. A projected radar picket version of the 1649A for the US Navy, the W2V-1, would have had four Allison T-56 turboprops plus two Westinghouse J-34 auxiliary jets in wing tip pods and the disc-shaped dorsal radome of the WV-2E with twin fins and rudders. The W2V-1 was cancelled in 1957.

Lockheed L-188 Electra

USA

Photo and Data: L-188A
Engines: Four 3,750ehp (max take-off) Allison 501-D13A turboprops
Span: 99ft 0in
Length: 104ft 5½in
Height: 32ft 9in
Wing area: 1,300sq ft
Basic operating weight: 61,500lb
Max payload: 22,825lb
Max take-off weight: 113,000lb
Speed: 450mph (max)
405mph at 22,000ft (max cruising)
Range: 2.200 miles with max payload
2,500 miles with max fuel

The Electra had its origins in a specification for a

short/medium haul airliner for US domestic routes drawn up by American Airlines, which announced an 'off the drawing board' order for 35 in June 1955, this was followed by a second order that same month from Eastern Air Lines for 40. Design work began in 1954 and, after revisions to meet changes in the specification, the Electra emerged initially as larger than the Viscount 800, but not as large or powerful as the Vanguard, seating 100 passengers and with a non-stop range of about 2,300 miles. Powerplants were four 3,750ehp Allison 501-D13 turboprops, a commercial version of the military T56, driving Aeroproducts or Hamilton Standard four-blade reversible props. The prototype first flew on 6 December 1957, by which time orders had reached a total of 144; maximum gross weight had

now risen to 113,000lb and up to 99 passengers could be accommodated in a high density interior. Three more prototypes flew in 1958, two of these later being sold to Cathay Pacific Airways after completion of the flight test programme, and one serving as the P3V-1 aerodynamic prototype. Lockheed had planned several military versions of the Electra for such roles as personnel transport and navigational trainer, but the only one to be developed was the P3V-1 (later P-3 Orion) anti-submarine aircraft; the YP-3A prototype, with full electronics, first flying on 25 November 1959.

FAA Type Approval was granted on 22 August 1958; Eastern flew the first Electra service, between New York and Miami, on 12 January 1959, and American inaugurated flights between New York and Chicago on the 23rd of that month. The Electra was also ordered by National Airlines, Braniff, Western Airlines, Northwest Orient and Pacific Southwest Airlines in the USA, but sales outside the States were disappointing, as airlines were turning increasingly to jets. Only KLM in Europe ordered the Electra and in Australia Ansett-ANA, TAA and Qantas bought the type, as well as TEAL (now Air New Zealand), Garuda Indonesian and Cathay Pacific being the only Asian customers. There were now two basic versions, the L-188A for US domestic operation, with a fuel capacity of 5,506 US gallons, and the L-188C, with 900 US gallons more fuel and a higher gross weight of 116,000lb, developed initially for Northwest Orient and Western, and intended mainly for overwater operations.

After two fatal accidents had occurred to a Braniff and Northwest Electra, in both of which a wing was lost in flight, the FAA imposed a speed limitation of 275 knots, very soon reduced to 225 knots, on the type in March 1960 while the cause of the accidents was investigated. The cause was finally found to lie in the structural strength of the engine mounting which, if damaged in, say, a heavy landing, would lead to an oscillation of the engine and airscrew developing, resulting in structural failure. The engine mounting structure was modified as well as the wing skin panels, and a previous change, made before the Braniff and Northwest accidents, had been to tilt up the engine nacelles slightly, resulting in improved vibration and noise levels in the forward cabin and reduced propeller stresses. FAA approval for the modifications, which also included reinforcing the front spar and strengthening 18 ribs in each wing, was given in January 1961, and as aircraft were modified the speed restrictions were lifted. The modification programme is estimated to have cost Lockheed some $25 million. Second-hand Electras have been acquired by US charter and supplemental carriers such as American Flyers and Evergreen International, intra-state carriers like Air California, and a number of Latin American airlines; TAME, the airline branch of the Ecuadorean Air Force, operates four on domestic routes. A number of second-hand Electras have been converted into freighters with large cargo doors. Altogether 174 of the type were built.

Below: *L-188C*

Lockheed L-100 Hercules

Photo and Data: L-100-30

Engines: Four 4,508eshp Allison 501-D22A
turboprops
Span: 132ft 7in
Length: 106ft 1in (L-100-20)
112ft 9in (L-100-30)
Height: 38ft 6in
Wing area: 1,745sq ft
Operating weight: 73,428lb (empty)
Max payload: 46,572lb
Max take-off weight: 155,000lb
Speed: 377mph at 20,000ft (max cruising)
Range: 2,130 miles with max payload
4,740 miles with max fuel

Designed to a specification issued in 1951 by the USAF Tactical Air Command for a medium/long-range assault transport, the Hercules first flew in prototype form as the YC-130 on 23 August 1954. A whole family of military C-130 versions was developed and the type is now in service with 30 military customers. The commercial possibilities of the Hercules were realised early on, but civil interest took a long time to reach the point of actual sales. The first civil version to be announced, in April 1959, was the Model GL-207 Super Hercules, a development of the C-130A and C-130B with an increase in length of about 25ft, a 12ft 6in greater span and four 6,500hp Allison 550-B7 turboprops, a civil version of the T-61, in place of Allison T56s. Provisional orders for 12 Super Hercules were placed by Pan American, and for six by Slick Airways, these being conditional on USAF backing for the Super Hercules, which was not forthcoming.

The next step was a straightforward civil version of the C-130E; on 21 April 1964 Lockheed flew a civil demonstrator based on the E and designated Model 382-44K-20. FAA Type Approval was received on 16 February 1965 and deliveries of the first commercial version, the Model CL-382B, began later that year to Continental Air Services Inc, who acquired two for its operations in Laos, Zambian Air Cargoes, which used five to fly copper shipments from Ndola to East African ports after Rhodesia's UDI, and Alaska Airlines, which flew three on oil exploration support work. Other customers for this variant, which was also designated Model L-100, were Interior Airways, of Fairbanks, Airlift International, Pacific Western and Delta Air Lines; Delta's three had a special cargo loading system. Powerplants were 4,050shp Allison 501-D22 turboprops, a civil version of the T56-A-7, and the L-100-10 was a projected variant, with 4,500shp Allison 501-D22A engines. The L-100-20, or CL-382E, which received FAA Type Approval on 4 October 1968, features an 8ft 4in fuselage extension; the 501-D22A engines are fitted, and the maximum take-off weight, at 155,000lb is the same as the CL-382B's.

Several Bs already in service, such as Delta's were converted to CL-382E standard but most Es were built as such, this variant being operated by Alaska International Air, Red Dodge Aviation Inc, Saturn Airways, Southern Air Transport, Pacific Western, SATCO of Peru and the Peruvian Air Force, Safair Freighters of Johannesburg, the Kuwait Air Force, Philippine Aerotransport and the Philippine Air Force. Two of the E version with the lower-powered 501-D22 engines were delivered as CL-382Fs. A further stretch of the E with the fuselage extended by 6ft 8in was produced, chiefly for Saturn Airways, which wanted to be able to ferry a complete aircraft set of three Rolls-Royce RB211 engines at a time from Derby to where the TriStar was being built in California. This was the CL-382G or L-100-30, and had the rear cargo windows, paratroop doors and provision for JATO removed. Saturn began services with the G in December 1970, using 12 of this version (some converted from Es), and Alaska International Air, Southern Air Transport, Safair, Uganda Airlines, and the Gabon Republic also operate the G. The L-100-50 is another stretched version proposed with a 30ft longer fuselage. By the end of 1978 71 of the L-100 civil versions had been ordered, including a number by CTA of Angola.

Martin 2-0-2 and 4-0-4

Photo: Martin 2-0-2
Data: Martin 4-0-4

Engines: Two 2,400bhp Pratt & Whitney R-2800-CB16 Double Wasp 18-cylinder 2-row radials
Span: 93ft 3½in
Length: 74ft 7in
Height: 28ft 5in
Wing area: 864sq ft
Weight: 29,126lb (empty equipped)
Max payload: 11,692lb
Max take-off weight: 44,900lb
Speed: 312mph (max) at 14,500ft
280mph at 18,000ft (cruising)
Range: 925 miles with max payload
1,070 miles with max fuel

Designed at the end of the war to meet the need for a DC-3 replacement airliner for major inter-city routes, and in particular the American Airlines specification of early 1945 for such a type, the 40-passenger Martin 2-0-2 was the first postwar twin-engined airliner to be given type approval by the Civil Aeronautics Authority, which it received on 13 August 1947. The prototype first flew on 22 November 1946 and in its original form had no dorsal fin and only 3° wing dihedral; a big dorsal fin was added to improve stability, especially in the engine out case, and dihedral was increased on the outer wings. The 2-0-2 had the same R-2800-CA18 Double Wasp engines as the Convair 240 and an unusual feature at the time (but also adapted by Convair for the 240) was the door incorporating ventral airstairs folding up into the rear fuselage. Unlike the 240, the 2-0-2 was unpressurised but another factor enabled the Convair 240 and its successors to capture most of the markets, especially overseas. This was a slump in US domestic traffic in 1946-47 which led to existing orders from Braniff, Pennsylvania Central Airlines (later Capital Airlines), Chicago & Southern, Colonial, Delta and United, totalling 165 of the 2-0-2 and 3-0-3 versions, being cancelled, and the Northwest Airlines' order being cut back from 50 2-0-2s and 3-0-3s to 25; the Convair 240 escaped much more lightly, with only 35 cancelled.

In the end, only 31 Martin 2-0-2s (plus two prototypes) were built, 25 for Northwest, four for the Chilean airline LAN, and two for Linea Aeropostal Venezolana. Northwest began 2-0-2 operations in November 1947 and later leased five of its fleet to the embryo Japan Air Lines to begin domestic services on 10 October 1951. The 3-0-3 was a pressurised version of the 2-0-2, but after United cancelled its order for 50 the 3-0-3 was abandoned, although a prototype was flown on 20 June 1947. The 3-0-3 was succeeded by the 4-0-4, also pressurised but with a 39 inch longer fuselage allowing an extra seat row to be installed; gross weight went up from 38,000lb to 44,900lb. The 4-0-4 prototype, modified from the second prototype 2-0-2, first flew in pressurised form on 21 October 1950 and 60 were ordered by Eastern Air Lines, 41 by TWA and two military versions, designated RM-1, by the US Coast Guard. As an interim version, while the 4-0-4 completed its certification tests, TWA acquired 12 of the 2-0-2A, these having the R-2800-CB16 Double Wasps of the 4-0-4, gross weight increased to 43,000lb and extra fuel tankage; the 2-0-2A was not pressurised. Northwest sold off its 2-0-2s from 1951 to Pioneer Airlines of Texas, California Central Airlines and Transocean Airlines, subsequent resales going to Southwest Airways (later Pacific Airlines), Allegheny Airlines, and to several smaller operators; a number went to executive owners. The 2-0-2As were disposed of in resales mostly to Pacific, Allegheny, Modern Air Transport and Southeast, and Allegheny had three of its 2-0-2s converted into freighters. The 4-0-4s were disposed of mostly to US local service airlines such as Piedmont Airlines, Southern Airways, Mohawk Airlines and Pacific, and in more recent years have been acquired by third-level operators such as Marco Island Airways and Shawnee Airlines. Some 4-0-4s have also been refurbished as executive transports.

McDonnell Douglas DC-8 Series 10 to 50   USA

Photo: DC-8 Series 55
Data: DC-8 Series 50

Engines: Four 17,000lb st (max take-off) Pratt &
Whitney JT3D-1 or 18,000lb st (max take-off) JT3D-
3 or JT3D-3B turbofans
Span: 142ft 5in
Length: 150ft 6in
Height: 42ft 4in
Wing area: 2,868sq ft
Basic operating weight: 132,325lb
Max payload: 46,500lb
Max take-off weight: 325,000lb
Speed: 579mph at 30,000ft (max cruising)
Range: 6,185 miles with max payload

Douglas had been studying various jet transport
projects since as far back as 1947, and preliminary
studies which led eventually to the DC-8 began in
1952. On 7 June 1955 the decision was taken to go
ahead with the DC-8 project and this, when revealed
that August, was seen to have the same basic
configuration as the Boeing 707, with four Pratt &
Whitney J57 (JT3C) turbojets in pods under a wing
with 30° sweepback, 5° less than that of the 707.
At this stage the gross weight was to be 211,000lb
for US domestic operation or up to 257,000lb for
long haul overwater versions. An important
difference from Boeing's sales approach with the
707 family was that Douglas decided to offer all
projected DC-8 versions with the same overall
airframe dimensions, and with uniform electrical,
hydraulic and other systems, structural modifications
for the higher operating weights and extra fuel of
intercontinental versions being confined to the use of
thicker skin and stronger materials in the wing
structure, rear fuselage and tailplane, together with a
strengthened undercarrriage. Pan American placed
its historic order for 20 each of the DC-8 and 707 on
13 October 1955, and this led to the big jet buying
spree, as it was called, with United, National, KLM,
Eastern, SAS and Japan Air Lines all ordering DC-8s
before the end of 1955. The Intercontinental
versions were now to have Pratt & Whitney JT4A
turbojets, a commercial version of the J75, or Rolls-
Royce Conways, these models being designated

Series 30 and 40 respectively. The series 10 was the
initial production model with JT3C engines for US
domestic use, and the Series 20 was the same with
more powerful JT4A engines. These versions could
seat up to 189 passengers in a one-class high-
density interior or 132 in a typical mixed-class
arrangement.

The first DC-8, a Srs 10, first flew on 30 May
1958 (there was no prototype as such) and was
followed by the first Srs 20 on 29 November that
year, the first Srs 30 on 21 February 1959 and the
first Srs 40 on 23 July. The Srs 10 received FAA
certification on 31 August 1959, being powered by
13,500lb st JT3C-6 turbojets and having an all-up
weight of 273,000lb. United and Delta Air Lines both
inaugurated DC-8 serivces on the same day,
18 September 1959, with Srs 10s. But flight tests of
this version had revealed an unexpected drag penalty
under normal cruise conditions, resulting in a
shortfall of some 24 knots in cruising speed at
30,000ft from the specified speed of 493 knots. This
led to a 27-point modification programme to reduce
drag and increase speed, which resulted in delivery
delays for some DC-8 customers. An extra 16in was
added to each wing tip to reduce drag and the tip
profile was changed, this 'mod' being made from the
30th DC-8. The Srs 20 was powered by 15,800lb st
JT4A-3 turbojets, and had an all-up weight of
276,000lb, whereas the Srs 30 had JT4A-3s or -5s
or 16,500lb st JT4A-9s or -10s initially, and fuel
capacity increased to 23,079 US gallons from the
17,600 US gallons of the Srs 10 and 20. Gross
weight was now 310,000lb initially and 315,000lb
after entering service. A new wing leading edge
which changes the wing profile and adds 4% to the
chord to reduce drag was introduced on later
production Srs 30s and also applied to other
versions, sometimes retrospectively. More powerful
17,500lb st JT4A-11 or -12 engines later became
available for the Srs 30, which first entered service in
April 1960 with Pan American and KLM on
transatlantic routes. The Srs 40 had 17,500lb st
RCo 12 Conway 509s and a gross weight of
315,000lb; TCA (now Air Canada) began Srs 40
services between Montreal and Vancouver on 1 April
1960, and Alitalia and Canadian Pacific (now CP Air)
also ordered Srs 40s.

The Srs 50 was the same as the Srs 30 but powered by 17,000lb st Pratt & Whitney JT3D-1 turbofans that gave considerable improvements in fuel consumption and range, especially when allied to the 4% wing. The first DC-8 Srs 10 was re-engined with JT3Ds and flew as the Srs 50 prototype on 20 December 1960; later, 18,000lb st JT3D-3 or JT3D-3B engines became available and with these the gross weight went up to 325,000lb, the version with -3B engines and aerodynamic refinements being known as the Srs 55. A number of earlier DC-8s were converted to Srs 50 standard by fitting the turbofans. The DC-8F Jet Trader announced in April 1961 is a passenger/cargo

Above: DC-8 Series 30

version of the Srs 50 with a 7ft 1in × 11ft 8in forward freight door, a strengthened freight floor and the same engines, 4% wing and gross weights. By the use of a moveable bulkhead, passenger capacities of from 24 to 114 people can be arranged with varying amounts of cargo space, a typical mixed load being six cargo pallets and 84 passengers. The DC-8F first flew on 29 October 1962, the DC-8F Srs 55 differing from the Srs 54 in having a gross weight of 325,000lb and many detailed improvements; including JT3D-3B engines. Altogether 293 DC-8s from the Srs 10 to the DC-8F were built.

McDonnell Douglas DC-8 Series 61, 62 and 63

USA

Photo: DC-8 Series 62
Data: DC-8 Series 63

Engines: Four 18,000lb st (max take-off) Pratt & Whitney JT3D-3 or -3B or 19,000lb st JTD-7 turbofans
Span: 148ft 5in
Length: 187ft 5in
Height: 42ft 5in
Wing area: 2,927sq ft
Basic operating weight: 153,749lb
Max payload: 67,735lb

Max take-off weight: 350,000lb
Speed: 583mph at 30,000ft (max cruising) 523mph (best economy cruising)
Range: 4,500 miles with max payload

When Douglas decided to go ahead with the DC-8 project in June 1955 they announced that all projected versions would have the same airframe dimensions, and the first five models differed chiefly in their fuel capacity and powerplants. While this simplified production planning, it made the DC-8 series less flexible in meeting varying airline

Above: *DC-8 Series 63*

requirements than the Boeing 707/720 family with its different fuselage lengths, and enabled Boeing to outstrip Douglas in big jet sales. To overcome this sales disadvantage, in April 1965 Douglas decided to offer three new DC-8 versions known as the Super Sixty Series, with different fuselage sizes and payload/range capabilities, and powered by the same JT3D-1 or JT3D-3 turbofans as the Series 50; all three also had repositioned double-slotted flaps and Hytrol anti-skid brakes. The Series 61 had a fuselage lengthened by 36ft 8in to accommodate up to 259 passengers, a maximum take-off weight of 325,000lb and 18,000lb st JT3D-3B turbofans; overall length was now 187ft 5in. The Series 62 was an ultra-long range version with a fuselage stretch of only 6ft 8in to accommodate up to 201 coach-class passengers, span increased by two 3ft wing tip extensions to reduce induced cruise drag, and increased fuel tankage. The engine pods were redesigned to reduce drag and increase thrust by ducting by-pass air through the entire length of the nacelle, and the engine pylons were also redesigned. The Series 63 had the longer fuselage of the Series 61, and the increased span and revised engine pods of the 62 for maximum flexibility of operation. The 63 could accommodate up to 259 passengers and had a maximum take-off weight of 350,000lb; some 63s were fitted with 19,000lb st JT3D-7 turbofans as alternatives to the JT3D-3s.

All three of the Super Sixties were also offered in

convertible and all-freight versions with a forward cargo door as on the DC-8F Jet Trader, the convertible models being designated Series 61CF, 62CF and 63CF and the all-freight ones Srs 62AF and 63AF. Some of the latter had the structural provisions for the freight door and strengthened freight floor but did not actually have them fitted, and these were known as the Srs 63PF. The Srs 61 made its first flight on 14 March 1966 and entered airline service with United Air Lines on 25 February 1967; the Srs 62 first flew on 29 August 1966 and began commercial services with SAS on 22 May 1967, while the Srs 63 first flew on 10 April 1967, entering airline service with KLM on 27 July that year. The Srs 61 and 63 freighters could carry up to 18 cargo pallets or some 59 short tons of bulk-loaded cargo. The Super Sixties filled the payload/range gap between existing 707s and DC-8s and the forthcoming Boeing 747, and they were ordered by many airlines that had bought the earlier DC-8s, by other operators such as Air Jamaica and Finnair that were moving into long haul operations, and by a number of the US all-freight, charter and supplemental airlines. Altogether 263 had been built when DC-8 production ended in May 1972, made up of 88 Srs 61s, 68 Srs 62s and 107 Srs 63s. Together with the earlier versions, this made a grand total of 556 DC-8s built.

McDonnell Douglas DC-9

USA

Photo: DC-9 Series 31
Data: DC-9 Series 30

Engines: Two 14,500lb st Pratt & Whitney JT8D-9 or 15,000lb st JT8D-11 or 15,500lb st JT8D-15 turbofans
Span: 93ft 4in
Length: 119ft 4in
Height: 27ft 6in
Wing area: 1,001sq ft
Operating weight: 58,500lb (empty)
Max weight-limited pay load: 29,860lb

Max take-off weight: 108,000lb
Speed: 572mph (max cruising)
496mph (long range cruising)
Range: 1,100 miles with max payload

The original Douglas project for a short/medium haul jet designated DC-9, announced in July 1959, resembled a scaled down DC-8 and was powered by four 8,250lb st Pratt & Whitney JTF10A turbofans in underwing pods; it seated up to 92 passengers. But following a reappraisal of the market, and no doubt influenced by the Braniff, American and Mohawk orders for the One-Eleven, Douglas from

1962 began to recast its ideas for a short haul jet into the present DC-9 (originally known as the Model 2086) with two rear-mounted engines and a T-tail. The decision to go ahead with the DC-9 was announced on 8 April 1963, rather unusually without a firm airline order, although Delta Air Lines soon signed for 15 with an option on 15 more. From the start a range of versions with different passenger capacities was offered, the first of these being the DC-9 Series 10 with two 12,000lb st Pratt & Whitney JT8D-5 turbofans and an initial gross weight of 77,000lb, or 83,000lb when extra fuel was carried in centre section tanks. The first DC-9 first flew on 25 February 1965, followed by two more in May, another in June and a fourth in July, all of these being Series 10s. FAA Type Approval was granted on 23 November 1965 and Delta inaugurated DC-9 services on 8 December, its Series 10s taking over a number of routes previously flown by Convair 440s. The Series 10 carried up to 90 coach-class passengers, or 72 in a typical mixed-class interior, and with 14,000lb st JT8D-1 or JT8D-7 engines fitted, this variant became known as the Series 10 Model 15, the gross weight going up to 90,700lb. The DC-9 Series 5 was a projected 60-seater version of the Series 10 with a 9ft 6in shorter fuselage, but was not built.

First customer for a stretched version was Eastern Air Lines in February 1965; this originally had a fuselage lengthened by 9ft 6in and was known as the DC-9B or DC-9 Series 20, but the fuselage stretch was increased to 14ft 11in, this now being known as the Series 30. Also featured were extended wing tips, adding 4ft to the span, triple-slotted instead of double slotted flaps and full-span leading edge slats, and the uprated 14,500lb st JT8D-9 engines. The Series 30 first flew on 1 August 1966 and was certificated in December, the first deliveries to Eastern beginning in February 1967. Up to 115 coach-class passengers could be carried, or 97 in a typical two-class interior, and the gross weight was initially 98,000lb. This was raised to 108,000lb with the fitting on later aircraft of 15,000lb st JT8D-11 or 15,500lb st JT8D-15 engines. In 1976 a longer range Series 30 with uprated JT8D-17s and extra fuel tankage was offered. The second stretched version was the Series 40, developed initially for SAS, which had a

further fuselage stretch of 6ft 4in enabling it to seat up to 125 passengers, more fuel tankage, a gross weight of 114,000lb and JT8D-9 engines initially; later, the uprated JT8D-15s were fitted. The Series 40 first flew on 28 November 1967 and deliveries to SAS began in February 1968; SAS eventually ordered 49 of this version and Toa Domestic of Japan 18. Also designed to meet SAS requirements was the so-called 'hot rod' Series 20, combining the Series 10's short fuselage with the Series 30's long-span wings and high lift devices for improved temperature/altitude performance. The Series 20 first flew on 18 September 1968 and had JT8D-9 or JT8D-11 engines and a gross weight of 100,000lb; 10 Series 20s were built for SAS. The third major stretched version was the DC-9 Series 50, with another 6ft 4in increase in fuselage length, which was now 27ft 7in longer than the original Series 10; this enabled up to 139 passengers to be accommodated. Initially powered by JT8D-15s, the Series 50 was later fitted with 16,000lb st JT8D-17s and has a gross weight of 120,000lb. The Series 50 first flew on 17 December 1974 and the first delivery, to Swissair, was made in August 1975.

With the final stretched version, the DC-9 Super 80 (previously the Series 55 and before that the DC-9-RSS) announced on 20 October 1977 with orders and options for 36, the DC-9 will have been stretched further than any other airliner; its length of 147ft 10in is 14ft 3in longer than the Series 50's and no less than 43ft 6in longer than the Series 10's. Wing span is increased to 107ft 10in by wing root and tip extensions, the wing area now being 1,279sq ft, and new 4-position leading edge slats are featured, as well as increased wing tankage and a longer-span tailplane. Refanned JT8D-209 engines of 18,500lb st will power the Series 80, and the gross weight goes up to 140,000lb, with a strengthened undercarriage to cater for the higher weights. Up to 160 coach/economy passengers or 137 in a two-class interior can be carried, and first deliveries, to Swissair, are due in March 1980. All versions of the DC-9 were offered with an 11ft 4in × 6ft 9in forward freight door for use in the all-cargo or convertible passenger/cargo roles, these being designated by the suffix F or CF to the Series number, or RC (Rapid Change) for the quick-change

variant. The first convertible, a Series 10CF, was delivered to Continental in March 1966, and the first all-freighter, a Series 30F, to Alitalia in May 1968. The C-9A Nightingale is an aeromedical version of the Series 30CF; 24 were supplied to the USAF and 14 C-9Bs to the Navy, three VC-9Cs (formerly C-9As) being used as staff transports. By the end of 1978 sales of all versions of the DC-9 had reached over 970.

Miles M57 Aerovan UK

Photo and Data: Mk IV

Engines: Two 155hp Blackburn Cirrus Major III 4-cylinder air-cooled in-line motors
Span: 50ft 0in
Length: 34ft 4in
Height: 13ft 6in
Wing area: 390sq ft
Weight: 3,000lb (empty)
5,400lb (normal gross)
5,800lb (max gross)
Speed: 127mph (max) at sea level
112mph at sea level (cruising)
Initial rate of climb: 575ft/min
Range: 400 miles

During the war Miles Aircraft Ltd, where George Miles was a staunch proponent of the powered glider concept, studied a number of glider and freighter projects, and these studies came to fruition with the M57 Aerovan, which made its first flight on 26 January 1945. This was, in fact, originally envisaged as a light transport for the Army in Burma in the troop- and vehicle-carrying or casualty evacuation roles, but the war ended before production could start, and Miles was officially rebuked for building the prototype without permission. The Aerovan's wooden construction and low power (two 155hp Blackburn Cirrus Majors) revealed its powered glider origins but it could carry a payload of one ton with a full load of fuel, and was unique among other transports of its size and weight in being able to carry such big loads as a racehorse

or small saloon car, which normally required a DC-3. The rear end of the pod-like fuselage hinged open to form a door, the tail being carried on a boom, and Miles high lift auxiliary flaps completed the Aerovan's distinctive appearance.

After the prototype Mk I and second prototype Mk II, which differed in having a lengthened nose and reduced tare weight, a few Mk IIIs were built. The main production version was the Mk IV, which featured an 18in extension of the fuselage rear end, round windows, revised engine cowlings and the central under-fin deleted. Its ability to carry up to nine passengers or a ton of freight made it popular with small charter operators in Britain and a number of other countries, and a total of 46 Aerovans were built up to the time Miles Aircraft ceased trading in 1948. The type could be converted into a flying showroom or workshop, and was used for aerial survey with cameras fitted, while an Aerovan IV was fitted experimentally with skis. Its inability to maintain height on one engine with a full load led to more powerful developments of the Aerovan, the Mk V with two DH Gipsy Major Xs and the Mk VI with two 190bhp Lycoming 0-435-A 'flat six' engines, the latter flying as a prototype before Aerovan production ended. A French company, Avions Atalante, was planning to build Aerovans under licence powered by two Mathis motors before it went out of business. In 1955-56 an Aerovan IV was experimentally fitted, as the Miles HDM105, with a Hurel Dubois all-metal high aspect ratio wing, giving a span of 75ft 4in, and this project was the ancestor of the Short SC7 Skyvan.

NAMC YS-11

Japan

Photo and Data: NAMC YS-11A Series 200

Engines: Two 3,060eshp (max take-off with water methanol injection) Rolls-Royce RDa10/1 Dart 542-10K turboprops
Span: 104ft 11¾in
Length: 86ft 3in
Height: 29ft 5½in
Wing area: 1,020sq ft
Operating weight: 33,945lb (empty)
Max payload: 14,508lb
Max take-off weight: 54,010lb
Speed: 291mph at 15,000ft (max cruising)
Range: 680 miles with max payload
2,000 miles with max fuel

The first Japanese airliner to be exported in some numbers, and the first postwar commercial transport to be designed and built in that country was the NAMC YS-11. The manufacture of a short- and medium-haul airliner was advocated by the Ministry of International Trade and Industry in 1956. With the Ministry's backing six major aerospace companies began initial design studies, at first separately and then collectively; the six companies were Mitsubishi, Kawasaki, Fuji, Shin Meiwa (formerly Kawanishi), Showa (which had built DC-3s before the war) and Japan Aircraft Manufacturing Co. These six firms later became participants in NAMC — the Nihon Aeroplane Manufacturing Co Ltd, formed in June 1959, in which the Government had a majority holding and production of the YS-11 was shared between them under NAMC's overall control. Japanese domestic air traffic was already growing fast enough to justify making the YS-11 a 60-passenger aircraft, larger than the Friendship, HS748 or Herald; and the Allison 501, Napier Eland and Rolls-Royce Dart were considered as powerplants, an uprated version of the latter, the RDa10/1 Dart 542-10K, being finally chosen. Four prototypes, two for structural tests, were built, the first making its maiden flight on 30 August 1962, followed by the second on 28 December that year. Type certification by the Japan Civil Aviation Bureau — JCAB — was granted on 25 August 1964, followed by FAA Type Approval on 7 September 1965. The first production YS-11 flew on 23 October 1964.

First operator of the YS-11 was Toa Airways (now Toa Domestic Airways) which began YS-11 services between Osaka and Hiroshima on 1 April 1965; Toa was closely followed by Japan Domestic Airlines in May and All Nippon in July that year. The first export order, from Filipinas Orient Airways, was for two (later doubled), and their first YS-11 was delivered on 20 October 1965. Hawaiian Airlines leased three YS-11s in 1966 from NAMC but did not place a firm order, and LANSA of Peru leased two. From the 49th production aircraft higher permitted operating weights and a payload increased by 2,800lb were introduced; this version known as the YS-11A, gained some important export orders, in particular 12 for the Brazilian airline Cruzeiro do Sul and 10 (later increased to 21) for the US local service carrier Piedmont Airlines. The YS-11A was offered in three variants: the 60-passenger Series 200, with no freight door, the mixed traffic Series 300, with a 98in × 72in cargo door forward and accommodation for 46 passengers, and the Series 400 freighter with a 120in × 72in cargo door aft. The first Series 200 made its initial flight on 27 November 1967 and over 90 of this variant were built, followed by some 16 Series 300s. Before production ended with 182 YS-11s built altogether, a few examples of the Series 500, 600 and 700 were produced, these being the same as the 200, 300, and 400 respectively, but with a 1,105lb increase in take-off weight. The YS-11 has also been used by Austral of Argentina, the Brazilian airline VASP, Reeve Aleutian Airways in Alaska, TransAir of Canada, Olympic Airways, Mey-Air of Norway, Air Ivoire (two leased from Air Afrique), SGA of Zaire, Bouraq Indonesia Airlines, China Airlines, Korean Airlines, Merpati Nusantara of Indonesia, Philippine Air Lines and Southwest Air Lines of Okinawa; several YS-11s are in executive or government use. In Japanese military use, as well as 14 YS-11As, are three modified for ECM training and known as the YS-11E, and six YS-11T ASW crew trainer variants for the Lockheed P-2J Neptune. Other users of the YS-11 include Pyramid Airlines and Pinehurst Airlines.

Noorduyn Norseman

Canada

Data: Mk V

Engine: One 600hp Pratt & Whitney R-1340-S3H-1 or R-1340-AN-1 Wasp 9-cylinder radial
Span: 51ft 8in
Length: 32ft 4in
Height: 10ft 1in
Wing area: 325sq ft
Weight: 4,250lb (empty)
7,400lb (loaded)
Disposable load: 3,150lb
Speed: 155mph (max) at 5,000ft
141mph at 5,000ft (cruising 66% power)
Range: 464 miles

Designed by RBC Noorduyn as a light STOL transport especially for Canadian bush operations, the eight-passenger Noorduyn Norseman made its first flight in 1935 powered by a 450hp (max take-off) Wright Whirlwind R-975-E3 radial. It went into production with this engine as the Norseman II and, like the later Beaver and Otter, could be fitted with floats or skis in place of the wheels. It was used before the war in Marks II, III and IV variants by bush operators such as Dominion Skyways Ltd and Mackenzie Air Service and by the Royal Canadian Mounted Police. The major production version, which followed in 1937, was the Norseman IV with a 600hp Pratt & Whitney R-1340-S3H-1 Wasp radial and in 1940 the Royal Canadian Air Force placed an initial order for 38 Mk IVs as radio and navigational trainers; this was followed by several subsequent RCAF orders. After service trials with seven YC-64s, the USAAF selected the Norseman in late 1942 and 746 were built as the UC-64A eight-passenger utility transport. Three of these were transferred to the US Navy as the JA-1, and six more were built as C-64B

floatplanes for the US Army Corps of Engineers; these seated only six passengers. Plans to produce UC-64As at the Aeronca factory in Ohio were dropped. The USAAF used its UC-64As in the European theatre for communications and ambulance work, and a few were employed by the US Navy Fleet Air Wing in England; the UC-64A was redesignated C-64A in 1945. In 1946 Noorduyn Aviation Ltd ceased aircraft manufacture, and its assets were acquired by the Canadian Car & Foundry Co Ltd, who continued to produce the Norseman at Montreal in an improved version known as the Mk V. Production continued until 1950, the final version being the Norseman VI.

A prototype Mk VII with a metal instead of wooden wing and a lengthened fuselage was test flown by the CCF but the manufacturing rights were later returned to Mr Noorduyn, who had formed a company providing spares and other items for the type. After the war Norsemans were acquired by many bush operators in Canada and Alaska, and by small airlines and air taxi operators in Chile, Colombia, Ecuador, Iceland, Norway and Sweden, Algeria and the Gabon, India and New Guinea/Papua; there were still about 100 in airline service in 1963. The Norseman was of mixed construction, with wooden fabric-covered two-spar wings and tailplane, and with the fuselage basically a welded steel tube framework with fabric covering, as were the fin, rudder and elevators. A Hamilton Standard two-blade airscrew was usually fitted, although a three-blade one was optional. Eight passengers on removable bench-type seats were usually carried, or six passengers in slightly more luxurious upholstered seats, or the cabin could be stripped for freight.

Nord 2501 Noratlas

France

Data: Nord 2501

Engines: Two 2,040bhp (max take-off) SNECMA-built Bristol Hercules 738 or 758 14-cylinder 2-row radials
Span: 106ft 7½in
Length: 72ft 0½in
Height: 19ft 10½in
Wing area: 1,089sq ft
Weight: 29,327lb (empty)
Capacity payload: 16,640lb
Max take-off weight: 50,700lb
Speed: 273mph (max) at 4,920ft
195mph at 9,840ft (continuous cruising)
Range: 790 miles with max payload
1,710 miles with max fuel

The Nord 2501 Noratlas orgininated in an official specification of 1947 for a medium tactical transport for l'Armée de l'Air (the French Air Force); design work began that year and a twin-boom high wing layout was chosen for ease of loading, wheeled or tracked vehicles. The first of two prototypes, the Nord 2500, made its maiden flight on 10 September 1949, and was powered by 1,600bhp SNECMA (Gnôme-Rhône) 14R engines, whereas the second prototype, the Nord 2501, had Bristol Hercules 739 radials. There were three pre-production aircraft, and the production Nord 2501, named Noratlas, had SNECMA-built Bristol Hercules 738 or 758 motors driving Breguet 4-blade airscrews; with the Hercules 758 these were reversible-pitch. Typically, 45 fully-equipped troops or 36 paratroops or 18 stretcher cases plus medical attendants could be carried in the hold, which had an unobstructed volume of 1,800cu ft and was 32ft 5in long. The clamshell-type rear doors could be removed for the air dropping of heavy loads. Extended dorsal fins were introduced in 1956, and fitted retrospectively to aircraft already built. Altogether 211 Nord 2501s were supplied to the French Air Force, and the type was also chosen as the standard medium transport for the Federal German Luftwaffe, 52 of these being French-built. The remaining 136 were built under licence in

Germany by Flugzeugbau Nord, the first German-built aircraft flying on 6 August 1958; German Noratlases were designated Nord 2501D. Those for the Israeli Air Force were the Nord 2501-IS variant, of which 12 went into service; these are believed to include three ordered by Arkia Israel Inland Airlines and delivered early in 1959.

The first civil customer was the French independent UAT, which acquired seven Nord 2502s; this version had two 880lb st Turbomeca Marboré auxiliary jets on the wing tips to improve take-off performance in high ambient temperatures. UAT's first Nord 2502 entered service on 10 September 1954 and the seventh on 7 March 1958; they were used for freighting in French Equatorial Africa and the Cameroons and passenger carrying, such cargoes as cotton, coffee, fresh meat, from the Lake Chad region, automobiles and dismantled helicopters being flown, and up to 45 passengers could be carried in four-abreast seating. UAT's Noratlases were sold to the Portuguese Air Force in 1960, that air arm eventually acquiring 24 Noratlases. Air Algerie also ordered three Nord 2502s, and the first of these went into service on 8 September 1957. Two ex-Luftwaffe Nord 2501Ds were acquired by the Nigerian Air Force and another has been used by a charter operator called Air Atlantic in the republic of Rwanda. Four more ex-Luftwaffe aircraft were disposed of to the Ecuadorean charter operator Aero Taxis Ecuatorianas SA, two more to West African Air Cargo and three to the Niger Republic Air Force. Other variants which did not go into production were the Nord 2503, with 2,500bhp Pratt & Whitney R-2800-CB17 Double Wasps; the Nord 2504, a trainer for anti-submarine warfare crews which had two Marboré tip jets and the Nord 2507 air-sea rescue variant, also with tip jets. The Nord 2506 (also known as the Nord 2500E) had a modified, adjustable height undercarriage to simplify loading, low pressure tyres, slotted flaps, two air brakes at the rear of the fuselage and Marboré tip jets. The Nord 2508, of which two were built, had R-2800-CB17 Double Wasps and Marborés and was intended as a civil version.

Piaggio P166

Italy

Photo: P166-DL3
Data: P166-DL2

Engines: Two 380hp (max take-off) Lycoming
IGSO-540-A1A 6-cylinder horizontally-opposed air-
cooled engines
Span: 48ft 2½in (with tip tanks)
Length: 39ft 3in
Height: 16ft 5in
Wing area: 285.9sq ft
Basic weight: 4,960lb (empty)
Max payload: 2,571lb
Max take-off weight: 9,039lb
Speed: 246mph (max) at 11,300ft
223mph at 15,000ft (cruising)
Range: 1,500 miles with max fuel

The P166 light executive transport was based on the
P136 five-seat amphibian flying boat which first flew
in 1948, and it retained the latter's high gull wing
layout with the same two Lycoming GSO-480
pusher engines driving Hartzell three-blade
airscrews. The first of three P166 prototypes flew on
26 November 1957, and production deliveries began
in April 1959. Although used mainly as a 6-8 seat
executive aircraft the P166, of which 32 were built in
all, also served as a feederliner seating up to 10
passengers, in which form it was used by the
German taxi operator Air Lloyd, Olympic Airways and
by Patair (Papuan Air Transport) several of the
Ansett group airlines and other operators in
Australia. Ambulance, light freighter and air survey
versions of the P166 could also be produced. The
P166M light military freighter, of which 51 were
built, 21 for the Italian Air Force for communications

and support of the Fiat G.91 tactical strike squadrons, and nine for the South African Air Force. This
version has a freight loading door in the port side
of the fuselage large enough to take a Bristol
Orpheus turbojet. Up to 10 people can also be
carried, and a strengthened floor for freight carrying
is featured. The P166M has Piaggio instead of
Hartzell three-blade airscrews. Next civil version was
the P166B Portofino, which had the more powerful
Lycoming IGSO-540-A1A engines, a lengthened
nose and a restyled cabin seating 6-10 passengers.
The Portofino first flew on 27 March 1962 and five
were built, followed by two P166Cs which differed in
having the main undercarriage members retracting
into new housings to give more cabin space enabling
up to 12 passengers to be carried. The P166S, of
which 20 were built, was a version equipped for
search and surveillance. Superseding the P166B is
the P166-DL2 which has increased fuel capacity in
integral wing tip tanks and a maximum take-off
weight increased by 662lb; a demonstration model,
designated P166-BL2, first flew on 2 May 1975.
Eight '-DL2s are being built, of which four are to be
equipped for photogrammetric survey work, and all
eight will have a new extra-large cabin door. Latest
variant is the P166-DL3 with two 587shp (max take-
off) Avco Lycoming LTP 101-600 turboprops
driving Hartzell three-blade airscrews; the structure
and systems are the same as the '-DL2 except for
changes associated with the installation of
turboprops. The '-DL3 is especially intended for
aerial work duties of various kinds such as
geophysical survey and aerial photography, and
features the big cabin door of the '-DL2.

Pilatus PC-6 Porter

Switzerland

Photo: PC-6/A Turbo-Porter
Data: PC-6/B2-H2

Engine: One 550shp Pratt & Whitney PT6A-27
turboprop driving a Hartzell 3-blade propeller
Span: 49ft 8in

Length: 35ft 9in
Height: 10ft 6in (tail down)
Wing area: 310sq ft
Weight: 2,678lb (empty equipped)
Max take-off weight: 4,850lb (normal)
Speed: 161mph at 10,000 ft (max cruising)

Range: 644 miles max (no reserves)
1,007 miles max with underwing tanks (no reserves)

One of the most versatile light STOL transports on the market, the Pilatus PC-6 Porter has appeared with a piston engine or three different types of turboprops, on wheels (oversize wheels and tyres are optional), a Pilatus wheel-ski gear, or on twin Edo floats, and can be used not only for passenger carrying but for freighting, supply dropping, air ambulance work (two stretcher cases can be carried), aerial survey and photography, parachuting, crop spraying and dusting, water bombing and target towing. Design work began in 1957 and the first of five piston-engined prototypes made its first flight on 4 May 1959; Swiss certification of the basic model, the PC-6/340 with a 340hp Lycoming GSO-480-BIA6, was given in December 1959 and the entire pre-series of 20 aircraft was built by the summer of 1961, FAA type Approval being received on 9 November that year. The PC-6/340 was followed by the PC-6/340-H1 and PC-6/340-H2 with successively increased all-up weights. The PC-6/350, the prototype of which first flew in December 1961, had a 350hp Lycoming IGO-540-A1A with fuel injection, and the same all-up weight (4,320lb) of the PC-6/340. The PC-6/350-H1 and PC-6/350-H2 likewise had successive increases in all-up weight. All aircraft delivered since mid-1966 have a forward-opening door each side of the cockpit, a large rearward-sliding door on the starboard side of the cabin and a double door on the port side.

The first turboprop version the PC-6/A Turbo-Porter, made its first flight on 2 May 1961 and was powered by a 523shp Turbomeca Astazou IIE or IIG driving a feathering and reversing Ratier-Figeac airscrew. The PC-6/A-H1 was similar to the PC-6/A, but with increased all-up weight, the PC-6/A-H2

having a further increase in all-up weight to 4,850lb. The PC-6/AX-H2 had a 630shp Astazou X derated to 523shp; a similar version had a 700 eshp Astazou XII. The PC-6/B-H2 Turbo-Porter had a 550shp Pratt & Whitney PT6A-6 driving a Hartzell three-blade prop. It first flew on 1 May 1964 and was produced by Fairchild Hiller at Hagerstown, as well as by Pilatus; the Fairchild-built ones were known as Heli-Porters at first, but are now called Porters whether piston- or turboprop-powered. The first Fairchild production aircraft, with a PT6A-20 engine, was rolled out on 3 June 1966. The 'B-H2 was the first version to introduce the new cockpit and cabin doors, and the current production version is the PC-6/B2-H2, certificated on 30 June 1970, with a 550shp (flat-rated from 680shp) PT6A-27. The PC-6/C-H2 was powered by a 575shp Garrett AiResearch TPE 331-25D turboprop driving a Hartzell three-blade prop, and the first prototype made its initial flight at the Fairchild Hiller works in October 1965, the first Pilatus-built 'C-H2 flying on 4 March 1966. By 1 April 1976 over 360 PC-6s of all versions had been built by Pilatus and Fairchild. Also optional on the Turbo-Porter are two 50 US gallon underwing tanks. Six quickly-removable passenger seats in the cabin are usually fitted, and a passenger can be carried beside the pilot; up to 10 people can be accommodated. The Fairchild AU-23A Peacemaker is a heavily armed COIN version for the USAF with a 650shp Garrett AiResearch TPE 331-1-101H turboprop. The USAF acquired 15 AU-23As, all but one of which were supplied to the Royal Thai Air Force, which later ordered 20 more. Porters and Turbo-Porters have been used by Air America and Continental Air Services on quasi-military operations in Laos, as well as by airlines in Alaska, the French and Swiss Alps, Nepal, Papua and Indonesia.

Piper PA-23-250 Aztec   USA

Data: Turbo Aztec F
Engines: Two 250hp Lycoming TIO-540-CIA
6-cylinder horizontally-opposed engines
Span: 37ft 2½in
Length: 31ft 2¾in
Height: 10ft 4in
Wing area: 207.56sq ft
Weight: 3,229lb (empty)
Max take-off weight: 5,200lb

Speed: 253mph (max) at 18,500ft
241mph at 22,000ft (cruising)
179mph at 10,000ft (long range cruising)
Range: 1,217 miles with max fuel and 45min reserves

A development of the earlier Piper PA-23 Apache, the Aztec, like its forebear, has been widely used by air taxi, charter and third-level or commuter

operators as well as by private and executive owners. Production deliveries of the first model, the five-seat Aztec A, began in December 1959 after FAA Type Approval had been received on 18 September that year, this differing only slightly externally from the latest model Apache, the PA-23-235, which it preceded. The six-seater Aztec B, production deliveries of which began in 1962 after FAA Type Approval was granted on 15 December 1961, featured an extended nose with more baggage compartment space, a modified instrument panel, improved maintenance accessibility and several other minor improvements. Twenty Aztec As were acquired 'off the shelf' in 1960 by the US Navy as U-11A (formerly UO-1) utility transports, while several South American air forces and military customers have also brought Aztecs, including the Peruvian Navy and the Argentine Army. The French and Spanish Air Forces have each bought two, the latter having also acquired six Turbo Aztecs which are used mostly for instrument training. The Aztec C, which appeared in 1964, features a modified landing gear, redesigned engine nacelles and Lycoming 10-540-C4B5 engines instead of the earlier 0-540-A1D5 powerplants of similar power.

The current version, which appeared in 1976, is the Aztec F which has a number of improvements as standard, including reduced control forces, flap and tailplane interconnection, a new easy-to-scan instrument panel, a redesigned fuel system, new brake assembly, new front seats and new interior styling. Like previous versions, the F is available in Custom, Sportsman, Professional and Turbo models, the latter being turbosupercharged, and having 250hp Lycoming TIO-540-C1A engines; an oxygen system with six outlets is optional on the Turbo Aztec F to allow operating at over 20,000ft. A stretcher, survey camera or up to 1,600lb of freight can be carried in the Aztec's cabin, and for such jobs as geological surveys or mineral prospecting more specialised equipment can be fitted. A floatplane version of the Aztec has been produced jointly by Melridge Aviation of Vancouver, Washington, and the Jobmaster Co Inc of Seattle; this has a door on the port side by the pilot's seat, instead of on the starboard side as in the landplane versions. About 4,000 Aztecs had been built by 1976.

Piper PA-31 Navajo   USA

Photo: Navajo Chieftain
Data: PA-31P

Engines: Two 425hp Lycoming TIGO-541-E1A 6-cylinder horizontally-opposed motors
Span: 40ft 8in
Length: 34ft 6in

Height: 13ft 1in
Wing area: 229sq ft
Weight: 4,990lb (empty)
Max take-off weight: 7,800lb
Speed: 280mph (max) at 18,000ft
266mph at 24,000ft (max cruising)
Range: 1,285 miles

The first of a larger series of Piper light twins for executive and commuter airline use, the PA-31-300 Navajo prototype first flew on 30 September 1964 powered by two 300hp Lycoming 10-540-K engines. It was made available with normally aspirated or turbocharged engines, and in Standard, Commuter or Executive versions with slight differences in seating arrangements and cabin interiors. The PA-31-310 Turbo Navajo has 310hp Lycoming T10-540-A engines with turbosuperchargers giving 75% power up to 23,500ft, an oxygen system as standard on the Executive version and an increased all-up weight. The Turbo Navajo C has six individual seats (two for the pilots) in the Standard version, with a seventh and eighth seat optional. The Commuter version of the Turbo Navajo C has eight individual seats for pilots and passengers, with an aft cabin dividing bulkhead with luggage shelf among the standard equipment. The Executive Turbo Navajo C has six individual seats, the four seats in the main cabin facing each other, with foldaway tables in between. A seventh and eighth seat may be installed in place of the refreshment unit and toilet at the rear of the cabin. The PA-31P Pressurised Navajo first flew in prototype form in March 1968, although it was not publicly announced until two years later. This has two 425hp Lycoming TIGO-541-E1A engines, and a take-off weight increased to 7,800lb from the 6,500lb of the Turbo. Pressurisation provides a cabin

altitude of 8,000ft up to 25,000ft and 10,000ft up to 29,000ft.

The PA-31P is offered in Standard and Executive versions, both with six individual seats for pilots and passengers; the Standard version has the four main cabin seats facing each other, and provisions for seventh and eighth seats at the rear of the cabin, while the Executive has four reclining chairs in the main cabin, with provision for seventh and eighth seats. The Spanish Air Force acquired a single PA-31P in 1972. The PA-31 Navajo Chieftain announced in September 1972 is a lengthened version of the Turbo Navajo with a 2ft 0in longer fuselage, and two counter-rotating Lycoming T10-540-J2BD engines of 350hp. This comes with Standard, Commuter and Executive interiors very similar to the earlier models, except that the Commuter version can seat up to 10 people, and the cabin floor is stressed for freight carrying; baggage can be carried in the rear of the engine nacelles. The PA-31 Turbo Navajo C/R is the same as the Turbo Navajo C but has the counter-rotating engines of the Chieftain. The Navajo has been widely used by commuter and feeder airlines in the United States and by air taxi operators, and has served in countries from Mexico to Madagascar and Papua/New Guinea; the type is employed by a number of British air taxi operators and the Argentine Army acquired five Turbo Navajos in 1969.

Rockwell Commander   USA

Photo: Commander 500B
Data: Strike Commander 500S

Engines: Two 290hp Lycoming 10-540-E1B5 6-cylinder horizontally-opposed engines
Span: 49ft 0½in
Length: 36ft 9¾in
Height: 14ft 6in
Wing area: 225sq ft
Weight: 4,635lb (empty equipped)
Max take-off weight: 6,750lb
Speed: 203mph at 9,000ft (max cruising 75% power)
Range: 797 miles with standard fuel (156 US gallons)
1,078 miles max with standard fuel (no reserves)

Better known as the Aero Commander light twin for

executive and feederline use, this design was later known as the North American Rockwell Commander and, from 1973, as the Rockwell Commander. It had its origins in the six-seat Model L3805 produced by Aero Design and Engineering Corp, the first of three prototypes of which flew on 23 April 1948 with two 190hp Lycoming 0-435-A engines. This went into production in 1951 in redesigned form as the Aero Commander 520 with two 260hp Lycoming GO-435-C2B engines and a larger fuselage; the first delivery was made on 5 February 1952 and three were supplied to the US Army as YL-26s (later U-9As). The 520 was succeeded by the Commander 560 early in 1954 with 280hp Lycoming GO-480-B motors and a slightly more swept fin and rudder; this was followed in May 1955 by the Commander 560A with Lycoming GO-480-D1A engines and a slightly longer fuselage and reduced span; 15 went to the

USAF as U-4A utility transports. The Commander 680 Super had 340hp supercharged GSO-480-A1A6 engines and appeared in September 1955, two going to the USAF as U-4Bs, four to the Army as U-9Cs plus two more as RU-9Ds with sideways-looking radar. The Commander 560E introduced in 1958 had an increased wing span and 295hp GO-480-G1B6 engines, the Commander 500 which appeared at the same time having 250hp Lycoming O-540-A1A motors, the same extended wing and only four instead of six seats. The Commander 680E was similar to the 560E but with supercharged GSO-480-B1A6 engines of 340hp. The first ever pressurised light twin for executive markets was the Commander 720 Alti-Cruiser announced in January 1958 and very similar to the 680E; only 13 were built.

The 1960 Commander models featured redesigned, extended and slimmer engine nacelles in which the main wheels turned through 90° to lie flat when retracted. These models were the Commander 500A, with 260hp Continental 10-470-M motors, the 500B (later redesignated 500U) with 290hp Lycoming 10-540-B1As, the 560F with 360hp Lycoming IGO-540 fuel injection engines and the 680F, with 380hp Lycoming IGSO-540 motors. The 680FP of 1962 was a pressurised version of the 680F, and the Grand Commander 680F/L, which first flew on 29 December 1962, was a stretched version of the 680F with a 6ft longer fuselage, seating from 5-7 executive passengers in a variety of layouts, or up to nine in a high-density version; a larger tailplane is featured and engines are 380hp IGSO-540-B1As. The 680FP/L is a pressurised version which first flew on 24 April 1963. Current production version of the 500 is the Shrike Commander 500S, with 290hp Lycoming 10-540-E1B5 engines, seating two in front with dual controls and two at the rear in the cabin; optional layouts for up to eight people are available. The Commander 685 announced in April 1972 is a pressurised 7-9 seater evolved from the Turbo Commander 690 but with 435hp Continental GTS10-520-F piston engines. The Turbo, which first flew on 31 December 1964, is basically a pressurised Grand Commander with two 605shp Garrett AiResearch TPE 331-43 turboprops driving Hamilton Standard reversible-pitch props. The Turbo Commander 690A, which first flew in June 1972, has two 700ehp TPE 331-5-251K turboprops driving Hartzell reversible props and an increased cabin pressure differential. Six passengers are usually carried, or up to 11 people in various optional cabin layouts.

Saab 90A-2 Scandia

Sweden

Engines: Two 1,800bhp (max take-off) Pratt & Whitney R-2180-E1 Twin Wasp radials
Span: 91ft 10in
Length: 69ft 11in
Height: 23ft 3in
Wing area: 922sq ft
Weight: 21,960lb (empty)
35,280lb (max gross)
Max payload: 9,350lb
Speed: 280mph (max at 8,500ft)
242mph at 10,000ft (cruising)
Range: 1,560 miles with max fuel

Svenska Aeroplan Aktiebolaget started design work on the Scandia, Sweden's first airliner, in 1944 and this twin-engined unpressurised monoplane was aimed at the DC-3 replacement market although, with accommodation for from 24 to 32 passengers, it was slightly smaller and less powerful than its US rivals the Convair 240 and Martin 2-0-2. The Scandia was designed to meet the then current ICAO and CAA requirements for transport aircraft and the prototype SAAB 90A made its first flight on 16 November 1946 powered by two 1,450bhp Pratt & Whitney R-2000-2SD13-G Twin Wasps. Production aircraft, the first of which flew on 12 November 1949, were powered by 1,800bhp R-2180-E1 Twin Wasp 14-cylinder radials, this larger version of the Twin Wasp being specially developed for the Scandia. The Swedish airline AB Aerotransport (later to become part of SAS) placed the first order, for ten, in 1948 and the Brazilian domestic airline VASP (Viacao Aerea Sao Paulo SA) ordered six, which entered service in July 1950

actually six months ahead of those of SAS. VASP's was destined to be the only export order for the Scandia because SAAB now needed all of its factory space for production of the new swept-wing J 29 fighter, deliveries of which had begun in April 1951. In 1952 production of the Scandia started to be transferred from SAAB's Linköping plant to Fokker at Amsterdam who, with Aviolanda and de Schelde as sub-contractors, completed four more Scandias for VASP and two for SAS, the first Dutch-assembled aircraft being flown in January 1954. Late in 1957

SAS sold its fleet of eight Scandias, now replaced by Convair 440s, to VASP, which thus became the only operator of the type, retaining its fleet in service until the mid-1960s, when they began to be retired in favour of Viscount 827s and 701s. Only 18 Scandias were built in all, and projected developments included a pure freighter version to carry a maximum payload of 10,000lb, the SAAB 90A-3 seating 30 to 38 passengers in a pressurised cabin and the SAAB 90B-3, also a pressurised version.

Saunders ST-27 and ST-28

Canada

Photo: ST-27
Data: ST-28

Engines: Two 783eshp Pratt & Whitney (UACL) PT6A-34 turboprops
Span: 71ft 6in
Length: 58ft 10in
Height: 15ft 7in
Wing area: 499sq ft
Operating weight: 9,284lb (empty)
Max payload: 4,216lb
Max take-off: 14,500lb
Speed: 232mph at 10,000ft (max cruising)
Range: 140 miles with max payload
970 miles with max fuel

For some years after the DH114 Heron had gone out of production with 148 built, several attempts were being made to extend its useful life and improve its performance by the installation of more modern piston engines than the 250bhp DH Gipsy Queen 30 Mk 2s which had powered it. De Havilland did not pursue this line of development, but both Jack Riley in the United States and Connair Pty Ltd, the Alice Springs-based Australian airline, produced versions with four Lycoming IO-540 'flat six' engines, while the Japanese carrier Toa Domestic Airlines produced the Tawron, a conversion of its Herons re-engined with Continental IO-470-Ds. A turboprop Heron was

a logical step, and the Saunders Aircraft Corporation of Gimli, Manitoba, produced the ST-27, a conversion of the Heron 2 with a 10ft longer fuselage to increase the passenger seating from 17 up to a maximum of 23, and powered by two 783eshp Pratt & Whitney PT6A-34 turboprops instead of four Gipsy Queens. The prototype ST-27 made its first flight on 28 May 1969 and Saunders, backed by loans from the Manitoba Government, began the conversion of existing Herons to ST-27As at its new Gimli facility. Thirteen such conversions were completed and sold to third-level airlines in Canada and also to Aerolineas Centrales de Colombia SA (ACES), but the supply of cheap surplus Heron airframes for conversion was limited and production from scratch of new aircraft as ST-27Bs began. One ST-27 was modified into the ST-28, first flying as such on 17 July 1974. This revised version features increased fuel tankage, more fin area, various interior improvements and a gross weight increased to 14,500lb. Seating 22 passengers, the ST-28 complies fully with American FAR Part 25 airworthiness requirements for third-level operations, and production of a batch was put in hand, 34 ST-28s being on order and option at the end of 1975. But early in 1976, further work on the ST-28 had to stop when the Manitoba Government withdrew its financial support.

Scottish Aviation Twin Pioneer

UK

Photo and Data: Series 3

Engines: Two 640bhp (max take-off) Alvis Leonides 531/8B radials
Span: 76ft 6in

Length: 45ft 3in
Height: 12ft 1in
Wing area: 670sq ft
Weight: 10,062lb (empty)
14,600lb (max gross)

Capacity payload: 3,550lb
Speed: 165mph (max) at 2,000ft
140mph at 8,000ft (cruising)
Range: 250 miles with max payload
789 miles with max fuel

Following the success of the Scottish Aviation Prestwick Pioneer CC1 in the casualty evacuation role with the RAF in Malaya, and also in Aden, development of a twin engined version was started intended to offer true STOL capability and the ability to operate into unprepared strips of restricted length often in places where runways of normal length were not available. The 16-passenger Twin Pioneer featured two Alvis Leonides radials and the same outer wings as the single-engined Pioneer with leading edge slats which opened when the big Fowler-type flaps in four sections were lowered; these enabled landings to be made at what came to be known as 'bicycle speed'. The prototype Twin Pioneer first flew on 25 June 1955 and the first production Series 1 on 28 April 1956; this version was powered by two 540hp Leonides 503/8 engines, later by Leonides 514s. Twin Pioneers entered service in small numbers with Borneo Airways, Sierra Leone Airways, de Kroonduif of Dutch New Guinea, British International Air Lines of Kuwait, Merpati Nusantara of Indonesia, Fjellfly of Norway and several government corporate or industrial owners. A special air and geophysical survey version for the Rio Tinto Finance and Exploration Co featured a 6ft 6in increase in wing span by the installation of large wing-tip pods carrying Mullard electro-magnetic equipment, the

large span enabling the transmitting and receiving coils of this equipment to be adequately separated; cameras and other special instrumentation were also carried. The Series 3 Twin Pioneer featured more powerful 640bhp Leonides 531/8B radials giving better engine out performance and a 600lb increase in gross weight to 14,600lb; up to 18 passengers could now be carried and some Series 1s were modified up to Series 3 standard. The five Twin Pioneers for Philippine Air Lines were fitted with 600hp Pratt & Whitney R-1340 Wasps as the airline's DHC-3 Otters already had these engines; they were known as Series 2s and were used on PAL's Rural Air Services to outback areas from 1959 to 1963 when they were sold, three of them being used by Continental Air Services Inc in Laos.

The Twin Pioneer CC Mk 1 was a light tactical/general purpose transport for the RAF which could carry 16 passengers, 13 fully-equipped troops or 11 paratroops, or nine stretcher cases, two sitting casualties and an attendant in the ambulance role, or up to 3,400lb of freight. A variety of external 'stores' could be carried under the stub wings such as two 500lb bombs, eight 20lb fragmentation bombs or four 500lb supply containers; vertical and oblique cameras could be fitted for PR work. A prone position for a bomb aimer was provided in the main cabin. The CC Mk 2 differed from the Mk 1 in having the more powerful engines of the civil Series 3, and all CC Mk 1s were later modified to Mk 2 standards. Altogether 32 Twin Pioneers were supplied to the RAF, serving with No 225 Sqn, and 14 were delivered to the Royal Malayan Air Force; total Twin Pioneer production numbered 78 aircraft.

Short S25/V Sandringham

UK

Data: Sandringham 2

Engines: Four 1,200hp (max take-off) Pratt & Whitney R-1830-92 Twin Wasp radials
Span: 112ft 9½in
Length: 86ft 3in
Height: 32ft 10½in
Wing area: 1,687sq ft
Weight: 41,370lb (empty equipped)
Capacity payload: 9,915lb
Max take-off weight: 60,000lb
Speed: 238mph (max) at 5,000ft
221mph at 9,000ft (max cruising)

Range: 1,890 miles with max payload
2,430 miles with max fuel

During the war a transport version of the Sunderland III was produced for BOAC, and the first of several such transport conversions with the nose and tail turrets replaced by fairings, entered service with BOAC in 1943, a total of 27 ultimately being delivered. During 1946 those in service were brought up to more usual peacetime standards of passenger comfort, and were given names as the 'Hythe' class. BOAC used three slightly different versions of the 'Hythe', the H1 and H2

accommodating 16 passengers and 3½ tons of freight, the H2 having a promenade deck, while the H3 carried up to 22 passengers and two tons of freight. Two 'Hythe'-type Sunderland transports were also used by New Zealand National Airways to operate services from Auckland to Fiji and other Pacific islands until 1950. One BOAC 'Hythe' was modified into the prototype Sandringham 1, which differed in having a more streamlined nose and tail shape due to the elimination of the turret fairings; the Bristol Pegasus 38 engines of the Sunderland were retained, but there was passenger accommodation for 24 by day or 16 in sleeping berths. Subsequent Sandringhams had the 1,200hp Pratt & Whitney Twin Wasp engines of the Sunderland GR5, and differed only in their cabin interiors. The 45-passenger Sandringham 2 and the 21-passenger Mk 3 were supplied to ALFA — Aviacion del Litoral Fluvial Argentino, a subsidiary of the Dodero shipping line that became part of Aerolineas Argentinas on 14 May 1949. Aerolineas continued to operate Sandringhams across the River Plate and from Beunos Aires up to Asuncion (Paraguay) until 1963, when five of the six Sandringhams were sold to a small Argentine independent. Tasman Empire Airways (now Air New Zealand) used four 30-passenger Sandringham 4s on its routes to Australia and also the 'Coral Route' to Fiji, Tonga, Samoa, the Cook Islands and Tahiti. Nine Mk 5s seating 22 day passengers were supplied to BOAC as the 'Plymouth' class followed by four 30-passenger 'Bermuda'-class Mk 7s with an all-up weight of 60,000lb. Two of the latter were later sold to CAUSA of Uruguay which used them, together with a third, for services across the River Plate until 1962. Five 37-passenger Mk 6s were supplied to DNL of Norway (which later became part of SAS) for operating domestic services down the Norwegian coast. Qantas used three ex-BOAC Mk 5s and an ex-Tasman Mk 4 for a time, while the French operator RAI (now Air Polynesie) acquired one in 1958 for local services from Tahiti. Aquila Airways used several ex-BOAC 'Hythes' and Solents for its services from Southampton to Lisbon, Madeira and Las Palmas, also to Marseilles, Capri and Genoa. Barrier Reef Airways Ltd, which flew two Sandringham 4s to the island holiday resorts off the Queensland coast, and Trans-Oceanic Airways, which flew 'Hythe' and Solent services from Sydney to Lord Howe Island, Norfolk Island, Hobart (Tasmania) and Port Moresby were combined to form Ansett Flying Boat Services Pty Ltd in 1952-53. This continued to operate two Sandringhams (one a converted RNZAF Sunderland produced in 1964) on the Lord Howe Island route until 1974, when they were sold to Antilles Air Boats Inc, who now fly them between the Virgin Islands and Puerto Rico. The Short S45A Solent was the civil version of the Seaford GR1 (originally the Sunderland IV) and BOAC used 18 Solents in the 34-passenger Mk 2 and 39-passenger Mk 3 versions, while Tasman Empire Airways operated four 42-passenger Solent 4s and an ex-BOAC Mk 3.

Short SC7 Skyvan

UK

Photo and Data: Mk 3

Engines: Two 755eshp (max take-off) Garrett AiResearch TPE-331-201A turboprops
Span: 64ft 1in
Length: 40ft 1in
Height: 15ft 1in
Wing area: 373sq ft
Basic operating weight: 7,297lb
Max payload: 4,600lb
Max take-off weight: 12,500lb
Speed: 190mph at 10,000ft (max cruising)
Range: 645 miles with max fuel and 3,000lb payload

The Short Skyvan light freighter had its origins in the Miles HDM106 Caravan and HDM107 Aerojeep projects bought by Short's from F. G. Miles in 1958, and which were developed from the HDM105 — a Miles M57 Aerovan fitted with a Hurel-Dubois high aspect ratio wing. The two Miles projects were used as a basis for the Short PD 36, as the Skyvan was initially known, on which design work started in 1959, and the Hurel-Dubois wing was discarded in favour of a more conventional wing with an aspect ratio of 11. This was married to a box-like fuselage with a hold cross-section of 6ft 6in square with a large rear loading door which could be opened in flight. The Skyvan 1 prototype first flew on 17 January 1963 with two 390bhp Continental GTSIO-520 piston engines, but proved to be underpowered in this form. It was re-engined with

two 520eshp Turboméca Astazou II turboprops, first flying with these as the SC7/10 Skyvan 1A on 2 October 1963. In March 1965 these engines were replaced by 637eshp Astazou Xs, producing the Skyvan 1A Series 2 which also had a lowered tailplane and some changes to the wing. That same month the first order, for two Skyvan 2s, was placed by the Italian operator Aer Alpi. The definitive production Mk 2 had a number of design changes, and uprated 730eshp Astazou XIIH-1 engines driving Ratier-Figeac FH76 airscrews; the nose was more streamlined, a single nosewheel replaced the previous twin ones, and larger cabin windows rectangular instead of round, were featured. From the ninth production Mk 2, total fuel capacity was increased from 175 to 225 Imperial gallons in four wing tanks, and the cabin length (excluding the flight deck) was extended by 31in to 18ft 7in.

Because the Astazou-powered Mk 2 could not meet performance specifications under certain 'hot and high' conditions, it was succeeded by the Skyvan 3 with two 755eshp Garrett AiResearch TPE-331-201A turboprops driving Hartzell props. The prototype Mk 3, a re-engined Mk 2, first flew on 15 December 1967, and the new version had a fuel capacity of 300 Imperial gallons, a lower empty weight and some detail changes. From 18 to 22 passengers could be carried, or 12 stretcher cases and two attendants, or up to 4,600lb of freight, including such loads as a jeep or small car. In the QC (quick change) version up to 4,400lb of cargo can be carried on four pallets with the lightweight passenger seats folded against the walls. The Mk 3

can also be used for aerial survey, as an executive aircraft or as an airborne workshop, fitted for such jobs as drilling, welding and serving remote construction sites or oil drilling rigs. The Skyvan 3M military version has weather radar in the nose and can accommodate 16 paratroops and a despatcher (who has a port-side blister window), or 22 troops or 12 stretcher cases or up to 5,000lb of freight. A roller conveyor system for loading or paradropping palletised supplies can be installed, and gross weight of the 3M is 13,500lb. First to order the 3M was the Austrian Air Force, which took delivery of its two on 12 September 1969; since then, the air arms of eleven other countries have acquired this version, which can also be fitted with survey cameras. The six Mk 3Ms of Singapore Air Defence Command's No 120 Sqn are specially fitted for search and rescue as well as transport duties, being fitted with advanced avionics and long range tanks; they can drop liferafts and other rescue equipment to a ditched aircraft.

A luxury version of the Skyvan 3 for third-level airlines also known as the Skyliner seats 19-22 passengers in a new cabin interior corresponding more closely to jet standards, with such features as individual passenger service panels and a washroom; a new low-entry passenger side door is featured, as well as Bendix weather radar and a Decca area navigation system. A quieter version of the Skyliner was later developed with low-speed engines and Hartzell four-blade instead of three-blade airscrews. More than 100 Skyvans have now been sold.

Sud-Est SE2010 Armagnac

France

Engines: Four 3,500bhp (max take-off) Pratt & Whitney R-4360-B13 Wasp Major radials
Span: 160ft 7in
Length: 129ft 10¾in
Height: 44ft 3in
Wing area: 2,542sq ft
Weight: 83,100lb (empty)
Capacity payload: 38,600lb
Max take-off weight: 170,860lb
Speed: 307mph (max) at 14,760ft
281mph at 143,000lb weight (cruising)

Range: 2,220 miles with max payload
3,580 miles with max fuel

Europe's nearest equivalent to the Boeing Stratocruiser, the SE2010 Armagnac long-haul airliner was powered by the same engines, four Pratt & Whitney R-4360 Wasp Majors, and could carry up to 84 first-class passengers six-abreast, or 107 in a tourist or economy layout. The Armagnac was an ambitious project for a French industry still recovering from the war; the prototype, which first flew on 12 January 1949, was assembled in a bomb-damaged hangar at Toulouse with the aerodrome still littered with Ju88s destroyed by the RAF. A production batch of 25 was planned in anticipation of an Air France order, and the latter's original requirement for sleeper accommodation had dictated the choice of a large diameter fuselage (no less than 15ft 5in maximum diameter), but this resulted in a low cruising speed and economics that compared unfavourably with such types as the Constellation and DC-6. The initial batch of 25 aircraft was cut back at first to 15 and then to eight, all built at Toulouse, the first production aircraft flying on 30 December 1950. Air France did not order the type, preferring the Constellation as first-line equipment, but the French independent TAI — Transports Aériens Intercontinentaux carried out proving flights with the Armagnac for the French government, flying freight services with it from Paris to Casablanca and Dakar prior to the award of a C of A. TAI operated four Armagnacs on routes from Paris to Casablanca and Las Palmas during 1952-53 before going over to DC-6As and DC-6Bs for its long haul routes.

The Armagnac came into its own as a result of the war in Indo-China which France was fighting; an airline known as SAGETA (Société Auxiliaire de Gérance et de Transports Aériens) was formed in 1953 jointly by the manufacturers, Air France and the leading French independents, TAI, UAT and Aigle Azure to operate seven of the eight Armagnacs between Toulouse and Saigon and Hanoi carrying military personnel on what came to be known as the 'Pont Aérien' ('Air Bridge'). By late 1955 SAGETA had made 130 flights on the Indo-China route and the Armagnacs eventually carried over 100,000 passengers and visited places as far apart as Santiago, Moscow and Melbourne on charter flights. But with France's withdrawal from Indo-China the airlift ended and SAGETA was grounded in 1958, the six remaining Armagnacs being cocooned. One Armagnac, designated SE 2060, was used as an engine test bed by SNECMA, at first with two SNECMA Atar turbojets mounted under the fuselage, and then with a 12,100lb st SNECMA Vulcain turbojet in this position; this engine did not enter production. In 1957 a 9,702lb st Atar 8 and a 13,230lb st (with reheat) Atar 9 were fitted under the wings, and more recently an Atar 9K50 (which powers the Mirage F 1C) and a Pratt & Whitney TF306 (which powered the swing-wing Mirage G) have been tested.

Sud-Ouest SO30P Bretagne

France

Photo: SO30P-1
Data: SO30P-2

Engines: Two 2,400bhp (max take-off) Pratt & Whitney R-2800-CA18 Double Wasp radials
Span: 88ft 2in
Length: 62ft 2in
Height: 19ft 4in
Wing area: 925sq ft
Weight: 29,357lb (empty)
44,370lb (loaded)
Capacity payload: 8,500lb
Speed: 288mph (max) at 16,000ft
267mph (cruising)
Range: 620 miles with max payload
1,930 miles with max fuel

The SO30P Bretagne was designed during the war by the Groupe Technique de Cannes, a group of 120 engineers and designers from the SNCA de Sud-Ouest who, refusing to work for the Germans in occupied France, moved to Cannes in May 1941 together with technicians from some of the other French nationalised companies. There they worked on several projects including the twin-engined SO90 which, on its first flight, took off from under the noses of the Italians and flew to Philippeville in North Africa with nine people aboard. The larger Bretagne first appeared in prototype form as the 23-passenger SO30N Bellatrix with a tailwheel undercarriage and two 1,260bhp Gnôme-Rhône 14N48/49 radials; it featured a pressure cabin and a mid-wing and was completed in November 1942 but, following the

SO90's escape, test flights were forbidden by the authorities. It remained in the SNCASO works near Marseilles until the Germans decided to occupy the Vichy zone and the French engineers, fearing the SO30N would be seized, dismantled it and hid the components in barns and farm buildings around Draguignan, some 20 miles from the coast. There it remained undiscovered until the Germans were driven out of southern France, when it was reassembled by SNCASO and, on 26 February 1945, became the first French prototype to make its maiden flight since the liberation.

It was followed by the 30-passenger SO30R with a nosewheel undercarriage, a single fin and rudder, increased wing area and two 1,650bhp Gnôme-Rhône 14R radials. The SO30P, which reverted to twin fins, was the production version of the N and R prototypes, and incorporated Air France's recommendations in its design. A batch of 40 was ordered, the first nine aircraft being SO30P-1s with

two 1,600bhp SNECMA (Gnôme-Rhône) 14R engines later replaced by 2,000bhp Pratt & Whitney R-2800-B43 Double Wasps driving 4-blade Curtiss Electric airscrews. The tenth and subsequent aircraft were the SO30P-2 version with 2,400bhp R-2800-CA18 Double Wasps driving 3-blade Hamilton Standard reversible airscrews. Thirty passengers could be accommodated in a de luxe interior, or up to 45 in standard seating; a VIP version was used by President Auriol of France and another by the French cabinet. The Bretagne served in small numbers with the French independents Aigle Azur and the Saigon-based Cosara, as well as with Air Algerie and Air Maroc but most were used by the Armée de l'Air (flown by 60e and 64e Escadres de Transport) and the French Navy on communications duties. The latter took over 20 Bretagnes originally intended for Air France in 1955 and some of these, together with one or two civil aircraft, were fitted with a Turboméca Palas auxiliary turbojet under each wing.

Sud-Est SE161 Languedoc

France

Engines: Four 1,200bhp (max take-off) Pratt & Whitney R-1830-92 Twin Wasp radials
Span: 96ft 5in
Length: 79ft 7in
Height: 16ft 10in
Wing area: 1,197.8sq ft
Weight: 27,890lb (empty)
Capacity payload: 8,650lb
Max take-off weight: 52,250lb
Speed: 217mph at 7,500ft (cruising)
Range: 1,240 miles with max payload
1,740 miles with max fuel

The SE161 Languedoc had its origins in the Bloch 160, a four-engined 12-passenger airliner designed in 1937 for the prewar French airline Regie Air Afrique for its African colonial routes, which stretched from Algiers down to the Belgian Congo and Madagascar. The 160 prototype first flew in 1938 and featured 720hp Hispano-Suiza 12X in-line engines and a span of 89ft 10in. It was succeeded in 1939 by a slightly larger development, the Bloch 161, which flew at Bordeaux that year, but the war delayed production plans and it was not until January 1942 that the 161 was able to complete its flight trials; it was powered by four 1,050hp Gnôme-Rhône 14N38/39 radials and could seat up to 33 passengers. By now it was known as the SO161 as

the Vichy Government had ordered it into production at the Toulouse plant of SNCA de Sud-Ouest in December 1941, and in June 1942 an additional order for 20 was placed with the SNCA de Sud-Est, of which 10 were for Deutsche Luft Hansa. After the Germans occupied Vichy France in November 1942 the order was taken over by Luft Hansa but later abandoned. The prototype SO161 was confiscated by the Germans, but the passive resistance movement among French workers successfully delayed any production deliveries until after the liberation, the first postwar aircraft flying on 17 September 1945. Altogether 100 were built by SNCA de Sud-Est as SE161s, early production aircraft having 1,200hp (max take-off) Gnôme-Rhône 14N68/69 radials. The French engines were soon replaced by 1,200bhp Pratt & Whitney R-1830-92 Twin Wasps, no doubt to ensure commonality with the DC-3 which also had these engines, and Air France, which had ordered 40 Languedocs, began services with them over the Paris-London route in 1947. Seating 33 passengers, the Languedoc was a very useful interim type for Air France in the early postwar years on short/medium haul European routes; the last scheduled service with the type was flown on 26 October 1952.

Five Languedocs were used by the Polish airline LOT for its longer routes such as Warsaw-Paris,

Warsaw-Belgrade via Budapest and Warsaw-Bucharest, and these were the first Western airliners to be sold to a Communist country postwar. Three ex-Air France Languedocs were acquired by the Spanish independent Aviaco in 1952, and five ex-Air France machines entered service with Misrair SAE of Egypt in 1950-51; the Lebanese operator Air Liban also used a few from 1951. Sixty Languedocs were supplied to the Armée de l'Air and the French Navy and a few of these were used as flying test beds. In particular, the Languedoc was used to launch the experimental Leduc 010 and 021 ramjet monoplanes; the 010, the world's first ramjet aircraft, made its first flight from the back of a Languedoc on 21 April 1949, and the 021 on 16 May 1953. The SE161SAR was a specially-modified air-sea rescue version that appeared in 1955, featuring an observer's position in a large, mostly transparent, fairing under the nose, search radar in a transparent ventral blister amidships and two smaller dorsal radomes. A few French Navy Languedocs were also fitted out to train radar operators for the Breguet Br1050 Alizé ASW aircraft; these SE161s had a nose and ventral radome.

Swearingen Metro   USA

Data: Metro 2

Engines: Two 940eshp Garrett AiResearch TPE331-3U-303G turboprops
Span: 46ft 3in
Length: 59ft 4in
Height: 16ft 10in
Wing area: 277.5sq ft
Weight: 7,450lb (basic)
12,500lb (max)
Speed: 294mph (cruising)
Range: 2,456 miles max

This very sleek mini-airliner was designed by Ed Swearingen to meet the requirements of the third-level or commuter airlines, and was in fact a stretched version of the 6-8 passenger Swearingen Merlin IIIA executive aircraft using the same wings, tail surfaces and powerplants. The Metro's longer fuselage seating from 19 to 22 passengers in single lightweight seats each side of a central aisle resulted in an increase in length from the Merlin's 42ft 2in to 59ft 4in, giving the Metro its distinctive appearance — its fuselage is almost one-third as long again as the wing span. The SA-226TC Metro made its first flight on 11 June 1970 and entered service early in 1971 but, in the effort to keep within the 12,500lb maximum weight limitation for third-level aircraft laid down by the US regulatory authorities, Swearingen found that the structure weight involved in a pressurised fuselage left too little margin for adequate fuel and payload. So although the Metro could carry two crew and 18 passengers, with safe fuel reserves its full-load range was no more than

200 miles, which would have meant refuelling at almost every stop on many third-level airline routes. As a result sales suffered for a time and the Swearingen company got into financial difficulties, but it became a wholly-owned subsidiary of Fairchild Industries in November 1971 and production was restarted at the San Antonio, Texas, plant. Fairchild had previously made the wings under sub-contract, and under its sponsorship the Metro's future was assured. Metros are now in service with a number of US commuter airlines, the largest operator being Air Wisconsin, with 12 ordered, while the Belgian operator Publi-Air uses one to fly certain third-level routes for Sabena. The Metro 2 introduced in 1974 featured square instead of round windows, and several internal improvements; as an optional 'extra' a small ATO rocket could be installed in the tail to improve the take-off performance from 'hot and high' airports. The basic Metro airframe is also offered as the Merlin IV and IVA executive aircraft with accommodation for up to 12 passengers. The Metro's seats can be quickly removed to allow freight to be carried. Some 40 Metros had been ordered by the end of 1977.

Transall C-160

International

Engines: Two 6,100eshp (max take-off) Rolls-Royce RTy20 Tyne 22 turboprops
Span: 131ft 3in
Length: 105ft 2in
Height: 38ft 3in
Wing area: 1,722.7sq ft
Weight: 61,110lb (empty equipped)
Max payload: 35,270lb
Max take-off weight: 108,250lb
Speed: 333mph (max) at 14,750ft
319mph at 18,050ft (max cruising)
Range: 1,070 miles with max payload

Intended as a medium tactical transport to replace the Nord 2501 Noratlas in the French Air Force and Federal German Luftwaffe, the Transall C-160 was designed from the start as a Franco-German co-operative venture to meet the two countries' requirements. The Noratlas had been built under licence in Germany, and this paved the way for the formation of the Transall group (the word means Transporter Alliance) in January 1959 by Nord Aviation, Hamburger Flugzeugbau — HFB and Vereinigte Flugtechnische Werke — VFW, design and production being shared between these firms with VFW as the overall manager of the project. The C-160 is very similar in size and configuration to the C-130 Hercules, with a smaller payload and take-off weight and two Hispano-Suiza-built Rolls-Royce Tyne turboprops; there was provision for two Rolls-Royce RB153 or RB162 auxiliary jets in underwing pods for STOL operations. The first prototype, assembled by Nord, made its initial flight on 25 February 1963, followed by the second prototype, assembled by VFW, on 25 May that year; the third prototype, assembled by HFB, flew on 19 February 1964. A pre-series of six aircraft, designated C-160A, followed, the first flying on 21 May 1965; these featured a 20 inch fuselage extension which became standard on subsequent aircraft. The C-160As were divided equally between the French and German air forces.

Main production consisted of 110 C-160Ds for the Luftwaffe and 50 of the C-160F variant for the French Air Force; the remaining ones currently equip two Luftwaffe tactical transport wings and three French Air Transport Command squadrons of No 61 Escadre (Wing). Nine of the C-160Z variant were supplied to the South African Air Force, where they equip (together with some C-130 Hercules) No 28 Squadron at Waterkloof. The Turkish Air Force has acquired 20 ex-Luftwaffe C-160Ds. C-160 production ended in March 1973 after 178 had been built, but the type is going back into production for the French Air Force, which has ordered another 25, the first of which for delivery in 1979; these have an extra centre-section fuel tank increasing range to 4,350 miles. The C-160 can carry up to 81 troops or paratroops or 62 stretcher cases and four medical attendants, or tanks, trucks or other military vehicles; the cargo compartment is pressurised, and loads of up to 17,640lb can be air-dropped. The first commercial version projected was the C-160C freighter, the same as the C-160D and F but with a floor capable of taking freight pallets on guide rails, and a flight crew of three instead of four. The Transall 161 Jet of 1967 was another civil freighter project with two 18,000lb st Pratt & Whitney JT3D-3B turbofans, a raised flight deck and upward-hingeing nose in place of the rear loading ramp. It

was not until 1973 that the C-160 entered airline service when four were leased to Air France for five years for use on its Postale de Nuit night air mail service linking French towns and cities. The third German prototype, now a C-160G, was sold to Air Affaires Gabon in 1977 for freighting in that country, and in August 1976 a water bomber version of the C-160 for fighting fires was demonstrated in southern France.

Tupolev Tu-104 USSR

Photo and Data: Tu-104B

Engines: Two 21,385lb st Mikulin AM-3M-500 turbojets
Span: 113ft 4in
Length: 131ft 5in
Height: 39ft 0in
Wing area: 1,975sq ft
Weight: 93,700lb (empty)
Max payload: 26,455lb
Max take-off weight: 167,550lb
Speed: 590mph (max) at 33,000ft
560mph (max cruising)
Range: 1,305 miles with max payload
1,925 miles with max fuel

Notable as being the first Russian jet airliner, and only the second in the world to enter regular airline service (the first was the DH Comet), the Tupolev Tu-104 was first dramatically revealed to western observers when the prototype, which had first flown early in 1955, visited London Heathrow on a VIP flight on 22 March 1956. The Tu-104 (NATO code-name Camel) was a straightforward adaptation of the Tu-16 Badger medium bomber with the same wings, tail unit (the tailplane being lowered), undercarriage (retracting into wing trailing edge nacelles) and powerplant — actually derated civil versions of the bomber's engines, while the nose and flight deck were similar to those of the Tu-16. The two Mikulin AM-3 turbojets of 19,180lb st were mounted in the wing roots in nacelles nearly 40ft long, the engines being attached behind the wing spar structure and 'toed out' to direct the jets away from the fuselage. The first Tu-104 of a series used for extensive proving flights made its initial flight on 17 June 1955 and the initial production version, which entered service with Aeroflot on 15 September 1956 on the Moscow-Irkutsk route, had an all-up weight of 156,525lb and a maximum payload of 11,460lb, made up of 50 passengers in an interior of rather old-fashioned styling by contemporary western standards, and 2,645lb of baggage and freight. When Aeroflot put the Tu-104 into service it was then the only airline operating jets, both the Comet 4 and Boeing 707 still being in the prototype stage. The Tu-104 marked a dramatic improvement in the quality of Aeroflot's service over major domestic routes, and it spearheaded the Russian airline's expansion into international routes, new Tu-104 services to Copenhagen, Paris, Brussels, Amsterdam and London being opened in 1958-60.

The Tu-104A entered service in 1958, this seating 70 passengers (16 first-class and 54 economy) in three cabins, plus 3,085lb of baggage and 2,205lb of freight, and featured more powerful and improved 21,385lb st Mikulin AM-3M-500 turbojets. In the spring of 1962 it was announced that some Tu-104As were being modified to carry 100 passengers, this increase in seating being achieved without lengthening the fuselage, by redesigning the wardrobes and toilets, and this version was designated Tu-104V; with the extra seating came an increase in maximum take-off and other weights. The only export customer for the Tu-104 series was the Czech airline CSA, which acquired six Tu-104As and used them to open the first international route of a Communist airline outside Europe, from Prague to Bombay, in the summer of 1959, this later being extended to Djakarta. The Tu-104B, which entered Aeroflot service in the spring of 1959, is similar to the A, but has a fuselage lengthened by 3ft 11in to accommodate 100 passengers five-abreast in three cabins, higher operating weights and increased flap area. Later an extra four seats were fitted to some Tu-104Bs, and a few 50-passenger Tu-104s were converted into 70-seaters. Altogether about 200 Tu-104s were built, and a few have been used by the Soviet Air Force, not only as transports but for experimental jobs such as zero gravity simulation for space flight.

Tupolev Tu-114

Engines: Four 14,795eshp Kuznetsov NK-12MV
turboprops
Span: 167,ft 8in
Length: 177ft 6in
Height: 42ft 0in
Wing area: 3,349sq ft
Weight: 200,620lb (empty)
Max payload: 66,140lb
Max take-off weight: 376,990lb
Speed: 540mph (max) at 26,250ft
478mph at 29,500ft (max cruising)
Range: 3,850 miles with max payload
5,560 miles with max fuel and 33,070lb payload

Noteworthy as being the largest and heaviest
commercial airliner ever flown before the advent of
the wide body jets, the Tupolev Tu-114 was
completed in the autumn of 1957, and because the
40th anniversary of the Russian Revolution was
celebrated that October, it was named Rossiya; The
NATO later gave it the code name of Cleat. The Tu-
144 was a straightforward development of the Tu-
20 'Bear' bomber with the same wings, engines, tail
unit, undercarriage and other features. The four
Kuznetsov NK-12MV turboprops, originally with a
maximum rating of about 12,000eshp but now
uprated to 14,795eshp, are the largest and by far the
most powerful turboprops ever fitted to an aircraft.
This huge NK-12 engine, designed with the
assistance of German engineers, drives eight-bladed
contra-rotating reversible-pitch Type AV-60N
propellers of 18ft 4½in diameter, and has a single
14-stage axial compressor and five-stage turbine;
the great swept wing has a normal fuel capacity of
16,540 Imp gallons in integral tanks. The engines in
particular, although obsolete (and no doubt pretty
uneconomic) by today's standards, were notable
technical achievements for the early 1950s. There
are two main versions of the Tu-114, the standard
one with accommodation for up to 220 passengers,

and normally seating 170 people, in which form it
entered service with Aeroflot on the Moscow-
Khaborovsk route on 24 April 1961 after undergoing
proving flights during 1960, and the Tu-114D. The
latter is really a transport conversion of the Tu-20
'Bear A' with a shorter and slimmer fuselage
essentially similar to that of the bomber; the D is
intended to carry just a few passengers, mail and
urgent freight over very long distances. The
prototype D made a non-stop 5,280 mile flight from
Moscow to Irkutsk and back in the spring of 1958 at
an average speed of 497 mph.

Before going into Aeroflot service the Tu-114 set
up a series of speed and payload records in March
and April 1960 over 1,000 and 2,000km closed
circuits, followed in April 1962 by a clean sweep of
all distance-with-payload records for propeller
aircraft, averaging 458.2mph over a 10,000km
closed circuit. The Tu-114 inaugurated Aeroflot's
first long haul over-water route, from Moscow to
Havana, on 7 January 1963, initially with only one
stop, at Conakry (Guinea). This was followed by a
Moscow-Montreal non-stop service on 4 November
1966, and the Tu-114 also operated several other
international routes from Moscow to Delhi, Conakry,
Accra (Ghana) and Brazzaville (Congo), as well as a
few long-haul domestic routes. The Tu-114s to which
JAL insignia were added began operating joint Japan
Air Lines/Aeroflot services between Moscow and
Tokyo across Siberia on 17 April 1967. The type was
finally retired from Aeroflot service in October 1976
and some 25-30 were built altogether. For long haul
routes normal accommodation is for 120 passengers
in mixed six-abreast and four-abreast seating; in the
170-seat interior there are three main cabins seating
42, 48 and 54 passengers six-abreast and four
'roomettes', each with two divans or six seats and
one folding bunk. There is also a lower deck kitchen
and two cooks are among the 10-15 crew.

Tupolev Tu-124

Engines: Two 11,950lb st Soloviev D-20P turbofans
Span: 83ft 9½in
Length: 100ft 4in
Height: 26ft 6in
Wing area: 1,281sq ft

Weight: 49,600lb (empty)
Max payload: 13,228lb
Max take-off weight: 83,775lb
Speed: 603mph (max)
540mph (max cruising)

Range: 760 miles with max payload
1,305 miles with max fuel and 7,715lb payload

The Soviet Union's first short-haul jet, the Tupolev Tu-124 entered airline service before either the BAC One-Eleven or the DC-9, and was the first airliner to go into service with turbofan engines. Although very similar externally to the Tu-104, it was a scaled-down derivative some 25% smaller and carrying fewer passengers than either the DC-9 or One-Eleven in their initial production forms. In its original 44-passenger form, the Tu-124 was closer in terms of seating capacity and overall power to the DH Comet 1A and, like the Tu-104, retained the wing root engine positions pioneered by the Comet. The prototype Tu-124 made its first flight in June 1960, and was followed by several more prototypes; the engines were two 11,023lb st Soloviev D-20P turbofans, this powerplant being specially developed for the Tu-124. The type was given the NATO codename Cookpot. The first production aircraft were delivered to Aeroflot at the end of 1961, differing from the prototypes in having a shortened nose to improve forward view; as on the Tu-104 the nose was transparent to provide a visual observation position for the navigator, and weather and terrain radar was housed in a chin fairing ahead of the nosewheel. The 44 passengers were accommodated in three cabins seating 12, 8 and 24 people, several of the seat pairs facing each other with tables in between. The standard version, the Tu-124V, seats 56 passengers with the removal of four tables in the middle and rear cabins; the three cabins now seat 12, 12 and 32 people.

Aeroflot flew its first Tu-124 scheduled service, and the first in the world by a turbofan-powered airliner, between Moscow and Tallinn (Estonia) on 2 October 1962. Tu-124s took over in due course many routes previously operated by Il-14s, and from the start the type was intended to operate from short runways and grass fields. Over 90 Tu-124s entered service with Aeroflot, other operators were the Czech airline CSA, with three, Interflug of East Germany with two and Iraqi Airways with two. Three VIP versions were supplied to the Indian Air Force for the use of government ministers. Fewer than 150 Tu-124s were built altogether. The Tu-124K is a 36-seater de luxe version seating four people in the forward cabin with revolving armchair seats, table, desk and other executive fittings, eight people in facing pairs in the second cabin, with tables, and 24 four-abreast in the rear cabin. The Tu-124K2 is another de luxe version for 22 passengers, the forward cabin seating four as in the Tu-124K, the second cabin seating two in revolving seats with table and divan, and the rear cabin seating 16 in facing pairs of seats with tables in between. Both the K and K2 can be quickly converted to the 56-passenger layout of the Tu-124V. Double-slotted flaps are fitted, and spoilers forward of the flaps act as air brakes to shorten the landing run; there is also a large under-fuselage air brake for steepening the approach. The four-wheel main undercarriage bogies retract into fairings on the wing trailing edge, turning through 180° and being housed inverted. There is a braking parachute in the tail for emergency use. VIP versions also serve the air forces of East Germany (3) and Iraq (2).

Tupolev Tu-134   USSR

Engines: Two 14,990lb st Soloviev D-30 turbofans
Span: 95ft 1¾in
Length: 114ft 8in
Height: 29ft 7in
Wing area: 1,370.3sq ft
Operating weight: 60,627lb (empty)
Max payload: 16,975lb
Max take-off: 99,200lb
Speed: 559mph at 28,000ft (max cruising)
466mph at 36,000ft (best economy cruising)
Range: 1,490 miles with 15,430lb payload
2,175 miles with 6,600lb payload

Although successful, the Tu-124 was really an interim type that would not, because of its smaller seating capacity, have been fully competitive against the DC-9 and One-Eleven, especially in their

stretched versions. A larger-capacity version with rear-mounted engines and a T-tail, similar to the two western jets, was being studied before the Tu-124 entered commercial service, and at first use of the latter's fuselage with minimum changes was contemplated, the resulting type being designated Tu-124A. But a complete redesign proved to be necessary, the resulting aircraft being the Tu-134, also known by the NATO codename Crusty. This had two more powerful Soloviev D-30 turbofans and a broad-chord fin and rudder with the variable-incidence tailplane mounted right at the top; the wing and undercarriage were very similar to the Tu-124's, the latter's wing spoilers and under-fuselage air brake being retained. The prototype first flew late in 1962 and was followed by five pre-production aircraft, production proper beginning at Kharkov in

1964. After a series of route-proving flights, Aeroflot began regular scheduled Tu-134 services between Moscow and Stockholm in September 1967. Standard seating is for 72 passengers four-abreast, 44 in the forward cabin and 28 in the aft cabin; alternatively, 16 first-class and 48 tourist passengers can be carried, the first-class ones in the front cabin, 20 tourists in the centre cabin and 28 in the rear one, while another mixed interior seats eight first-class and 56 tourists.

The Tu-134A, introduced by Aeroflot in the latter half of 1970, is a stretched version with a 6ft 10½in longer fuselage, Soloviev D-30 Series II engines with thrust reversal, and an auxiliary power unit. Maximum take-off weight is increased to 104,000lb. Some later production aircraft dispensed with the transparent nose containing a navigator's station in

favour of a conventional 'solid' nose containing weather radar. Standard seating was for 76 passengers four-abreast, with up to 80 at reduced seat pitch or 68 in a mixed-class layout (12 first-class and 56 tourists) as alternative arrangements. This was still some way below the maximum seating capacities of its chief western rivals (119 passengers for the One-Eleven 500), but both the Tu-134 and Tu-134A proved to be popular with other Eastern bloc airlines, being operated by the Jugoslav charter carrier Aviogenex (6), Balkan Bulgarian Airlines (12), CSA of Czechoslovakia (13), Interflug of East Germany (29), LOT of Poland (12), Malev of Hungary (9) and Hang Khong of Vietnam. Aeroflot itself has just about 350 of both versions in service. Recently, the vental air brake has been removed from Tu-134s in service.

Tupolev Tu-154   USSR

Engines: Three 20,950lb st Kuznetsov NK-8-2 turbofans
Span: 123ft 2½in
Length: 157ft 1¾in
Height: 37ft 4¾in
Wing area: 2,169sq ft
Operating weight: 95,900lb (empty)
Max payload: 44,090lb
Max take-off weight: 198,416lb
Speed: 605mph at 31,150ft (max cruising)
560mph (optimum cost cruising)
Range: 2,150 miles with max payload
3,280 miles with max fuel

Russia's equivalent of the Boeing 727-200 and Trident 3B, the Tupolev Tu-154 was intended as a replacement for the Tu-104, Il-18 and An-10 on domestic and international routes, and carries slightly fewer passengers than the Advanced 727-200, at a slightly lower maximum gross weight, but is considerably more powerful. The extra power leads to better take-off performance and, combined with a strengthened landing gear, make it suitable for operation from the many Russian Class 2 airfields with surfaces of gravel and packed earth and none-

too-elaborate terminal facilities. Each main-gear unit consists of a bogie made up of three pairs of wheels and retracts into fairings on the wing trailing edge. The Tu-154 has triple-slotted flaps, like the 727, and five-section slats on each wing leading edge to ensure good field performance, and there are four-section spoilers the inboard sections of which can be used as air brakes and lift dumpers, and the middle sections as air brakes in flight. The Tu-154 first flew on 4 October 1968, six prototype/pre-production aircraft being used for the flight test programme. The first delivery to Aeroflot was made early in 1971 and from May of that year route-proving flights with freight and mail were undertaken, together with a few *ad hoc* passenger services; full scheduled services beginning on 9 February 1972 on the Moscow-Minrealnye Vady route. Accommodation is for 158 or 164 passengers in a one-class interior, seated six-abreast in two cabins separated by the galley amidships. A 128-seat mixed traffic interior seats 24 first-class passengers four-abreast in the forward cabin and 104 in the rear one, and up to 167 people can be seated in a high-density layout.

The Tu-154's avionics and flight control system permit ICAO Category II automatic approaches to be

made, with development continuing toward fully automatic Category III landings. After several fatal accidents occurred in 1973-74, production was temporarily halted while the lessons from them were incorporated; the crash of one of Egyptair's eight Tu-154s in 1974 and technical difficulties experienced with the type led to the return of the Egyptian aircraft to the Soviet Union in 1975. The Tu 154A, which entered Aeroflot service in April 1974, is an improved version incorporating the lessons of operational experience, and powered by uprated 23,150lb st Kuznetsov NK-8-2U turbofans which allow the maximum take-off weight to be increased to 207,000lb. A disadvantage of the initial version was that it needed to carry nearly seven tons of ballast to trim the aircraft with full tanks; the Tu-154A and B have a centre-section fuel tank which serves the same purpose, although this fuel cannot be fed to the engines while the aircraft is in flight. The A has now been succeeded in production by the

further improved Tu-154B, which introduces some major changes to controls and systems, including the use of spoilers for lateral control at low speeds, these now being extended in span. Other unspecified changes to the controls have apparently cured the longitudinal control problems of the original version, and the centre-section fuel tank used as ballast on the Tu-154A can now be used in flight. The take-off weight has been raised to 211,500lb, and passenger capacity has been increased to 169. A Tu-154 flew in 1974 with the Soloviev D-30-KU turbofans which power the Il-62M, and versions with greater weights and range are being studied; the new Kuznetsov NK-86 turbofan is another possible engine for a future version. Over 260 Tu-154s have now been delivered to Aeroflot, and the type has also been supplied to the Jugoslav charter operator Aviogenex (2), Balkan Bulgarian Airlines (12), the North Korean airline CAAK (3), Malev of Hungary (8) and Tarom of Rumania (8).

Vickers (BAC) VC10 and Super VC10 UK

Photo: VC10 Type 1101
Data: Super VC10

Engines: Four 21,800lb st (max take-off) Rolls-Royce RCo43D Conway 550 turbofans
Span: 146ft 2in
Length: 171ft 8in
Height: 39ft 6in
Wing area: 2,932sq ft
Operating weight: 158,594lb (empty)
Max payload: 60,321lb
Max take-off weight: 335,000lb
Speed: 581mph at 31,000ft (high speed cruise) 550mph at 38,000ft (long range cruise)
Range: 4,720 miles with max payload 7,128 miles with max fuel

Initial design studies of the VC10 were started in 1956 by Vickers-Armstrongs at Weybridge, and the type was intended to meet a BOAC requirement for an aircraft for the Commonwealth routes carrying a 32,000lb payload over ranges of up to 2,500 miles and at speeds of more than Mach 0.8. Particular attention was paid to the ability to operate into existing airports without having to extend the runways; on the routes to Africa and the Far East these often had fairly short runways and/or were located several thousand feet above sea level in high ambient temperatures. The VC10 was intended to have a better airfield performance than any other long-haul jet, and one of the ways this was achieved was the choice of the rear-engined layout to give a clean wing, the first time this configuration had been used on a long-haul jet. On 22 May 1957 BOAC

announced its intention of ordering 35 VC10s for entry into service from 1963, and the contract, which also featured an option on 20 more VC10s, was signed on 14 January 1958, being at that time the largest order ever placed for a British airliner. It seemed all the larger because the Britannia had only just started services, and BOAC had hardly started to sell off all its piston-engined types; so from the start there was speculation that BOAC had too many VC10s on order. As then projected, the type had accommodation for up to 135-152 passengers and four 20,250lb st Rolls-Royce RCo42 Conway turbofans. Subsequent development of the design for the transatlantic routes resulted in the Super VC10, as well as an increase in payload to 40,000lb for the standard version.

As originally conceived the Super VC10 had a fuselage stretch of some 27ft, and could seat up to 212 passengers, and on 23 June 1960 BOAC signed a contract for 10 Supers with 10 more on option. But before the end of the year the airline had asked Vickers to reduce the size of the Super and to make it available on the production line as the 16th aircraft, and in 1961 BOAC's orders were changed to 15 (later 12) standard VC10s and 30 Supers, deliveries of the latter to start in October 1964. In its final form the Super had a fuselage 13ft longer than the standard VC10, accommodating 163-187 economy passengers, higher operating weights, uprated 22,500lb st RCo43 Conways, a fuel tank in the fin and the 4% chord leading edge extensions from wing root to fence already fitted to some standard VC10s. Payload was increased to 58,000lb and in 1963

BOAC asked for eight of the Supers to be convertible passenger/freighters with a side-loading cargo door. The prototype VC10 first flew on 29 June 1962 followed by the first production aircraft for BOAC on 8 November that year. ARB Certification was granted on 23 April 1964 and, as an aircraft of rear-engined T-tail configuration, the VC-10's stalling characteristics took some time to get right. BOAC operated its first VC10 service, from London to Lagos, on 29 April 1964 and the type was soon demonstrating its outstanding passenger appeal on this and other routes, as well as consistently achieving higher load factors. This should have enhanced the VC10's sales prospects but, shortly after it had begun services, BOAC decided to cut back the number of Supers it had on order and to order more 707-320Cs instead. Originally the airline wanted to cancel all 30 it had on order but, after a good ideal of unfortunate political controversy, the number was cut back to 17, three of the surplus ones yet uncompleted going to the RAF, which had already ordered 11 similar to the standard VC10, but with forward cargo door and the RCo43 Conways and fin tank of the Super. BOAC's first Super flew on 7 May 1964 and entered service with the airline on 1 April 1965.

Vickers identified VC10 variants by Type numbers,

Above: *Super VC10 Type 1154*

the Type 1101 being BOAC's standard version and the Type 1151 its Super VC10; the Type 1152 was the convertible passenger/freighter which, in the end, was not built. The Type 1101s had an all-up weight of 312,000lb and thrust reversers on the outboard engines. The prototype, originally Type 1100, became Type 1109 after being converted to airline use, and was sold to Laker Airways, being leased to Middle East Airlines during 1968-69. Three Type 1102s were ordered by Ghana Airways, two of which had the large cargo door and the 4% wing leading edge of the Super; the third one was sold to BUA before delivery, the latter having ordered three Type 1103s with cargo doors and the extended leading edge. BUA VC10s reopened the South American route previously flown by BOAC on 5 November 1964. The RAF's 14 Type 1106s seated 150 passengers and could have a flight refuelling nose probe. East African Airways had five Type 1154s with a large freight door to port and a strengthened forward freight floor. By 1975 British Airways had sold five standard VC10s to Gulf Air and British Caledonian had sold one to Air Malawi. British Airways has 15 Supers in service and is now the sole airline operator of the type.

Vickers Viking

UK

Photo: Mk 1A
Data: Mk 1B

Engines: Two 1,675 bhp Bristol Hercules 634 14-cylinder radials driving de Havilland or Rotol 4-blade airscrews
Span: 89ft 3in
Length: 62ft 10in
Height: 19ft 6in
Wing area: 882sq ft
Weight: 23,250lb (empty equipped)
Capacity payload: 7,120lb
Max take-off weight: 34,000lb
Speed: 263mph (max) at 10,000ft
209mph at 10,000ft (continuous cruising)
Range: 1,150 miles with max payload
2,242 miles with max fuel

Designed as a replacement for the DC-3, the Vickers-Armstrongs VC-1 Viking was a straightforward development of the Wellington bomber and was at first named 'Wellington Transport Aircraft' in the project stage. Three prototypes to Spec. 17/44 were ordered in 1944, the first of these flying on 22 June

1945, being the first British postwar commercial airliner to fly. The first 19 production aircraft had fabric-covered outer wings and tailplanes of geodetic construction, like the Wellington, and the latter's engine nacelles and undercarriage; this 21-passenger version was known as the Viking 1A. Because geodetic construction and fabric covering were not considered suitable by civil operators, subsequent Vikings, known as the Mk 1, had metal-covered wings and tailplane of conventional stressed skin construction; both Mks 1 and 1A had Hercules 630 or 631 engines. The Viking 1B, of which 113 were built, had the same wings and tailplane as the Mk 1 and a 28in fuselage extension allowing an additional row of seats in the cabin, which now seated 24-27 passengers; Hercules 634 engines were fitted. First and by far the largest Viking customer was BEA, which took delivery of 14 V498 Viking 1As, nine V614 Viking 1s, and 44 V610 Viking 1Bs; BEA in 1952 also acquired eight more V635 Viking 1Bs from South African Airways. The Corporation flew its first regular Viking service from Northolt to Copenhagen, on 1 September 1946 and Vikings flew the major European routes until

replaced by Elizabethans and Viscounts. From 1951 they became known as the 'Admiral' class, and seating capacity was increased to 36 and all-up weight to 36,712lb.

Other major export customers, mostly for the Mk 1B, were, in addition to SAA, British West Indian Airways, Central African Airways, Indian National Airways, Air India Ltd, DDL of Denmark, Misrair of Egypt, the Argentine Government (mostly for their Air Force), Aer Lingus and Iraqi Airways. Three Mk 1As acquired military serials and were used, as the Viking C1A, for such jobs as research flying on radio installations, while 12 Mk 1s became Viking C 2s with the Ministry of Supply. These included four delivered to the King's Flight, one as a C Mk 2 (VVIP) for use by the King, a second of this variant for use by the Queen, one as a C Mk 2 (VIP) for passengers accompanying the Royal party, and for the Flight's ground crews, and one C Mk 2 fitted out as a 'flying workshop' and freighter. Three of the King's Flight aircraft were finally disposed of to Tradair in 1958.

Other Mk 1Bs were used by the Pakistan Air Force, the Royal Australian Air Force and Jordan's Arab Legion Air Force. The V 618 Nene-Viking was fitted with two 5,000lb st Rolls-Royce Nene 1 turbojets under the wings as a test bed, first flying on 6 April 1948 — it was the world's first jet airliner to fly. In 1954 it was sold to Eagle Aviation Ltd and converted back to a standard piston-engined Mk 1B freighter with a 5½ft square cargo door; it was used for trooping and finally scrapped in 1962. Another Viking flight-tested two Napier Naiad turboprops. Vikings were extensively used from the mid-1950s by many British independents and a few German, especially the smaller ones, for trooping, charter work and inclusive tour flights. Altogether 166 Vikings were built. Retrospective modifications devised by Eagle, primarily for the cooling system of the Hercules 634 engines, produced the Viking 3 which could carry up to 1,200lb extra payload in conditions of WAT (weight, altitude, temperature) limitations.

Vickers Viscount 700   UK

Photo: Viscount 754
Data: Viscount 700D

Engines: Four 1,780ehp (max take-off) Rolls-Royce RDa6 Dart 510 engines
Span: 93ft 8½in
Length: 81ft 10in
Height: 26ft 9in
Wing area: 963sq ft
Weight: 36,859lb (empty equipped)
Capacity payload: 11,600lb
Max take-off weight: 64,500lb
Speed: 310mph at 20,000ft (optimum cost cruising)
Range: 1,780 miles with max payload
2,000 miles with max fuel

The Viscount made history by being the first turbine-powered airliner ever to carry fare-paying passengers, the first British airliner to be ordered on a large scale by operators in the USA and Canada, and by becoming Britain's best-selling commercial transport, with which many of the world's airlines gained their first experience of gas turbine operations. It had its origins in the Brabazon Committee's Type IIB requirement of March 1945 for a 24-seat aircraft, powered with four gas-turbine engines driving airscrews for European and other short-to-medium range services'. A payload of

7,500lb and range of 1,000 miles were soon specified, and, known as the VC-2, the design was considered with four Rolls-Royce Darts, with Armstrong Siddeley Mambas or Napier Naiads as alternatives; two Napier E128D Double-Naiad coupled power units were also considered at one time. The VC-2 was named Viceroy, but this was changed to Viscount when India became independent, and two Mamba-powered V609 prototypes (later V630s) were ordered with a longer fuselage than originally planned as BEA now required seating for 32 passengers; in August 1947 choice of powerplant finally fell on the Dart, and the two V630s were converted accordingly. The first prototype made its initial flight with RDa1 Darts on 16 July 1948 but BEA began to have increasing doubts about the economics of the 32-seat V630, which now seemed too small, and when the order for 20 Airspeed Ambassadors was confirmed at the end of 1947 the Viscount seemed to be doomed. The second prototype was diverted for use as a test bed for the 6,250lb st Rolls-Royce RTa1 Tay turbojet, eventually flying with these engines on 15 March 1950.

Meanwhile Rolls-Royce had come up with the uprated 1,550ehp RDa3 Dart and this combined with a 6ft 9in fuselage stretch and 5ft increase in wing span to produce the Viscount 700, seating 40-53 passengers, which first flew on 28 August 1950.

The economics of this enlarged version were much more attractive, and BEA ordered 20 (plus seven more later) V701 Viscounts on 3 August 1950, seating 47 passengers. The V630 prototype operated the world's first turbine-powered scheduled services with BEA, between London, Paris and Edinburgh, during July-August 1950. BEA's Viscount 701s, which had a gross weight of 56,000lb initially and RDa3 Dart 505s instead of the Dart 504s in the 700 prototype, began scheduled services between London and Nicosia on 18 April 1953. Viscounts soon established that turboprop power had a major competitive appeal, and orders for the type started to build up. In November 1952 TCA (now Air Canada) had placed its first order, eventually buying 51 V724s and V757s, and in June 1954 Capital Airlines signed its first contract, eventually buying 60 V745s. Adapting the Viscount to North American requirements called for a major design effort, some

of the 250 changes required by TCA including a flight deck restyled for two-crew operation and a new four-tank fuel system of increased capacity; the gross weight was raised to 60,000lb. Capital's V745s were very similar, the first batch having Dart 506s but later ones had the 1,780ehp RDa6 Dart 510 engines and provision for two 145-gallon slipper tanks on the outer wing leading edges. Carry-on luggage racks, airstairs, and provision for weather radar were also featured and the eventual gross weight was 64,500lb. Viscounts for other airlines were fitted with Dart 510s and these were known collectively as V700Ds, having more fuel and increased take-off weight. BEA's Viscounts were later converted to a high-density layout seating 63 passengers and fitted with airstairs. Altogether 287 Viscount 700s were built, of which over 30 are still in airline service and others are used as executive and VIP transports.

Vickers Viscount 800 UK

Photo: Viscount 832
Data: Viscount 810

Engines: Four 2,100ehp de-rated to 1,990ehp (max take-off) Rolls-Royce RDa7/1 Dart 525 turboprops
Span: 93ft 8½in
Length: 85ft 8in
Height: 26ft 9in
Wing area: 963sq ft
Basic operating weight: 41,565lb
Max payload: 14,500lb
Max take-off weight: 72,500lb
Speed: 350mph at 20,000ft (cruising)
Range: 1,725 miles with max payload
1,760 miles with max fuel

Development of a stretched version of the Viscount with improved payload/range capabilities had been started by Vickers and BEA even before the V701 began airline services with the latter, and BEA orderd 12 Viscount 801s on 11 February 1953, this version having a 13ft 3in longer fuselage seating up to 86 tourist passengers, and four 1,690ehp Rolls-Royce RDa5 Darts. This version was abandoned because it was felt to be too large for the traffic then foreseen, and it was succeeded by the Viscount 802, of which 24 were ordered by BEA, with a fuselage stretch of 3ft 10in which, combined with moving back the rear pressure bulkhead by 5ft 5in, gave an extra 9ft 3in of usable cabin length, enabling 65-71 passengers to

be carried. The same 1,740ehp RDa6 Dart 510 engines as in the Viscount 700D were fitted, and gross weight was now 64,500lb. A slipper tank could be fitted on each outer wing. The Viscount 802 first flew on 27 July 1956 and entered service on BEA's London-Paris route on 18 February 1957. BEA also ordered 19 Viscount 806s, this being the same as the 802 but with 2,100ehp RDa7 Dart 520s de-rated to 1,890ehp for maximum take-off. As with the Viscount 700, each customer variant for the 800 series was given a different type number, ie Viscount 803s for KLM, 804s for the British independent Transair, 805s for Eagle Aviation, 807s for New Zealand National Airways Corp and 808s for Aer Lingus. The latter's were later converted into freighters with a forward cargo door, which variant was known as the Viscount 808C.

Largely to meet Continental Air Lines's requirements for an 800 with more power to cope with such 'hot and high' mid-Western airports as Denver, the Viscount 810 was evolved with 2,100ehp RDa7/1 Dart 525s de-rated to 1,990ehp for maximum take-off, a strengthened structure for a gross weight increased ultimately to 72,500lb, a higher landing weight and an ultimate cruising speed of 400mph. The Viscount 840 would have been the true 400mph cruise version because it was intended to have 2,350ehp RDa11 Dart 541s, which engines could have been fitted to 810s to bring them up to 840 standard. But in the end there were no orders

for the 840 and this version was not built. A prototype 810 flew on 23 December 1957, and Continental began Viscount 812 services between Chicago and Los Angeles on 26 May 1958. The basic 810 was ordered by South African Airways, Lufthansa, TAA, Pakistan International and a number of other airlines, the last customer being CAAC of China, which bought six Viscount 843s as its first western equipment, flying its first Viscount service,

from Peking to Shanghai, on 25 March 1964. The three Viscount 833s of Hunting-Clan Air Transport (later part of BUA) had non-standard Dart 530 engines which, unlike the Dart 525s, were not derated for take-off so as to cater for 'hot and high' airports on the African Safari routes. Of 444 Viscounts built, 151 were 800s and 810s, and some 70 of these are still in airline service, while several have been used as executive transports.

Vickers Vanguard   UK

Photo: Vanguard 953
Data: Vanguard 952

Engines: Four 5,545ehp (max take-off) Rolls-Royce RTy11 Tyne 512 turboprops
Span: 118ft 0in
Length: 122ft 10$\frac{1}{2}$in
Height: 34ft 11in
Wing area: 1,529sq ft
Weight: 82,500lb (empty equipped)
Max payload: 37,000lb
Max take-off weight: 146,500lb
Speed: 425mph at 20,000ft (max cruising)
Range: 1,830 miles with max payload
3,100 miles with max fuel

The Vickers Vanguard was designed to a very detailed BEA specification of 1954-55 for a bigger turboprop-powered successor to the Viscount, capable of operating with the greatest economy on any route sector of between 200 and 2,500 miles in length. About 60 separate design studies, all designated V870, were considered before the final design was arrived at, and these included several high wing layouts. BEA's highly seasonal traffic pattern, with under-utilisation of its fleet in winter, led to the development of the Vanguard's double bubble fuselage with exceptional freight capacity (1,350cu ft) in the two lower deck cargo compartments, which could take up to 17,000lb of freight; this meant that a full payload could be

carried when only 30% of the seats were filled, thus greatly improving the off-peak economics. The 20 Vanguards ordered by BEA in October 1955 were originally to have been of the V901 version, but this was succeeded by the V951 which had increased range, a maximum weight of 135,000lb and four 4,985ehp Rolls-Royce RTy1 Tyne 506 turboprops; six of BEA's 20 were V951s and 14 were V953s with the same engines, maximum weight increased to 141,000lb and increased payload. The first Vanguard, built on production jigs, made its initial flight on 20 January 1959, followed by the second, which was the first for BEA, on 22 April that year. In the certification programme a fault in the Tyne compressor discovered by Rolls-Royce on the test bed, and the subsequent modifications, led to the award of a C of A for the type being put back to December 1960, the first Vanguard passengers being carried by BEA between London and Paris on the 17th of that month, full Vanguard services beginning on 1 March 1961.

Up to 139 passengers could be accommodated in an all-economy interior, and BEA's aircraft seated at various times 114 passengers, 132 in an all-tourist layout or 119 (30 first-class and 89 tourist). The only other airline to place an order was Trans-Canada Air Lines (now Air Canada), which signed for 20 of the V952 version in January 1957; this had higher design weights than the V951, a higher cruising speed, a higher payload and uprated 5,545ehp RTy11 Tyne 512 engines. TCA began Vanguard

services to the Caribbean on 1 April 1961, and almost a year earlier had placed a repeat order for three V952s; in TCA service up to 149 passengers were carried. The Vanguard's sales prospects were eclipsed by the advent of short/medium-haul jets such as the Caravelle, DC-9 and One-Eleven, and larger types such as the Trident and Convair 880. Air Canada had converted the first of several of its V952s to freighters by 1967, and BEA had some of its Vanguards similarly converted, nine going in service as V953C Merchantmen, with a large upward-opening side-loading cargo door, a strengthened floor and a conveyer system for loading; the first Merchantman conversion flew on 10 October 1969. Air Canada withdrew its Vanguards from 1969, and used examples of V951s, 952s and 953s have been sold to Air Viking of Iceland, Air Bridge Carriers, Europe Aero Service, Indonesia Angkasa Civil Air Transport, Invicta International and Merpati Nusantara of Indonesia.

Yakovlev Yak-40 USSR

Engines: Three 3,300lb st Ivchenko AI-25 turbofans
Span: 82ft 0¼in
Length: 66ft 9½in
Height: 21ft 4in
Wing area: 753.5sq ft
Weight: 20,140lb (empty)
Max payload: 5,070lb
Max take-off weight: 32,410lb
Speed: 373mph (max) at sea level
342mph at 19,685ft (max cruising)
Range: 900 miles max (no reserves)
590 miles with max fuel

Although western manufacturers such as Lockheed, de Havilland and Dassault pioneered and developed the executive jet, it was the Russians who were the first in the field with the logical step-up from the bizjet, namely the truly short-haul jet airliner. The Yak-40 was the first venture into the airliner field of the Yakovlev design bureau, better known for fighters and trainers. The bureau undertook the difficult task of designing a small, economic short-haul jet that could replace the many Lisunov Li-2s (Russian-built DC-3s) used on Aeroflot's multi-stop routes in the remoter parts of the Soviet Union. The new jet had to be able to operate from Class 5 (grass runway) airfields, and instead of a twin-engined layout three small turbofans were chosen for good field performance and high thrust-to-weight ratio — the 3,300lb st Ivchenko AI-25 especially developed for the Yak-40 — and with three engines runway lengths and take-off weights could be calculated on the basis that only one-third, not one-half, of take-off power would be lost with an engine failure. A ventral airstair provides the main access to the cabin, and for engine starting at remote airfields an auxiliary power unit is mounted above the rear fuselage. Standard seating is for 27 passengers three-abreast, and alternative interiors provide for 33 seats at reduced pitch, an executive layout with 11 seats and mixed-class interiors for 16 or 20 passengers.

The first of five Yak-40 prototypes made its maiden flight on 21 October 1966, and Aeroflot, which flew its first scheduled services with the Yak-40 on 30 September 1968, now has over 750 of the type. Realising that the Yak-40 had no equivalent in the west, the Russians mounted a major sales effort which led to full certification to western standards in Italy and Germany, the Yak-40EC being the export version with Collins avionics. The Italian third-level airline Aertirrena SpA was the first export customer to put Yak-40s into service when it began domestic services at the end of 1970 using three aircraft, but ceased operations in 1976; two of them were then acquired by another Italian third-level operator, Avioligure. General Air GmbH took delivery of five Yak-40s in 1972 for German third-level routes, but this operator also went out of business late in 1975. Yak-40s are also operated by Cubana (6 at least), Balkan Bulgarian Airlines (12), CSA and its domestic associate Slov-Air (17), Air Guinee (1), TAAG Angola (4), Bakhtar Afghan Airlines (2) and the Pathet Lao airline in Laos (2). The Yugoslav Air Force has two, and a few others serve with other Communist air forces or government agencies. Several modifications have been made to the Yak-40 since it went into service, in particular the addition of a clamshell-type thrust reverser on the centre engine and the removal of the acorn fairing at the fin/tail-plane leading edge junction. During 1974 a new export version, the Yak-40V, was offered with 3,858lb st AI-25T engines, increased fuel capacity and gross weight increased to 35,274lb for the 27-seater or 36,376lb for the 32-passenger variant. British CAA certification of the type may be obtained with certain modifications, and ICX Aviation of Washington, DC, intends to market the Yak-40 in the States with Garrett AiResearch TFE 731-2 turbofans and US avionics fitted to modified American-built airframes, this version being known as the X-Avia.

Index